Online Assessment and Measurement:
Case Studies from
Higher Education, K-12
and Corporate

Scott L. Howell
Brigham Young University, USA

Mary Hricko
Kent State University, USA

Information Science Publishing

Hershey • London • Melbourne • Singapore

Acquisitions Editor:	Renée Davies
Development Editor:	Kristin Roth
Senior Managing Editor:	Amanda Appicello
Managing Editor:	Jennifer Neidig
Copy Editor:	Eva Brennan
Typesetter:	Larissa Zearfoss
Cover Design:	Lisa Tosheff
Printed at:	Yurchak Printing Inc.

Published in the United States of America by
      Information Science Publishing (an imprint of Idea Group Inc.)
      701 E. Chocolate Avenue
      Hershey PA 17033
      Tel: 717-533-8845
      Fax: 717-533-8661
      E-mail: cust@idea-group.com
      Web site: http://www.idea-group.com

and in the United Kingdom by
      Information Science Publishing (an imprint of Idea Group Inc.)
      3 Henrietta Street
      Covent Garden
      London WC2E 8LU
      Tel: 44 20 7240 0856
      Fax: 44 20 7379 3313
      Web site: http://www.eurospan.co.uk

     Library of Congress Cataloging-in-Publication Data

Online assessment and measurement : case studies from higher education,
  K-12, and corporate / Scott L. Howell and Mary Hricko, Editors.
   p. cm.
  Summary: "This book features case studies detailing online applications and
uses of assessment and measurement methodologies, systems, and practices
across three broad educational or training areas"--Provided by publisher.
  Includes bibliographical references and index.
   ISBN 1-59140-720-6 (hc) -- ISBN 1-59140-721-4 (sc) -- ISBN 1-59140-722-2
(ebook)
   1. Educational tests and measurements--United States--Data processing--Case
studies. 2. Educational tests and measurements--United States--Computer
programs--Case studies. 3. Employees--Rating of--United States--Computer
programs--Case studies. I. Howell, Scott L. II. Hricko, Mary.
  LB3060.55.O65 2006
  371.26'0285--dc22

                         2005013552

British Cataloguing in Publication Data
A Cataloguing in Publication record for this book is available from the British Library.

Online Assessment and Measurement:
Case Studies from Higher Education, K-12 and Corporate

Table of Contents

Section I: Higher Education

Foreword

The 18 chapters in this volume feature a number of case studies detailing online applications and the uses of assessment and measurement methodologies, systems, and practices across three broad educational or training areas, namely elementary and secondary (K-12), higher education, and corporate. Although the experiences of those who experimented with the varied forms of online assessment and measurement are individual, they are also generalizable. Their stories of migrating old assessments and introducing new ones to the online environment have been frustrating and challenging but also exhilarating and rewarding. This volume makes significant contributions to the growing body of knowledge and experience in the burgeoning academic and applied areas of online assessment and measurement.

Even though the authors of and settings for each of these case studies are diverse, their experiences are common. They have identified the foundational need for widespread stakeholder inquiry, communication, and professional development and the importance of counting financial costs and not underestimating information technology (IT) requirements up front. The case studies capture newness and an early unfamiliarity with online assessment and measurement in both attitude and approach and summarily declare findings as premature and systems as experimental. They agree that any systems they adopt or processes they develop have not become a panacea. They also observe that the greatest challenge for online assessment and measurement is change itself. Administrators, instructors, and learners are all affected by the most important change that new online technologies, theories, and models make possible: the tight and inextricable integration of learning and assessment. Clearly, this phenomenon appears to have opened up so many possibilities that the newness and largeness of it all is still overwhelming and unsettling to many.

The future of online assessment and measurement is in the hands of the early adopters and hardy pioneers who are determined to overcome the challenges and help push forward and out the learning and assessment paradigm. All these pioneers know-even if they can't prove it yet-that teaching, training, operational, learning, and assessment advances can only be realized as online assessment and measurement, and all that it represents, is better understood. Surely online assessment and measurement promises to revolutionize the way that corporate, K-12 and higher education institutions and professionals approach and realize their educational missions.

Now we provide brief summaries of and introductions to each of the eight higher education, five K-12 and five corporate chapters.

Preface

Section I: Higher Education

Chapter I. *"Continuous Assessment for Improved Student Outcomes: Examples from WebCT's Exemplary Course Project"*

In the late 1990s a widespread instructional technology explosion occurred with the development and advancement of Internet and computer technologies. One scholar has referred to this period of time as being as important and significant to learning as was the invention of the Gutenberg press, turning the educational world upside down in so many ways. This phenomenon was brought to the common educator by instructor-friendly learning content management systems (LCMS) such as WebCT, Blackboard, eCollege, and many others. This chapter reveals the remarkable impact that online assessments and measurements embedded in LCMS tools are having on teaching and learning and leaves the reader with a desire for much more than the word limit on chapters in this volume allows. It is clear from this chapter and the many examples identified from the WebCT Exemplary Course Project that the innovative and best online assessment strategies made possible by LCMS in recent years are redefining not only the way instructors assess but also, more significantly, the way teachers teach and students learn. These authors briefly introduce many of the numerous online assessment features available in WebCT and illustrate the best practices through examples provided by instructors now using WebCT for online assessment. One of the most notable and unique features of an online assessment system such as WebCT is its capacity to provide immediate and quality feedback to the learner on quizzes and exams and also allow him or her to self-check exercises introduced throughout the LCMS environment. The authors acknowledge that the dream of assessment being more closely integrated with learning and even being indistinguishable from each other is a step closer because of LCMSs such as WebCT.

Chapter II. *"Coordinating a Distance Learning Software Rollout with the Needs and Visions of a Mature Test Organization: Political and Technical Lessons Learned"*

Any university or college seriously considering the adoption of a large LCMS (e.g., WebCT or Blackboard) with its online assessment and measurement capability for not only its campus and testing center but also its distance education programs will benefit from this chapter. The sometimes difficult and costly lessons learned by one university promise to inform the strategic planning efforts of other like institutions, especially if they already have an established testing center. The competing needs and interests of faculty in the classroom, administrators in the testing center, and both in the distance education context are best addressed before, not after, the integration of an expensive, enterprise-wide LCMS for online assessment and measurement purposes.

Chapter III. *"Assessing the Relationship between Learner Satisfaction and Faculty Participation in Online Course Discussions"*

This chapter is written by senior administrators from one of the largest and most well known for profit international distance education institutions: Capella University. The brief history of this successful "dot edu" university-provided by the authors as context for their case study-is as fascinating as the case study itself. This specific case study focuses on the assessment and evaluation of the instructor and adult learner interaction in an online setting by using the Capella-developed Faculty Development Feedback System (FDFS). The authors explain how FDFS is used to assess online instructor immediacy within a course by measuring the frequency and quality of instructor and learner interaction in online course discussions. The authors also examine the intersection of FDFS results and course evaluation ratings with the surprising conclusion that the learner-content relationship may be more important than the learner-instructor relationship. This finding further validates a claim by distance education researcher Terry Anderson that "sufficient levels of deep and meaningful learning can be developed as long as one of the three forms of interaction (student-teacher; student-student; student-content) is at very high levels. The other two may be offered at minimal levels or even eliminated without degrading the educational experience" (Anderson, 2002, p. 4).

Chapter IV. *"Authentic Online Assessment: Three Case Studies in Teacher Education"*

This chapter reminds readers of the importance of aligning objectives, activities, and assessment. Three diverse teacher education programs at the Hong Kong Institute of Education undertook an initiative to update their assessment strategy by using technology-mediated tools unavailable to the teacher and student just a few years ago. This effort not only realized new insights about and experience with online assessment but also resulted in a redesign of the whole curricular package to ensure full alignment and integrity among all the pieces. The authors extol the benefits of online assessments, especially in promoting more timely and helpful peer collaboration and review. They note the value of using online assessments to better prepare students for high tech jobs, where online assessment and measurement are commonplace and to succeed in lifelong learning opportunities that will increasingly rely on online assessment and measurement strategies. The three case studies also showcase, through the eyes of students, the impact that formative-not summative-online assessments and feedback had on their learning process.

x

Chapter V. *"Electronic Tools for Online Assessments: An Illustrative Case Study from Teacher Education"*

The chapter highlights the creative use of common software tools by teacher education professors in a university course at Eastern Michigan University to facilitate and automate elements of online assessment involving student papers and portfolios while modeling the same for their students-soon to be teachers themselves. The authors introduce the use of rubric-building and-customizing software, databases, and the track changes feature in word processors with the help of a number of illustrative figures. Even though the tools described are common and accessible to both instructors and university students alike, their use, particularly in concert with each other, appears less common. Some benefits and advantages for use of these tools identified by the authors include *more* valid measurements, efficient grading, and modeling of online assessment methods to future teachers. The authors also note the importance of formative online assessments in helping students improve the educational product (e.g., paper or portfolio) and the instructor in improving the overall teaching, assessment, and feedback process.

Chapter VI. *"Online Assessment of Foreign Language Proficiency: Meeting Development, Design, and Delivery Challenges"*

The author of this chapter has taken a very complex subject involving an elaborate model of computer-adaptive testing for language placement and proficiency and explained the process and issues confronted in converting the exam to a Web-based format in a very lucid and engaging manner. The author's endnotes are not to be overlooked either, as she defines in a simple and straightforward way three terms or phrases that help explain semi-adaptive or hybridized computer-adaptive tests developed specifically for this language testing context. This case study focuses on the adaptation of two less commonly taught languages (LCTL), Arabic and Russian, from a traditional to online format while introducing the reader to the many issues and challenges confronted by the team-some of them unique to online language assessment and measurement. As part of this project, the Center for Applied Linguistics and Georgetown University conducted an analysis of online assessment vendors by using predefined characteristics, for example, security, adaptability, price, and so forth, that will be helpful to other institutions looking for the right vendor fit. This chapter concludes with five pragmatic lessons that will generalize to other online assessment initiatives not exclusive to LCTL online assessment.

Chapter VII. *"Using Web-Enabled Technology in a Performance-Based Accreditation Environment"*

This chapter, written by five engineering faculty members from Penn State University, touts the role that two different online assessment systems played in helping their college prepare for professional engineering accreditation. Much of this volume, and most online assessment and measurement efforts themselves, focuses on the student and not the instructor; this case study features the instructor's role and participation in online assessment and measurement systems. The first system developed by these engineers is clearly an example of using technology as a lever for change to build consensus and foster democratization so that their accreditation effort is not perceived as only a top-down mandate. Because outcomes are the focus of new engineering accreditation standards, the 17 engineering programs of the 12 campus university system turned to a simple Web-based tool to build outcome consensus from a dispersed faculty. This online self-assessment instrument captured on a weekly basis three types of class level data from the faculty: learning goal(s), learning activities to support each goal, and performance summary. The authors speak of the benefits that accrued from this exercise, including the use of the aggregated data to make and build program level decisions and outcomes. They also remind the readers throughout the chapter about the importance of online assessment systems being scalable-stretchable and shrinkable-according to need. The second online assessment system developed focused on three data sources or measurements that would provide further evidence to the accreditation agency that outcomes were being met. Those three data targets included student performance on each outcome (as determined by the faculty member), faculty perception of course effectiveness, and students' perception of their own degree of mastery at the outcome level. This triangulation of data clearly provides the multilevel, outcomes-based measurements critical for not just accreditation but, even more importantly, continuous improvement and advancement of student learning.

Chapter VIII. *"Moving Beyond Objective Testing in Online Assessment"*

The Scottish Centre for Research into online Learning and Assessment is taking online assessment where it has never gone before. Many of the questions that educational institutions are asking today about online assessment are in the past for this university research center, as they look into the future and beyond the constraints of today's assessment theory and technology. Although the six authors of this chapter are constrained by space limitations, they still succeed in engaging those educators who read this chapter with an eye to the future of online assessment and measurement. This chapter emphasizes the importance of aligning multimedia teaching methods with multimedia assessment methods; it also challenges educators to not so quickly dismiss the capacity of online assessments to test higher order skills and highly symbolic subject areas (e.g., mathematics). This case study also provides some interesting background and history on where United Kingdom computer-aided assessments (CAA) have been and where the authors predict they are going. These authors and the research coming from their institute portend a day when rich multidimensional and authentic simulations/animations/presentations are commonplace in both formative and summative assessments, and where reporting and feedback along the instructional way is both rich and immediate. The overriding theme of this chapter is the need to blur the line between learning and assessment because technology allows a total integration of the same and a redesigning of the educational paradigm.

Section II: Elementary and Secondary Education (K–12)

Chapter IX. *"Development of a Computerized Adaptive Test for a Large-Scale Testing Program: A Case Study of the Development of the North Carolina Computerized Adaptive Testing System"*

The five authors of this chapter provide any state office of education considering computer-adaptive testing (CAT) in reading and math a helpful case study that examines large-scale CAT administration with suitable accommodations for disabled students. This study and pilot over 3 years touches on a number of online CAT issues through the accessibility perspective. These five authors are as conversant with the legal and moral responsibility of accommodating their disabled students as they are with the complexities of item response theory-the foundation of CAT. These practitioners and researchers alike have arguably taken CAT where it has not been before as they modify and adapt typical CAT delivery to accommodate content domain coverage and the atypical learner. This pilot exposes, as have other case studies in this volume, the importance of not overlooking technical requirements, best testing practices, and political nuances for rolling out a new testing paradigm on a large scale while accommodating students with special needs on a small scale. The authors categorize lessons learned from this experience under six headings: usability, comparability, development of the item pool, test security, state/local infrastructure, and buy-in from test consumers. Finally, the authors raise both important and provocative questions about the intersection of online assessment with federal/state/local regulations, including "No Child Left Behind."

Chapter X. *"Introducing a Computer-Adaptive Testing System to a Small School District"*

Computer-adaptive testing (CAT) in a K-12 smaller school district setting is the focus of this chapter. This small district successfully introduced this "new" type of online assessment using a relatively "new" type of testing theory-item response theory-and at the same time documented critical issues and questions that other districts need to address before they make a similar adoption. Although the authors do their best to keep this chapter as nontechnical as possible and demonstrate that CAT can be more efficient and reliable than traditional testing methods, some background in CAT would be helpful. However, even those without a rich background in CAT will benefit from a discussion of issues emerging from the case study. Although many of the benefits and drawbacks of CAT are similar to those of the more linear and traditional forms of online assessment, many are unique to this format: different levels of examinee familiarity with computers, shorter exam lengths, few items that are really easy or hard, lack of item review capacity, and examinees missing about half of the items before the algorithm brings the test to an end. This case study also emphasizes the important role of professional development and in-service in helping teachers and administrators better interpret results at the individual, class, and district levels and then make just-in-time curricular adjustments for their students. Furthermore, the authors posit the use of CAT data to identify trends in student achievement that can then be associated with best practices that are worthy of dissemination to other teachers. Finally, the authors give reasons why this CAT should supply just one of the measures of student progress and that its best use in the school district setting is "to support student learning by providing timely information to teachers in the classroom, and school administrators".

Chapter XI. *"A Computer-Adaptive Mathematics Test Accommodates Third Grade Students with Special Needs in the Pacific Northwest"*

This case study examines the use of a computer-adaptive mathematics test administered to 250 third grade students in the Pacific Northwest with limited reading and writing skills. Out of fairness to the students and as a matter of integrity in reporting test results, it was important that no students who understood math but struggled with reading and writing be misrepresented in ability or otherwise left behind by the online assessment. The researchers endeavored to incorporate recent findings and recommendations from APA's Task Force on Psychological Testing on the Internet in ensuring that this online assessment was in compliance. The authors examine issues of reliability and validity for this online assessment that include appropriate item development as well as what they call "structural development." With item development, they employ "read-aloud and simpler vocabulary strategies"; with structural development, they go to great lengths to ensure consistent access and presentation of 10,000 learning assessment objects across an inconsistent computing environment or infrastructure, for example, varied platforms, browsers, screen sizes, color depths, and so forth. This chapter briefly introduces the many software tools used to develop the exam with some rationale for their selection and place in the entire process. The authors appear to have made every reasonable effort to anticipate and manage the many challenges and variables inherent in accommodating not only disabled students but also digitally disadvantaged schools. While the authors herald the benefits of online assessment and measurement, especially for providing accommodations that are otherwise not as readily available, they also acknowledge the phenomenon that sometimes occurs in solving one problem and then introducing a new one.

Chapter XII. *"Designing an Online Formative Assessment that Helps Prepare Students and Teachers for a Summative Assessment: A Case Study—A Two Year Pilot Pairing an Online Classroom Assessment with a Statewide High-Stakes Test"*

This case study showcases the role of online assessment and measurement in better preparing elementary students and their teachers for a mandated statewide test. Even though the statewide test is paper-based, the Gates Foundation and the Washington State Education Department piloted an online initiative to assess students along the way so that teachers could better respond to areas of concern in a more timely fashion. This experience highlights some of the advantages of online assessment and measurement, particularly in a diagnostic role, while at the same time exposing some of the practical and technical challenges that are frequently overlooked in the transition to more automated and computer-based testing environments.

Chapter XIII. *"Online Assessment in the K–12 Classroom: A Formative Assessment Model for Improving Student Performance on Standardized Tests"*

The importance of formative assessment along the instructional path is at the heart of this chapter. Much of this book (and much of assessment itself) focuses on the final or summative test that determines placement, certification, grade, and/or level. However, the real opportunity of online assessment may be in uniting its technical capacity with the instructional theory of continuous feedback in providing formative feedback to students and instructors along the way. Even though these case studies have been conducted in the K–12 context, the use and application of formative assessment methods similar to these generalize too many other instructional instances.

The three specific examples used to demonstrate the multiple student and instructor effects of using an online formative assessment system include (a) the No Child Left Behind (NCLB) initiative with 223 elementary schools in Kentucky and Tennessee, (b) 35,300 students in grades three through eight in Tennessee preparing for the Tennessee Comprehensive Assessment Program (TCAP), and (c) several elementary schools in Alabama identified as "priority" schools with some other brief examples of similar efforts in Kentucky and elsewhere. The authors also look ahead at the increasing need for and interest in the use of online formative assessment in K–12 schools nationwide; they identify reasons for predicted increases in the use of online formative assessment. They also include limitations of the current model, for example, not enough constructed response item types, and so forth. Finally, the authors briefly address the age old debate of "teaching to the test" in the context of these formative assessment systems.

Section III: Corporate and Government Training

Chapter XIV. *"Online Assessment Distribution Models for Testing Programs: Lessons Learned from Operational Experience"*

This first part of this chapter provides a brief but fascinating review of the evolution of online assessment and measurement since the 1970s. Many readers will be surprised to learn of the origins and milestones of computer-based or online assessment chronicled in this chapter. The author, vice president of testing services for Pearson VUE, then proceeds to define and describe three major categories of online assessment delivery entitled (a) controlled, (b) global, and (c) ubiquitous. The controlled model is as its names implies-very controlled. Online assessments that are controlled are usually administered by organizations that consider the results sufficient to make high-stakes decisions, for example, employment, advancement, and so forth. The characteristics of a controlled model generally include restricted access (as contrasted to global outreach), tight security, careful authentication, complete standardization, and a proscribed testing environment. At the other end of the delivery model continuum is the ubiquitous model (also known as Web based), and somewhere in between is the global model. The author emphasizes, regardless of model selection, the need for test owner, developer, and deliverer to work carefully through the many issues involved in the successful distribution of online assessments. He also shares some creative but effective data mining strategies used to detect possible security breaches and promote tighter security. At the conclusion of the chapter the author looks into the future and predicts more sophistication and capacity in all dimensions of distribution that will better enable online assessment sponsors to satisfy their goals with fewer of the current constraints.

Chapter XV. *"From Paper and Pencil to Computerized: A Dental Board's Perspective"*

A large testing company, Thomson Prometric shares its experience in helping the Dental Board shift its certification testing approach for dentists, hygienists, and dental assistants from paper to the Web (computer based over secured networks and Internet based) after a security breach occurred in 2001. The author reviews previous concerns with online assessment, focusing on general access to computers, unfamiliarity with computers, and computer anxiety, and then points out how few, if any, of these historical concerns still exist today. This case study reminds any company looking to transition its assessment model of the current and relevant issues executives should consider in their analysis of whether they transition from paper to the Web, to what degree, and how quickly. Some of the online assessment and measurement issues addressed through this case study and discussion include security, a more authentic testing experience, exam availability and distribution, automated scoring, additional respondent data, item and form functionality, administrative efficiencies, technical considerations, data storage, and costs. After the Dental Board case study considered all these issues, one exigency was emphasized as probably more important than them all: "selling the idea to the candidates." Change does not always come easy, and even though it is evident that online assessment is the wave of the future, many test takers would still prefer the former way.

Chapter XVI. *"Assessment Elements in Web-Based Training"*

The online training and assessment company, Imedia.it, was contracted by the U.S. Army to develop simulated instruction and assessment. This chapter recounts the experience of the army and Imedia.it in transitioning classroom training and assessment to an online setting. The specific instructional and assessment need that the army brought to Imedia.it was how to more efficiently train counterintelligence military personnel in effective interviewing techniques and strategies. Historically, this training module required such intense trainer involvement with learners that one instructor could train only two learners at a time, creating a tremendous training backlog. The new model of training and assessment reduced the trainer/learner ratio from 1:2 to 1:10–15 by using computer-based instruction and assessment. This performance-based training and assessment approach appears successful from a number of perspectives, including administrative efficiency, interrater reliability, and learner mastery; it also introduces creative and diverse approaches to maintaining online assessment security—a nagging challenge for online assessment and measurement. The case study also highlights the use of customized learning based on the results of diagnostic or pre-assessment exercises to create customized or adaptive learning for each soldier. Finally, the author examines the future prospects of merging CAT with computer-enabled individualized and adaptive learning.

Chapter XVII. *"The Seven C's of Comprehensive Online Assessment: Lessons Learned from 36 Million Classroom Assessments in the Cisco Networking Academy Program"*

In a day of corporate nondisclosure and secrets, this chapter is a welcome and refreshing addition to the growing body of knowledge concerning online assessment and measurement from a large corporation. Arguably, Cisco Corporation and its Networking Academy Program have had more experience in online certification assessment with its 36 million assessment instances than any other institution. The seven *C's* described herein are best practices as much as they are overarching principles for anyone involved in online assessment and measurement, including certification testing. Although some people may consider the seven *C's* as common sense, invariably one or two of the *C's* have been overlooked in many institutional assessment strategies and have become the Achilles heel in an otherwise successful experience. The seven *C's* are claims, collaboration, complexity, contextualization, computation, communication, and coordination. In context, each of these terms becomes a story unto itself and represents the critical and somewhat discrete dimensions of online assessment that, when combined, enjoy a synergistic and successful interaction. The authors share glimpses of the genius of their proven but innovative model by briefly introducing their use of networking-literal and figurative-to link instructional objectives to learning activities to assessment and then back; to provide a worldwide collaboration in instrument design and development, including language and cultural translation for over 150 countries and nine languages; and to just-in-time prescripted computations that enable the assessment professional to customize and interpret the results according to unique institutional needs. The third *C,* complexity, while referring to the capacity of technologies to accommodate new and more complex item types, for example, simulations and other performance-based assessments, also represents the many complexities and exciting opportunities associated with online assessment and measurement.

Chapter XVIII. *"Feasibility Studies on Transitioning Assessment Programs from Paper and Pencil to CBT Delivery."*

Yes or no—should the paper-based assessments be converted to online assessments? What are the factors to be considered? The costs? Although some problems will be solved or at least mitigated and some efficiency introduced, will new problems and inefficiencies result? The experiences of these authors in conducting feasibility studies for clients considering the transition from paper to electronic are profound; this chapter promises assistance and insight not readily available to committees tasked with the transition from paper to electronic assessment feasibility study. As profound as these findings may be, they are just as frank and honest. The authors' experience reveals that the transition actually costs more-at least net cost is more after accounting for net gains and losses. One of the biggest challenges introduced is determining actual costs of the current paper-based program to be used as a benchmark for comparison and analysis. Five phases for a feasibility study are discussed: Phase 1: Strategic Planning with the Sponsor, Phase 2: Extended Data Gathering, Phase 3: Integration of Data Gathered and Analysis of Costs and Timeframes, Phase 4: Integration and Interpretation of Data to Identify Deal Breakers, and Phase 5: Development and Presentation of Feasibility Report. Threading their way through all these phases are stakeholder support and buy-in, which the authors emphasize as the most critical aspect of any feasibility study. Finally, three exhibits are included that are ready-made checklists or questions to gather information about the existing examination program, expectations of the stakeholders, and vendor characteristics that best match up with institutional objectives.

One of the authors of this volume may have best summed up the excitement, optimism, and outlook associated with this book and its discussion about online assessment and measurement: "We are just beginning to have a small idea of the real extent of the possibilities for online assessment." Unquestionably, all the authors, researchers, and practitioners herein wish that they had had the benefit of this volume's collective experience and knowledge before beginning their experiments and adventures with online assessment and measurement. It is the hope of these editors that this book series will encourage and inform the practical and scholarly inquiry and application of online assessment and measurement for many years yet to come.

Scott Howell
Mary Hricko
December 2004

Acknowledgments

As senior editor for this volume, I would like to give special thanks and acknowledgement to my coeditor, Mary Hricko, who first envisioned this project and then so graciously invited and encouraged my involvement. I will always cherish the opportunity that Mary and the publisher for this volume, Idea Group, have given me to work so closely with the 47 authors of and 26 reviewers for the 18 chapters included in this volume. They have collectively raised the body of theoretical and applied knowledge in this burgeoning field. These professionals are truly pioneers who have helped chart the way for many administrators, teachers, trainers, learners, and online assessors to follow.

All the authors join me in acknowledging again each of the 26 reviewers whose expertise, insights, and suggestions have added so much to the quality and value of the chapters in this volume. I have listed alphabetically by last name all reviewers who generously contributed to this volume: Scott Bergstrom, Tim Bothell, Bryan Bradley, Paul Byrd, Susan Clark, Luke Fernandez, Lee Glines, Justin Johansen, Paul Jones, Jerry Larson, Barbara Lawrence, Duane Lemley, Alan Meredith, Adisack Nhouyvanisvong, Jim Olsen, Leslie Pelton, Tim Pelton, Hal Sanderson, Lynn Sorenson, Steve Taggart, Ron Terry, Jon Twing, Nancy Wentworth, David Williams, Peter Williams, and Bud Wood.

Special appreciation is also due to Dianne King and Chellae Brooks of Brigham Young University, Division of Continuing Education, for the numerous and invaluable editing contributions they and their staff have provided to the chapter authors and volume editors. Special thanks also go to Jan Travers, managing editor for the publisher, and her team at Idea Group for their professional support and personal encouragement.

This project would not have been possible without the generosity and support of the dean of the Division of Continuing Education at Brigham Young University, Dr. Richard Eddy, who enthusiastically made possible my involvement and that of others within the division to make this project a reality. To Brianne Gillespie, my assistant, thank you for organizing the many details of this endeavor and for making sure I did not overlook anything. To my mentors over the years who instilled within me a love and respect for assessment and instructional science, I give heartfelt acknowledgement, in particular to my former faculty advisors, Dr. Richard Sudweeks and Dr. Paul Merrill, and my professional colleagues Dr. Dwight Laws and Ron Malan. Finally, I thank my wife, Lori, and our seven children for their constant love and encouragement.

Scott L. Howell, PhD
Brigham Young University
Provo, Utah, USA

Section I

Higher Education

Chapter I

Continuous Assessment for Improved Student Outcomes:
Examples from WebCT's Exemplary Course Project

Daniel Volchok, WebCT, USA

Maisie Caines, College of the North Atlantic, Canada

David Graf, Nova Southeastern University, USA

Abstract

WebCT views assessment as an activity that is integral to the full scope of the learning process. A variety of methods and strategies are available to course designers and instructors to assess student performance before, during, and after a course has taken place. WebCT provides three major categories of assessment tools (self-tests, quizzes and surveys, and assignments within these tools) and seven types of questions (multiple choice, including true/false; combination multiple choice; matching; calculated; short answer; jumbled sentence; and paragraph). The layout, design, and administration of assessments is flexible through selective release, timed assessments, and the sequencing of questions. Through examples from the WebCT Exemplary Course Project, this chapter reviews the many tools and methods available and describes the assessment, grading, and reporting capabilities of WebCT.

Introduction

Assessments can be an effective way to gather critical information about student and course performance (WebCT, 2001). A variety of assessment methods and strategies are available to course designers and instructors in WebCT. This chapter reviews the many tools and methods available and describes the assessment, grading, and reporting capabilities through examples from the WebCT Exemplary Course Project.

Assessment is often thought of as a tool that measures a student's knowledge of the course content. In contrast, WebCT views assessment as an activity that is integral to the full scope of the learning process. The advent of online learning has opened new methods to assess student performance before, during, and after a course has taken place.

Precourse Assessment

The assessment tools in WebCT can be used in orientation or precollege courses to assess in a diagnostic fashion the students' abilities in specific subject areas. The University of Alberta, for example, is using WebCT Vista to deliver online placement testing for students. Students are given a test prior to coming to campus to determine which course level is most appropriate. This approach is very effective because it helps ensure that the students are in the right courses, and it uses the distance learning aspect to begin the semester effectively. Course pretests can be administered and used to customize the course content and coverage (Vallone, 2004).

Assessment During the Course

Faculty can choose to assess students through a number of methods. Quizzes and other tools can be embedded within the course content to gauge students' knowledge of the material. Subsequent or remedial material can then be selectively released based on the outcome of the assessment. Self-tests and surveys can be used throughout the course to aid instructors in the delivery of course material.

Postcourse Assessment

At the conclusion of the course, traditional assessment methods such as quizzes and exams can be administered. In addition, posttests can then be correlated with pretests to measure student learning. Course evaluations can also be administered to evaluate the effectiveness of the course and the instructor. Finally, the instructor has a number of reports available to evaluate the effectiveness of the assessments.

Assessment Tools in WebCT

WebCT's assessment tools fall into three major categories: self-tests, quizzes and surveys, and assignments.

Self-Tests

The self-test tool in WebCT allows the creation of simple multiple choice tests that students can use as a risk free assessment of their knowledge of specific information, concepts, and ideas. Students can take them an unlimited number of times and receive immediate and detailed feedback on their answers. No marks are assigned or recorded. Self-tests are often added to specific pages of related content to reinforce the concepts, terms, and other information that students should learn.

Dr. Robert Sanders of Portland State University makes exemplary use of the self-test tool in Spanish 101. Every module in the course contains a series of graded self-tests that assess all language building skills: grammar, structure, listening, comprehension, and writing. Self-tests allow students to practice concepts and skills and receive immediate feedback prior to taking a graded quiz.

The question types used in the assessment consist of multiple choice, short answer, matching, and paragraph. The questions often include audio and/or video elements to test student comprehension and listening skills. Figure 1 and Figure 2 show samples of some of the question types used.

In the *Linear Systems and Control* course at the University of Texas at San Antonio, Cheryl Schrader provides two review quizzes on prerequisite material to students throughout the semester. These self-tests are designed as self-assessments and can be

Figure 1. Multiple choice example

Figure 2. Short-answer example

accessed and taken as often as the students wish. Feedback embedded in the answer to each question directs students to additional resources for further learning. The assessment ends with a question to students on how prepared they feel in that particular content area. The students' answers are then analyzed and used to determine balanced discussion groups among the students for solving complex mathematical problems.

Other uses of the self-test include the creation of chapter, unit, or module summaries, similar to traditional textbook chapter questions that ask students to recall important ideas and concepts. These self-tests give students an opportunity to review course materials in preparation for formal assessments, such as quizzes, midterms, and final exams. They also allow students who are unfamiliar and inexperienced with online quizzing the opportunity to practice answering questions in a nonstressful environment within the online course.

Quizzes and Surveys

The quiz and survey tools in WebCT allow for the creation of robust, time sensitive quizzes and anonymous surveys. Both may contain various question types, such as multiple choice, matching, short answer, and essay. Quizzes can be automatically graded by the WebCT system, and both quizzes and surveys provide detailed reporting of statistics and student responses. Surveys and quizzes are identical in the way they are added to a course, populated with questions, and released to students. The essential differences between a survey and a quiz are that surveys are programmed to be anonymous and do not have any point value or grade associated with them. The results of the quiz or survey can be e-mailed to a third party source for review and tabulation. Quiz grades are automatically recorded in the student management area, but the instructor can manually edit a quiz grade if necessary.

The quiz and survey tools can be used in many ways throughout an online course. Some more innovative quizzing methods include providing a quiz at the beginning of each unit or chapter to determine whether students have completed reading assignments, releasing quizzes only to students with a specific grade on a previous assignment, or releasing content only when a student scores a certain passing grade on a quiz. Surveys can be used to allow students to register their opinion without fear of an attack on their personal opinions or to post data tabulated from the survey in the course to allow discussions or debate. Many institutions also use the survey tool in WebCT for instructor and course evaluations.

Cheryl Schrader's *Linear Systems and Control* is designed as a blended learning environment. In addition to the self-tests discussed earlier in this chapter, Schrader also uses the quiz tool to deliver weekly multiple choice quizzes as homework assignments. These quizzes consist of five questions designed to reinforce the concepts covered in class and in the assigned readings.

In the *Measurement and Evaluation in Education* course at the University of Central Florida, Dr. Robert Paugh uses the WebCT Survey tool extensively to collect feedback on course activities. Upon completion of an assigned activity, students are required to complete a feedback form that asks questions such as "Describe difficulties you encountered in completing this activity," "How were difficulties overcome?", "How would you revise the assignment and/or its instructions?", "Were the objectives of the assignment clear?", "Did the assignment help you obtain the course objectives?", and

Figure 3. Assignment feedback form

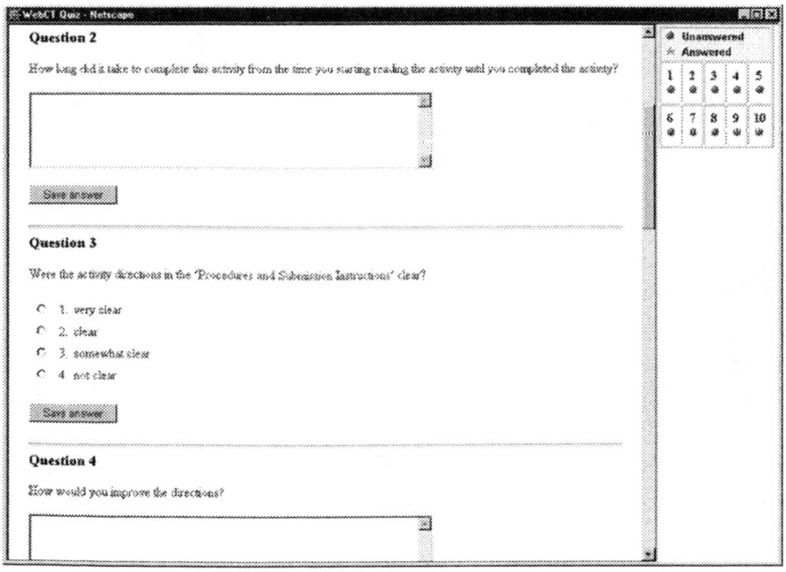

so forth. This feedback is then analyzed, and revisions to the course and activities are made accordingly. Figure 3 shows a small portion of an assignment feedback form (WebCT, 2002–2004).

In the *Clinical Calculations* course at Middle Georgia College, students apply formulas and mechanics of calculating and preparing accurate medication dosages. Marilyn Halaska, facilitator, uses the quiz tool in an "Earn While You Learn" activity, in which students are required to complete a quiz the end of each unit to test their knowledge and skill in calculating dosages. As an optional activity, students can use the results of the quiz to generate a Medication Occurrence Report. Students become engaged in detailed risk analysis by reviewing errors made on the test, identifying personal errors and error sources, and developing a safety plan to prevent the recurrence of similar errors. These optional Medication Occurrence Reports provide students the opportunity to regain up to 50% of the points lost on the quiz.

Assignments

In face to face courses, assignments and homework are typically distributed to the students, completed, and then returned to the instructor for review and grading. The Assignments tool in WebCT creates an online area for students to view and download assignments, instructions, and files as well as a space for students to submit their work. Essentially, the assignments tool is a shared folder inside the course where any type of file can be exchanged between the instructor and the students. Students can receive their assignments anytime after the instructor has uploaded and released them. Instructors can collect completed assignments and grade them at their convenience.

Instructors have the flexibility to program assignments in WebCT to be released based on a date and time and for a specified length of time. The instructor can allow late submissions of assignments or specify a cutoff date for each assignment; the date and time that each assignment is submitted are recorded in WebCT. To save instructors time, each time an assignment is created, a column for grading is automatically added to the student management database. Comments on graded assignments are displayed automatically when students view their grades. This provides students with rich, rapid feedback on their work while alleviating the administrative burden on faculty.

Faculty use the Assignment tool in WebCT in a variety of ways to assess students, including the following:

1. **Written review or summary:** An article is uploaded to the assignments tool for students to read and then returned with their review or summary included.
2. **Problems to decipher:** A page of math, engineering, or word problems is distributed and then returned. Assignment instructions can relate whether the students can work collaboratively or individually.
3. **Spreadsheet to complete:** Students can complete a spreadsheet and produce related graphs and reports.

4. **Gather resources and list them comprehensively:** Students search for resources on the Internet- geographically, within a document, library, or computer program- and then create a comprehensive list of resources.

5. **PowerPoint presentation to create or edit:** A template or rubric for presentations is distributed. A completed presentation, including original material, is then returned.

6. **Creation of a graph or diagram:** Students are asked to produce an original graph or diagram from data that is distributed to them or gathered by them.

7. **Formation of a bibliography or reference sheet:** Bibliographic or other styles can be uploaded for students to use as a guide to produce their own reference sheets.

8. **Written research paper:** Outlines, drafts, and finished papers can be edited and exchanged (WebCT, 2003).

Michael Danchak, a professor at Renssalaer Polytechnic Institute, makes extensive use of the assignment drop box tool in his *GUI Building* course. Students are required to submit exercise files and homework assignments regularly that demonstrate their ability to apply, analyze, and synthesize course material. Michael is able to provide files necessary for completing the assigned work to his students using the assignment drop box. Files, such as executable jar files, zip files, and pdf files that students need to modify or peruse to complete the assignment, are "handed out" to the students through this tool. In return, students are also required to submit their files to the instructor through their individualized drop box area.

The following figures show a sample of the assignments available in *GUI Building*.

Figure 4. Assignments Example 1

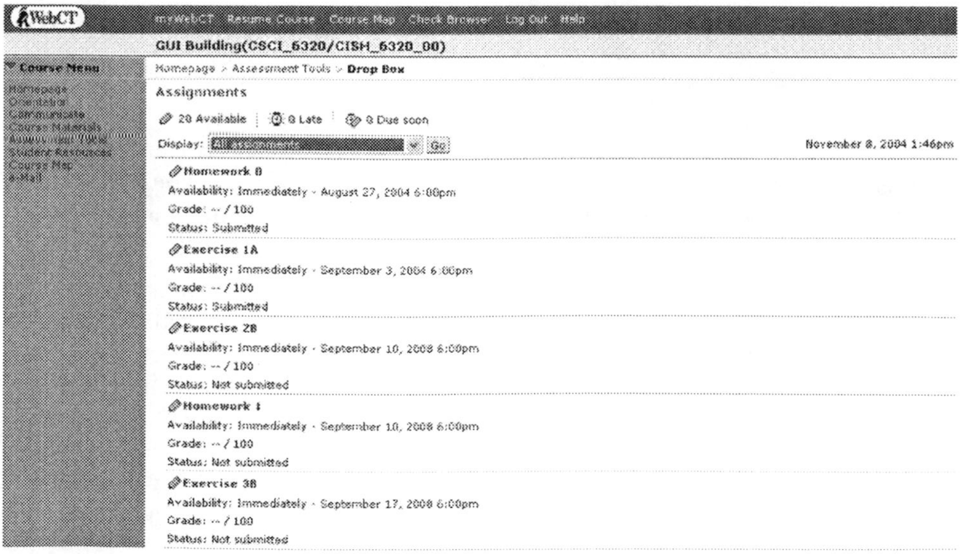

Figure 5. Assignments Example 2

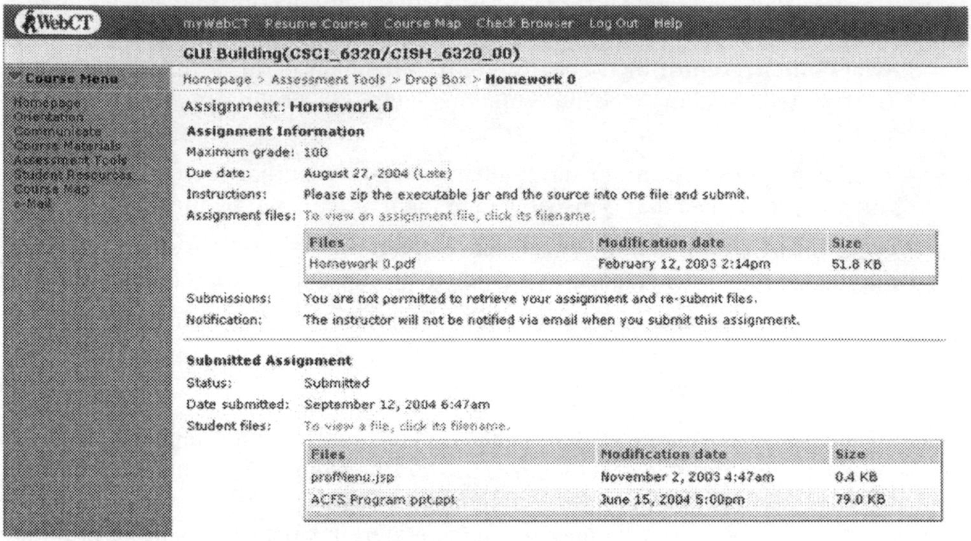

Students in Dan Barnett's *Eastern Religions* course at Butte College complete three collaborative writing projects throughout the semester. Students are divided into groups of three for each project. Private discussion areas are created for each group, where students share their ideas and work together to create the writing project. The group's facilitator (a rotated role) uploads the finished Word document to the assignment drop box. The instructor provides extensive feedback to the students in the Word document and then returns it to the group facilitator through the drop box. The assignments, in turn, are distributed to the remaining group members by the group facilitator.

In addition to using WebCT's self-test, quiz and survey, and assignment tools, instructors have been assessing student learning in a number of creative ways. For example, students in the University of Victoria's Supervised Practicum course facilitated by Michelle Koroll are assessed on how well they construct their own learning experience. In this constructivist, problem-based learning environment, assessment activities consist of formative and summative practicum performance evaluations, critical documentation and self evaluation of their practicum experience, and participation in assigned online discussions.

The critical documentation is one of the main assessment pieces within the course. As students translate theory into practice, they are required to document their learning journey through the practicum experience. According to Koroll, "Students are expected to set learning goals at the beginning of the course for themselves in eight prescribed practice areas and then to document their progress toward these goals" (WebCT, 2002–2004). Students create a learning plan that the instructor and practicum supervisor review. At the end of the course and practicum experience, students compile a learning portfolio that documents their plans and evidence of knowledge and skills development. They critically evaluate and reflect on their learning process by using the documentation compiled.

In her *Ethics for Health Care Professionals* course at the Medical College of Georgia, Kathleen Hernlen requires students to complete a number of "quandary" assignments. By completing these assignments, students self assess their ethical decision making skills. Within each quandary, the student is given a real life health care dilemma and a choice to make. The students are allowed the opportunity to see the consequences of the choice and may repeat each quandary as many times as they like, choosing different paths and observing the consequences each time.

For example, a Web Quest assignment causes students to explore the cultural implications involved in ethical decision making. The students are given the beginning of a story and asked to finish it, exploring all possible options for the characters in the story. In completing the assignment, students apply what they have learned about the culture to the solution. They are also required to develop two epilogues to the story: a best case scenario and a worst case scenario.

At the University of Maryland, students in *Water and Nutrient Management Planning* for the Nursery and Greenhouse Industry work collaboratively in project management teams composed of a resident student, an extension professional, and a nursery or greenhouse crop grower. The ultimate objective of the course is to write a site-specific nutrient management plan for the nursery or greenhouse as represented by the grower in each team.

The project management teams engage in problem solving activities to obtain or create information and data that they then apply to the nutrient management planning process. Students obtain some information by the use of hyperlinks to Web-based resources outside the course, such as federal and state government Web sites. Students also visit the offices of state agricultural agencies to obtain soil maps not available on the Internet. As a result, they become familiar with agency resources and personnel who can assist them in their project efforts.

In addition, required on-site research activities encourage collaborative team efforts and student participation. Each team utilizes the resources and specific crop production methods of the nursery or greenhouse that they are assigned to study and develops nutrient management plans. Students conduct on-site evaluations of the physical layout and operational management of the nursery or greenhouse. They are required, as a team, to perform a series of tests of specific crop production practices. Students then incorporate data obtained from these tests, along with data from the physical layout and operational management of the site, into the planning process.

Authoring and Delivery of Assessments

WebCT offers faculty and designers the capability for easy and flexible authoring and variable delivery methods to impact learning. For example, a repository of questions can be used in multiple assessments. Questions can be created either within an individual WebCT course assessment or within the database. Either way, all questions are available to use for any assessment in any WebCT course. Within the database, questions can be categorized, modified, or even developed offline. Statistics on each question are maintained over the life of the question.

WebCT allows for seven different question types: multiple choice (including true/false), combination multiple choice, matching, calculated, short answer, jumbled sentence, and paragraph. Within each question type are numerous available settings to allow the faculty or designer to customize the performance of the question.

Multiple Choice Questions

Multiple choice questions are by far the most common form in use. WebCT can automatically score these questions, making them easy to grade. There are two types of traditional multiple choice questions: pick-one and pick-multiple answers. *Pick-one* questions ask the student to choose one correct answer from multiple selections, including true or false. *Pick-multiple* questions ask the student to pick one, some, all, or none of the selections, and are good for making a series of related judgments.

Combination Multiple Choice Questions

Combination multiple choice questions are a variation on the traditional pick-one multiple choice questions. Here, students are presented with a question and a list of answers from which they must choose the combination of items that is correct. The list of possible combinations can include "all of the above" or "none of the above."

Matching Questions

Matching questions ask students to associate items in one list with items in another. Items may have more than one correct match or no match at all. WebCT allows faculty to create three types of matching lists: (a) short answer matching, which consists of one to three words; (b) long answer matching, which consists of several words or phrases; and (c) images.

Calculated Questions

Calculated questions allow faculty to generate mathematical questions based on a random set of variables. Calculated questions begin with the question in text form and the variables identified within the text in brackets. The same variables are then added to a formula box. A series of questions is then created by using the identified formula and variables, so students will receive different questions and have to figure out different answers, all based on the single application of a formula. For example, if students are asked to calculate the perimeter of a yard, the yard size will vary with each test, but the formula for calculating a parameter will always be a constant.

Short Answer Questions

Short answer questions require the student to type in specific answers to questions, usually in a fill-in-the-blank format. In automatically grading short-answer questions, WebCT allows for the responses to be exact words or phrases, contain the targeted word or phrase, or specify a regular Perl expression, which WebCT uses to evaluate a student's answer. It is also possible to program a percentage of points for responses that are within the range of acceptability but not the exact response. Short answer questions can contain one or more answer boxes, which the student uses to fill in their answers.

Jumbled Sentence Questions

Jumbled sentence questions present students with a sentence from which words are missing. Drop-down lists containing several word selections appear for the missing words, and students must select the correct word. This question type is popular in foreign language courses.

Paragraph Questions

Paragraph questions, or essay questions, test the breadth and depth of a student's understanding and application of ideas, concepts, beliefs, and attitudes. Students have the opportunity to organize their thoughts and demonstrate their abilities to think, analyze, and persuade. Paragraph questions are the only question type for which WebCT cannot create an automatic grade, for obvious reasons.

Quiz Structure

In conjunction with the many types of questions available, there are a variety of ways to design and administer assessments within the WebCT course environment. The structure of the quiz, or its *architecture,* can have a great impact on what the quiz measures and how it is measured. How the question is asked is just as important as the question itself. The design of a quiz should consider three main factors: (a) the sequencing of the questions, (b) how much time is allowed to answer the questions, and (c) how many attempts a student is allowed to pass the quiz (WebCT, 2004a).

Question Sequencing

WebCT allows the instructor to deliver all the questions at once or release each question one at a time. Instructors can also decide whether to allow students to revisit any question or force them to answer or skip a question without the ability to revisit. As instructors decide upon a sequence, it is valuable to vary the form of the questions and answers. They can design each question to quiz for a common concept in a different way, mix different forms of questions within the quiz, vary the way a question is posed, and change the position of the correct answer.

Timed Exams

WebCT provides the opportunity to offer quizzes for a specified period of time. The instructor can disallow answer submission if the time limit has expired. A timed exam can lessen the likelihood of cheating, help measure how rapidly students can perform a task or recall facts, and assist students in using their time effectively.

Quiz Retakes

WebCT can permit student's multiple quiz attempts. The instructor can program up to five retakes, set the retakes to "unlimited," and set the time duration between retakes for a set number of minutes, hours, or days. Students retaking quizzes are given a second chance to show mastery of the material. WebCT can score and assign a final grade on multiple attempts by using the first attempt, the latest attempt, the highest attempt, or an average of all attempts.

Selective Release of Assessments

WebCT also provides a number of other settings to control the availability and management of the assessment. The availability of the assessment can be based on a date or time or other criteria, such as user ID or grades. The selective release functionality in WebCT can be used to accommodate accessibility issues, such as longer quizzing time. Questions can be randomized within the quiz or survey so that no two students receive the same set. Access to a quiz or survey can be password protected or be released to specific computers, such as those in a quizzing center, using the IP address mask feature.

For all question types that can be autograded, WebCT allows the instructor to give feedback to the students on their response. If they give the incorrect response, the correct answer can be displayed, along with an explanation why the choice they selected is not correct.

Grading Options

Instructors also have a wide range of options for how questions are graded. For example, in matching questions, instructors can opt for three different scoring schemes: *equally weighted,* where points are equally distributed among all correct answers; *all or nothing,* where all answers must be correct to receive points for the question; or *right less wrong,* where the point value for incorrect matches is subtracted from the point value for correct matches. Use of the latter two schemes cuts down on guessing. Similarly, in multiple choice questions where the student can select more than one correct response, scoring for the question can be cumulative; that is, if some of the correct answers are selected, partial credit will be awarded, or all or nothing, meaning that all correct answers must be chosen to receive points. Allowing a negative score means that students will be penalized for guessing wrong answers by the value of the wrong answer being subtracted from the value of the correct answers.

In order to prevent answer sharing, WebCT provides the ability to present different questions within a single assessment. A question set is a group of questions from which one question is randomly selected and presented to students. Instructors can create question sets by selecting a set of questions from the repository of questions or by adding question alternates. They can then indicate the number of questions to be randomly selected from the set and presented to students.

Grading and Reporting

WebCT allows for a number of options when grading assessments. When a student submits an assessment, all responses except for questions requiring a paragraph answer are automatically graded. The grades for an assessment are automatically added to the gradebook, which saves time and effort for instructors. Instructors are also given the option to manually grade assessments. They can choose to grade assessments by student (similar to traditional paper-based marking, where the instructor views and grades the entire assessment by a student) or to grade assessments by question (where instructors see each student's answer to the same question in succession). Instructors may opt to hide students' names for anonymous grading to reduce the risk of bias. Instructors are also given the option to regrade and autograde questions. For example, instructors can choose to globally modify quiz grades, where the grade of an entire quiz, rather than just individual questions, is changed (WebCT, 2004b).

A number of reports are available to determine how well students are performing on quizzes and surveys. For quizzes, the reports can break out individual student statistics by name. Because surveys are anonymous, student names are replaced with randomly assigned numbers in survey reports.

Performance reports provide each student's answer to quiz questions and also provide statistics on which answers students selected. For example, in multiple choice questions, a breakdown is provided on how frequently each of the possible answers was selected.

Instructors can also display the performance for individual questions while comparing the performance of selected students to that of the entire class. *Item statistics reports* can be generated for the class as a whole or for all individuals in a class. Available statistics include the percent of students who answered correctly, the mean, the standard deviation, and a comparison to the whole class's performance. *Summary statistics* are similar to the item statistics report but are at the assessment level, showing the mean score either by person or by class on a particular assessment. *Class statistics* show a question by question analysis of the performance of an entire class or section on a quiz. One class value for each question is displayed for each of attempts, percent answering correctly, discrimination, mean, and standard deviation.

Assessment in WebCT involves more than just providing quizzes and exams to measure students' knowledge of the subject matter. Rather, assessment is integrated into the entire course from the beginning to the end, encompassing self-tests, graded and ungraded surveys and quizzes, and individual and collaborative assignments. Students are given immediate and developmental feedback on their assessments, and instructors are provided numerous reports to evaluate the effectiveness of the assessments. The WebCT Exemplary Course Project provides many examples of outstanding uses of the assessment capabilities of WebCT. Additional examples from selected exemplary courses and further information about the project are available at www.webct.com/exemplary.

References

Vallone, C. (2004, July). Online learning's impact on global education. *Proceedings of the Sixth Annual WebCT User Conference,* USA.

WebCT. (2001, November). Online assessment—What's good for the instructor is good for the student. *WebCT Newsletter.* Retrieved December 6, 2004, from *http://www.webct.com/service/ViewContent?contentID=8318910*

WebCT. (2002–2004). *WebCT exemplary course project.* Retrieved November 15, 2004, from *http://www.webct.com/exemplary*

WebCT. (2003). *Quizzing and assessment with WebCT.*

WebCT. (2004a). *Creating quizzes, self tests, and surveys in WebCT Vista 3.x.*

WebCT. (2004b). *Managing and evaluating assessments in WebCT Vista 3.x.*

Chapter II

Coordinating a Distance Learning Software Rollout with the Needs and Visions of a Mature Test Organization:
Political and Technical Lessons Learned

Luke Fernandez, Weber State University, USA

Abstract

As online education programs expand across the country, many universities are adopting course management software (CMS) such as Blackboard or WebCT. Although these out-of-the-box solutions may simplify the administration of online classes, they do not comprehensively meet the needs of mature testing organizations. This chapter describes the process that has led Weber State University to reconsider whether an out-of-the-box implementation of WebCT actually is a sensible strategy.

It looks at both the political and technical issues involved in choosing a test technology, examining how institutions can best balance and meet the needs of both distance-learning organizations and testing centers.

Introduction

University administrators who are contemplating or presently engaged in rolling out learning management systems (LMSs) face ponderous technological and political logistics. Weber State University is currently one year into its LMS rollout and plans on having the LMS implementation completed by the spring of 2005. In most respects, this rollout has been successful and has moved forward relatively smoothly. However, in respect to online assessments, the LMS initiative continues to experience problems. These problems have resulted from incomplete knowledge about assessment needs on the part of the organizations initiating the rollout, a lack of dialogue between the distance learning organizations and test organizations, and inchoate approaches for achieving consensus on test related issues.

This chapter elaborates on these problems, broaches the main questions that should have been tackled by the initiative in order to forward a smoother rollout, and lists some strategies that may be worth implementing in order to build consensus on assessment issues as the rollout moves into its concluding stages. In doing so, it seeks to offer a model for how other institutions may coordinate distance learning software with the needs of a mature test organization.

Background

At Weber State University, over 110,000 departmental tests are delivered each semester through a home grown, Web-enabled assessment tool. This tool has evolved over the years in close coordination with the expanding needs of Weber's testing centers and faculty. The technologies and organizational structures that deliver departmental testing at Weber State have grown in such close concert that they appear at times almost inextricably attached. The needs of the testing centers are served by the software, and the policies and practices that give expression to a testing center's identity are in turn defined by what the software can and cannot do.

Although this organic relationship has been in place for over five years, it has recently been challenged by Weber State's burgeoning, and very profitable, distance learning organization, which has purchased and begun implementing Vista-WebCT's most advanced distance learning software. The Vista product has a built-in assessment tool, and the distance learning organization has signaled that its ultimate goal has been to replace the home grown solution with the Vista product in the interest of promoting efficiency, system integration, and standardization. The WebCT product promises to realize many of these goals because:

- It provides easy session and navigational integration across the student portal and all course management tools.

- It provides easy data integration with student information systems, thereby facilitating enrollment and identity management across semesters.

- It provides standardization by dint of the fact that it is a technology that is documented and supported by an established company with a large community of users.

Sold and promoted largely on the basis that it is more capable of realizing integration, efficiency, and standardization than the technologies that have been around until now, WebCT promises much, and the groups promoting the technology on campus have worked zealously to be the handmaiden to this promise. However, after a year of use, and after more than $350,000 has been expended on training and marketing WebCT on the Weber State campus, a core set of faculty and test administrators are continuing to resist the replacement of the home grown assessment tool with the WebCT assessment technology. According to these users, the Vista assessment tools:

- Are not able to cater to the needs of testing organizations as effectively as to distance learning organizations

- Are not unequivocally superior to the assessment technologies they were meant to replace

- Will not necessarily streamline the work processes of every user group who switches to them

- Do not clearly serve the interest of every campus constituency

- Lack security features that are necessary for the delivery of so called high-stakes tests. These security features include the ability to configure a test so it is deliverable only at certain specified testing locations, the ability to prevent students from navigating around the World Wide Web while taking a test, and the ability to easily disseminate test passwords to targeted proctors.

Because so much money has been invested in promoting the WebCT product and because a vociferous contingent of users resist this promotion, a certain amount of polarization has occurred. It is difficult to establish clarity or consensus on testing issues because the technology is no longer perceived as something that resolves a problem that is common to all. Instead, it is perceived as an initiative that promotes some interests at the expense of others. When the evaluation of technology is colored by interest, as it has been at Weber State, technology assessment becomes a more challenging task. How, in the face of this challenge, can clarity and consensus be achieved?

One possible way to achieve this is to avail oneself of outside literature. After all, if internal parties are not considered disinterested, then perhaps a review and evaluation of assessment literature generated by outside parties can produce more objective perspectives. There are several repositories for this literature. Among the most obvious is Web literature published by MIT's open knowledge initiative, the IMS Global Learning Consortium, the National College Testing Association, and for profit testing companies. However, all these resources have limitations. MIT and the IMS Global Learning Consortium have been developing and promoting specifications for learning technology for a number of years. The adoption of these standards helps make learning technology more interchangeable, and these standards should be attended to when selecting or developing an assessment tool. In this chapter those needs fall under the aegis of the term *standardization*. But while modularity and interchangeability are important technical considerations, they are not the only campus needs that deserve to be considered when choosing an assessment tool.

As an organization that is chartered to focus "on issues relating to test administration, test development, test scoring, and assessment"[1] the National College Testing Association (NCTA) is also an important resource. Currently, however, the main energies of this organization are devoted to delivering and administering certification and placement exams like the LSAT, the MCAT, or Compass. The NCTA is beginning to attend to the technical and administrative challenges associated with the delivery of tests managed and created by faculty, but this subject has not been the NCTA's primary focus. Because of this, at this point they are not a repository of literature that can help a campus wisely choose an online testing technology.

In addition to these resources, some literature is published by for profit testing companies. Questionmark, for example, publishes a white paper entitled "Delivering Computerized Assessments Safely and Securely," which reviews some of the security concerns that need to be considered when choosing an assessment tool that can deliver tests securely. However, their account lacks scholarly integrity because it promotes their own software, neglects to cite competing software technologies, and overlooks important security features, including features that allow faculty to restrict test delivery to one or more test centers and those that facilitate the distribution of passwords to remote proctors. Although literature generated by for profit companies can sometimes be illuminating, its pecuniary orientation often compromises its credibility.

A review of the literature suggests that although off campus parties may cast some light on the controversies that have bedeviled Weber's LMS rollout, there doesn't appear to be a technology or body of technological information that can obviate all political difference. Online testing technology, and its associated literature, is still evolving. At this point in time, it is not so refined that it is capable of anticipating every competing testing need or transcending and eliminating the political controversies that are fueled by these competing needs. The rest of this chapter spells out some of these concerns as well as some strategies that can mitigate their more invidious effects. These concerns, which are political, technical, and procedural in nature, revolve around the need to:

- Include more voices in the rollout process
- Find technologies that scale to testing center needs

- Find technologies that ensure the secure delivery of high-stakes tests
- Develop procedures that can comprehensively identify campus testing needs and the constituencies that are associated with those needs

The technical and political challenges that arise in meeting these needs are addressed in detail in the following section.

Political and Financial Concerns

Over the course of the last eight years, more and more Weber State faculty members have been delivering their tests online at the campus testing centers and off campus through distance learning programs. As Weber State has discovered, on-campus and off-campus online testing needs may be similar, but they are not the same. Moreover, the university bureaucracies that deliver these tests are not the same, either. These differences have fueled two problems of import: What should be the relative influence of each organization in choosing a campus assessment technology, and what role should revenue play in deciding who has influence?

The Weber State testing centers bring in about $120,000 a year in fees from for fee testing services. However, no fees are charged for the departmental testing, which is delivered through the homegrown assessment software. Although this arrangement allows the costs of departmental testing to be defrayed by for fee test revenue streams, it has put the testing centers at a disadvantage vis-à-vis the distance learning organizations when exercising influence over the choice of departmental testing software. The revenue streams controlled by distance learning are far larger than those controlled by the testing center, and as a result of controlling these purse strings, the distance learning organizations have been able to exercise disproportionate influence over the choice of departmental testing software. Although 30% to 40% of departmental testing is being delivered through the testing centers, the testing centers were not accorded any formal voice when it came time to make decisions about what technology the university should use for online testing. The disproportionate influence exercised by distance learning appears to have impeded the Vista rollout because the process failed to consult key stakeholders.

The committee steering the rollout is realizing that a successful plan for moving forward with assessment technologies has a greater possibility of success when the criteria for deciding who to bring to the table is broadened. In addition to asking, "Who controls the purse strings?", the committee is beginning to ask, "Who has the most technological and managerial expertise with regard to assessment issues?" and "What organization on campus is actually delivering the bulk of online tests?"

Political and Financial Concerns: Lessons Learned

Inclusion in Rollout Strategies

Some of the problems articulated in the preceding section are undoubtedly specific to the particular constellations of organizational power that exist at Weber State. But any university that is contemplating an upgrade to their distance learning software and has mature and autonomous testing and distance learning organizations on campus may stand to benefit from Weber State's experience. On a concrete level, the needs and protocols of the distance learning organization have differed from those in the testing organizations. Although discrepancies in financial power have allowed the Vista initiative to subordinate (and almost exclude) the needs of one of these organizations, this subordination has been costly. A more effective strategy would have ensured that both organizations had been brought to the strategizing table. Even if the technological outcomes end up being the same, at the very least this approach would have been good for public relations and consensus building. It would mitigate perceptions that the initiatives are being imposed from above, that they are failing to consult with assessment experts, and that there is an intentional attempt to exclude.

Financial Strategies

Whether a test organization chooses to charge for departmental testing can have an impact on organizational influence vis-à-vis distance learning organizations. Although secure departmental testing through the testing centers may constitute a plurality of testing at Weber State, this has not given the testing organizations commensurate influence in strategizing about Weber State's future assessment technologies. It may be sensible to provide a free service to instructors and to the distance learning organizations (who have fielded a plurality of their tests through the testing centers). But testing center directors may want to make sure that the service is formally recognized by the university and accorded appropriate recognition when it comes time to make technology decisions that should fall, at least in part, under the testing center's jurisdiction.

Technical Concerns

Scalability Concerns

As test taking has grown at the campus testing centers, so too has demand on test center resources. In order to supply enough resources to meet demand, Weber State testing centers have begun to look for procedures and technologies that exact as much efficiency as possible from limited numbers of testing center personnel and limited numbers of Web-enabled computers. The quest for greater efficiency in the face of growth and the concomitant rollout of the LMS has fueled two important questions: What testing technologies adequately accommodate growing testing loads, and which ones can facilitate the types of efficiencies needed in testing centers?

On any regular given school day during the fall or spring semester, about 1,700 tests were delivered through the home grown assessment tool. However, during finals week, this number spiked to as many as 2,500 tests, of which 67% were delivered in testing centers. These spikes in demand created long lines in the testing centers as students queued up for testing terminals that were in short supply.

With exponential growth in online test taking, Weber State's most pressing concern in the last two years was to find an assessment technology that could continue to smoothly accommodate more users as testing demand increased. The pilot semester with WebCT's assessment tool did not live up to expectations, because the system actually was inoperable for a significant portion of finals week, even when assessment was confined to a small number of pilot students. However, these scalability problems have largely been solved in the home grown technology, which uses a clustered architecture, allowing more servers to be plugged into the system as loads increase. Given the resources and expertise available to WebCT, it is expected that scalability questions will eventually be resolved, even if the initial experience was not always a happy one.

It is worth bearing in mind, however, that the ability to accommodate increased load constitutes only one dimension of testing scalability. As can be seen at Weber State, the resolution of the technological bottleneck (e.g., the ability of the servers to smoothly accommodate load) has revealed a new bottleneck that is epitomized by the long student queues that form when students wait for secure testing terminals during peak demand periods. Weber has implemented or needs to implement a number of organizational and technological strategies in order to scale effectively to this problem. These strategies include the following:

- Creating flexible testing centers that can expand and contract the number of terminals that are available as demand expands and contracts throughout the semester.
- Creating integrated scheduling software that will:
  - Track how many minutes, on average, a student needs in order to take a test
  - Allow students to reserve a secure terminal for authorized tests so that they do not have to wait in lines at the testing center
  - Allow faculty members to reserve a bank of terminals for a given time period so that they can be assured that their students will be able to take the test during a given time period
  - Allow testing administrators to track and forecast test taking demand so that they act proactively

Notably, WebCT Vista does not appear to have features that cater to these needs. In some ways, this is not surprising. The WebCT software was designed primarily as a tool for delivering distance learning tests; it is not designed around the needs of a testing center.

Scalability Concerns: Lesson Learned

When the WebCT tool was initially promoted on campus, it was touted as a piece of software that could address the needs of the distance learning organization and the testing center. However, after two semesters of use a number of technological lacunae have been encountered in the product, it has not only failed to scale to very nominal testing loads, but it also has not incorporated the sort of integrated scheduling tools that are necessary for a testing center to act proactively or to use its terminals in a fashion that efficiently caters to changing demands. These features are a critical component in assessment scalability-at least if the university plans on allocating resources in as efficient and cost effective a fashion as possible. Because scheduling is not currently a component in LMS software, universities, at least for now, need to look elsewhere for technologies that can cater to the scalability needs of testing centers.

Security Concerns

Currently, the test delivery mechanisms of WebCT and Blackboard are not as secure as they could be-at least when they are not used in conjunction with technologies like Questionmark, home grown assessment tools, and/or secure browsers. This was not apparent when Weber State initially contracted with WebCT. However, when the security issue did become manifest, many parties on campus began to wonder whether the technology could be imposed wholesale on test organizations that were accustomed to delivery mechanisms that offer more security.

When WebCT came to town, it was hailed as a comprehensive solution that could address not only the needs of distance learning but those of the testing centers as well. However, two semesters of use and a gap analysis study have revealed that WebCT fails to cater to basic testing security needs. In fact, according to one WebCT representative, the WebCT assessment tool was never designed for high-stakes testing or proctored testing. To cater to these demands, a testing tool needs the following features:

- It must be able to provide a comprehensive list of passwords that a proctor administrator can access and deliver to proctors when proctor requests are received from students.
- It must be able to allow faculty members to configure tests so that they are only deliverable at specified testing locations. Moreover, these locations should be specifiable by a faculty member by selecting from a list rather than by inputting a set of IP addresses.

- It must provide an interface that an administrator can easily configure so that a test-taker is confined to the test interface. In other words, the testing utility must prevent test takers from being able to access the World Wide Web or other course content.

Security Concerns: Lesson Learned

WebCT advocates at Weber have placed a great deal of faith in the merits of outsourcing and LMSs. The general attitude was that a company as large as WebCT must have been aware of the scalability and security needs of testing organizations and that through the use of effective change management, Weber could use an out-of-box solution to meet its testing needs. The perception was that the obstacles impeding a full embrace of the WebCT solution were cultural rather than technological in origin. Although WebCT had suggested the commission of a formal gap analysis during the pilot phase, these were not encouraged, presumably because they would impede rather than inform the WebCT rollout.

However, after two semesters of use, it is becoming obvious that some of the obstacles that had been minimized by advocates should not have been. Significant security and scalability needs are not adequately addressed in the current Vista product, and glossing over them, rather than requisitioning formal gap analysis, has made it more difficult for the steering committee to strategize in as informed a fashion as possible. It also has increased the perception that the committee has failed to engage in full disclosure.

Customization Concerns (Should Pedagogy Drive Technology, or Should Technology Drive Pedagogy?)

Although LMS assessment tools are fairly flexible, faculty members are inevitably going to score and deliver tests in ways that are not accommodated in out-of-the-box solutions. The move toward generic campus-wide technology and the move away from technology that is customized and precisely fitted to testing centers have raised two questions of import: What level of customization should testing centers provide in appealing to the particular assessment needs of faculty, and what are the costs and benefits associated with this customization and how are they measured?

WebCT's Vista software, like any ERP solution, promises to centralize and integrate systems that had hitherto been decentralized. Centralization initiatives, whether they occur in the realm of politics or in the realm of information technology, are touted for a variety of reasons. These include the potential to make administration more efficient, the potential to standardize procedures, and the potential to reduce costs and to coordinate systems or organizations that had hitherto worked at cross-purposes. Although these potentials are all compelling, it is important to recognize that system and organizational integration are not always panaceas or unequivocally salutary in their effects. Put another way, if federated systems and autonomy are principles that have a place in politics, they may also have a place in the world of campus information technology and, more specifically, in the rollout of distance learning software, especially when it impacts departmental testing.

Customization Concerns: Lesson Learned

At Weber State, the tensions between initiatives that promote centralization and traditions that esteem a degree of organizational autonomy are being played out in a miniature but nonetheless illustrative scale. On one hand, the parties rushing forward with the Vista implementation argue that a "vanilla implementation" is in order and that requests for assessment features that fall out of the vanilla implementation have to go through an extended review process. This approach may seem sensible from the standpoint of administrators who want to move toward more centralized administration. But it comes at significant cost to faculty and testing organizations who, previous to the WebCT initiative, had been able to streamline work processes by getting changes made to assessment software through a relatively autonomous testing organization.

From an administrative perspective, centralization appears to be a cost-effective solution, because it means that less money needs to be spent on customized programming. But from a more comprehensive perspective, what appears as cost cutting may only be the devolution of cost. Costs that at one time were shouldered by administration are now devolved to faculty and to testing organizations, who are forced to use software that fails to expedite their business processes as effectively as more customized solutions. So far, there hasn't been a clear calculus or method for determining whether the move toward centralization is creating a situation where benefits exceed costs. Very likely, the decrease in autonomy and the ability of testing organizations to innovate and customize is merely devolving costs from administration onto faculty and the testing organizations that support them.

Procedural Concerns

In the previous two sections ("Political and Financial Concerns" and "Technical Concerns"), I highlight some of the more central constituencies that Weber State needed to include in an LMS as well as some of the more central technical needs that deserved consideration at Weber State. In retrospect, Weber's rollout would have gone much smoother had it taken care to more clearly identify campus testing needs and the constituencies associated with those needs. Weber's experience suggests that LMS rollouts are facilitated by:

*   Recognizing the critical role that testing plays in LMS technology
*   Creating comprehensive lists of a campus's testing needs

- Identifying the constituencies that are associated with those needs
- Creating a clear formula for prioritizing those needs

Other institutions are likely to have different combinations of needs and constituencies than those of Weber State. However, the procedures for mitigating the political discontent that is generated when needs are left unmet may not be so unique-in this respect, all software rollouts are the same. Needs and technical concerns should be identified, and the political challenges that may be associated with those concerns should be researched in order to gauge the import of those needs. In the references section of this chapter, I include a Web citation that links to a spreadsheet (Fernandez, 2004b). This spreadsheet enumerates Weber's testing needs as well as the Weber constituencies that are associated with those needs. Institutions that are interested in implementing some of the procedures enumerated may find this spreadsheet to be a helpful tool.

Conclusion

Weber State's move toward WebCT's Vista product was initiated because it promised to integrate disparate e-learning systems. Theoretically, this system would be easier to administer and would be more intuitive for faculty to use. In many ways these promises have been realized by the pilot rollout. Administration is significantly easier, course design and teaching are simpler, and students can navigate between course content and teaching tools more seamlessly than they could when these utilities were served by disparate technologies. Long term, these trends should contribute to better distance learning.

Although the rollout promises significant advantages in most respects, there are significant problems in using a vanilla implementation of WebCT's assessment technology. This area of the product:

- Doesn't allow faculty members to easily configure their tests so that they are available only at selected testing centers
- Cannot deliver closed-book tests in an effective fashion
- Does not allow proctors to easily access passwords that they need for administering tests

Although Weber State test organizations were aware of most of the technological problems in the WebCT product from very early on, this expertise could not be effectively conveyed to the steering committee because the test organizations did not have any formal representation. The testing organizations may have been marginalized because they were not seen as a party that added significant revenue streams to the university. But given that they deliver more than 40% of Weber's online tests (and sometimes up to 70%), they are a significant stakeholder in any initiative attempting to move the campus toward a particular Web-based assessment solution.

Other universities may not have the same organizational constellations that Weber State has,[2] nor may they be interested in rolling out WebCT's Vista product. Nevertheless, general lessons can be culled from the Weber State experience. The successful rollout of distance learning software depends on informed decision making and consensus building. To forward these ends, distance learning initiatives should consider very carefully whether it is sensible to marginalize testing organizations from the decision making process or whether the political and technical concerns raised here need greater consideration during an LMS initiative. Perhaps, in some future iteration, LMS technology will come closer to comprehensively meeting all testing needs on campus. Until that time arrives, administrators may be able to profit from the political and technical strategies that have been elaborated herein.

References

Fernandez, L. (2004a). *NCTA departmental testing survey*. Retrieved July, 2004, from *http://chitester1.weber.edu/misc/DTSR/Survey%20description.htm*

Fernandez, L. (2004b). *Needs spreadsheet*. Retrieved July, 2004, from *http://chitester1.weber.edu/misc/DTSR/Needs_vf.xls*

Shepherd, E., Kleeman, J., Phaup, J., Fair, K., & Martin, B. (2003). *Delivering computerized assessments safely and securely*. Retrieved July, 2004, from *http://www.questionmark.com/us/whitepapers/index.htm*

Endnotes

[1] Quoted from the main page of the National College Testing Association Web site: http://www.ncta-testing.org

[2] Results from a recent poll of National Collegiate Test Association members indicate that only a very small portion (i.e., less than 5%) of NCTA test centers deliver more than 5,000 online departmental tests per semester. More than half the centers deliver fewer than 100 online departmental tests per semester, which suggests that departmental and high-stakes online testing is hardly even a peripheral activity at many testing centers (Fernandez, 2004a). Given these numbers, Weber State is in a minority. However, online testing is growing. Weber's experiences may indicate where other schools will be going.

Chapter III

Assessing the Relationship between Learner Satisfaction and Faculty Participation in Online Course Discussions

Dana Offerman, Capella University, USA

Kimberly Pearce, Capella University, USA

Christopher Tassava, Capella University, USA

Abstract

Faculty-student interaction in online courses heightens student satisfaction and success. Capella University studied the relationship between learner satisfaction with faculty (as reported in end-of-course evaluations) and faculty participation in online courses (as measured by monitoring faculty interaction). Learners appear to be more responsive in courses led by instructors who seem committed to learner success and dedicated to improving learner engagement with the subject matter and other learners. Some instructor behaviors, including certain messages and feedback on assignments, improved overall learner satisfaction. However, these faculty behaviors did not improve other learner perceptions, such as increased professional value. Instructor-learner interaction with respect to projects and course content may be more important to learner satisfaction and realization of professional value than other kinds of faculty-student interaction.

Introduction

Most online courses are highly dependent upon frequent interaction—often in the form of threaded discussions between students and faculty. Research suggests that faculty interaction with students in an online course is an indicator of student satisfaction and success, as well as a means to overcome the inherent sense of isolation that can characterize online learning and teaching. Therefore, online courses are developed to emphasize recurrent interaction between faculty and students and between students in an attempt to emulate the dialogue that occurs in a conventional classroom. However, our ability to assess the value of these discussions to student learning (both perceived and actual) has been problematic.

This chapter provides a case study of Capella University's attempt to understand the relationship between learners' self-reported satisfaction levels and actual measurements of faculty participation in online courses. This study addressed several issues crucial to online assessment, including the development of standards and methods for measuring both the quantity and quality of faculty-to-learner interaction in online courses, the obstacles to effective measurement of faculty-to-learner interaction, and the application of the results of online measurement to ongoing faculty development and to setting performance expectations for faculty. The results of Capella's investigation promise to shed light on the qualitative measures of online interaction, furthering that literature and complementing the larger literature on quantitative measures.

The chapter begins with a discussion of some of the relevant literature on interaction within online courses and explains how the theoretical framework of this literature has influenced Capella University's online course development model and faculty expectations. The chapter then discusses two aspects of an attempt to understand learner satisfaction with online interaction: Capella's Faculty Development Feedback System (FDFS) and an internal Capella study on the relationship between the faculty feedback and learner satisfaction (as measured by course evaluations). The chapter concludes with an analysis of the assessment project, a description of actions taken as a result of the research, and a summary of implications for further research, institutional practice, and instructional design.

Founded in 1993, Capella University presently enrolls over 12,900 adult learners and offers bachelor's, master's, and doctoral degrees as well as certificate programs in five schools: Business & Technology, Education, Human Services, Undergraduate Studies and Psychology. In 1997, Capella was accredited by the Higher Learning Commission of the North Central Association of Colleges and Schools. Since 2000, the university has maintained its accreditation with the commission through the Academic Quality Improvement Program, a continuous quality improvement approach to reaccreditation.

As of April 2005, the university's active enrollment comprised:

- 15% undergraduate learners
- 39% master's learners
- 45% doctoral learners
- 1% nondegree certificate learners

Demographics of Capella learners include the following:

- 86% are part-time
- 61% are female
- 97% are at least 25 years of age, with the average age being 40 years old
- 68% receive financial aid
- 33% of all learners are persons of color

Capella has 760 faculty members, 15% of whom are *core faculty,* meaning that they are full-time, salaried employees of the university with both instructional and administrative responsibilities. The remaining 85% of the faculty are *adjuncts*—independent contractors who serve as instructors in the "courseroom" (Capella's name for the online course environment), who act as dissertation mentors and committee members, and who develop new courses. Seventy-five percent of all faculty members have earned doctorates.

Capella's online courses are developed collaboratively by faculty and instructional designers. In the first phase of this process, subject-matter experts drawn from the core and adjunct faculty conceptualize course content, identify course objectives, and align those objectives with program objectives. Faculty select appropriate course materials and resources for the course media center; write requirements, including weekly discussion questions, for weekly learning units and for the course as a whole; and develop rubrics to assess course assignments. In the second phase of the course development process, instructional designers—specially trained curricular and technical specialists—work with faculty course developers to apply sound instructional design principles to the courses, assure that the courses adhere to Capella's pedagogical model, edit the content and check technical features such as hyperlinks, and provide specialized services such as graphic arts, Web design, and audiovisual resources.

After school administrators approve a developed course, qualified instructors—including an experienced lead instructor—are assigned, and the course is opened to enrollment. Instructors teaching individual sections adhere to the preset course schedule and conduct the course by using the prepared discussion questions, assignments, and due dates. Changes to discussion questions or assignments must be approved by core faculty. Capella maintains this administrative control over course structure to ensure that all learners have a consistent experience, regardless of section or instructor. Instructors do enjoy flexibility in that they can post new content to evolving discussions. In addition, any instructor can suggest a course change to the lead instructor, who evaluates the change, decides whether to implement the change, and assures that the change is made in subsequent course revisions.

This course production system works very effectively to develop and launch completely new courses and to revise existing courses. In both cases, the system helps Capella address internal and external issues, such as the need to develop clear course competencies aligned with program outcomes, demands for programs or courses to meet emerging or new standards, and so forth.

Essential to Capella's course delivery process are faculty development activities, which continuously train faculty members for online instruction. The faculty development system is directed by staff in the office of the provost. Three sequential courses orient and train faculty members for their numerous roles: performing online instruction, acting as mentors to doctoral learners, and serving on comprehensive examinations and dissertation committees. The faculty development courses culminate with a weeks-long shadowing experience, in which a novice faculty member observes a seasoned instructor in an actual online course. Shadowing is the final step before a new faculty member is approved to serve as an online instructor. However, faculty development activity does not cease after initial training and shadowing. Working together online, face-to-face, in conference calls, and via e-mail correspondence, both core and adjunct faculty share best practices, discuss important issues, update each other on current activities, and build a coherent Capella faculty community. This work complements and extends the faculty development courses themselves. Capella ensures that active instructors continue to receive useful feedback from learners and fellow faculty members alike. Capella's FDFS was developed to assess the success of instructors in the courses.

Capella's Learning Model: Theoretical and Philosophical Basis

Both the course development and faculty development systems rest on Capella's commitment to a learner-centered model of instruction that is informed by best practices in adult learning theory and andragogy (Brookfield, 1986; Cross, 1981; Hase & Kenyon, 2000; Knowles, 1980; Merriam, 1993). For instance, Knowles's theory, which has particular import for Capella, contends that adult learners display the following characteristics:

a.   They are self-directed and expected to take responsibility for decisions.

b.   They need to know why they are expected to learn something.

c.   They need to learn experientially.

d.   They approach learning as problem solving.

e.   They learn best when the topic is of immediate value.

As Capella applies these characteristics of andragogy to its adult learning programs, the focus of instruction has shifted from theoretical *content* to *process* and *practical application*. Process is emphasized through threaded discussion; practical application of content is emphasized through course assignments that frequently include case studies, applied projects, and learner self-assessment. The andragogy model also has implications for the role of faculty in an online course: it shifts an instructor's responsibilities from lecturing or grading to facilitating discussion or serving as a resource. The instructor-as-facilitator role is also consistent with andragogical principles regarding adults' need to be invested in their own learning and self-directed, instead of being directed by faculty (Brookfield, 1986).

As Capella has continued to refine its learning model, the university has recently incorporated the scholar-practitioner concepts developed by Ernest Boyer (1990) and Donald Schon (1987). Capella's learning model guides the philosophies and activities of both learners and faculty. Learners are placed on a continuum of learning experience that demonstrates their development and growth as reflective practitioners at the certificate and baccalaureate levels, as practitioner-scholars at the master's and MBA levels, and as scholar-practitioners in doctoral programs:

> *Capella's scholar-practitioner model includes the recognition that learners bring valuable life knowledge and experience to their programs and course work. Capella builds on that experience by facilitating the creation of communities of learners and providing regular opportunities for collaborative work, learners with peers as well as learners with faculty. The scholar-practitioner framework reinforces the idea that learners in all programs move along the same continuum, with their instructors, helping to build a sense of community as well as fostering a commitment to lifelong learning.* (Capella University, 2004, p. 6)

Capella has endeavored to incorporate these learner-centered and adult-centered models into its course design and expectations for faculty and learners in the courseroom. A key feature of the course model is interaction between learners and instructors and among learners. Research suggests that high-quality faculty interaction is a key indicator of learner satisfaction and success (Paloff & Pratt, 2001; Rossman, 2000; Swan, 2002). Holmberg (1995) postulated a theory of distance education that values explicit interaction personally involving the student, occurring continuously, and emulating a didactic conversation. Bischoff (2000) suggests that instructor visibility in course interaction is key to student satisfaction and success. The research of Palloff and Pratt (2003) asserts that interaction in the online course is critical to building a learning community. Muilenburg and Berg (2000) promote teaching strategies in the online classroom that promote critical thinking within a constructivist framework. They assert that online instructors must carefully attend to discussion questions to facilitate high-quality online threaded discussions.

Issues and Problems: Assessing Faculty Feedback and Learner Satisfaction

Borrowing from the literature of adult learning theory and interaction in online courses, Capella has placed significant emphasis on threaded discussions in the courseroom, striving to emulate a dialogic, or even Socratic, learning environment within each online course. This model emulates the traditional course or classroom in that it aims to encourage faculty to engage in intellectually stimulating, Socratic dialogue with students. Capella's approach, to date, is consistent with the adaptation of new technologies in other spheres; that is, Capella has preserved aspects of older technologies, such as presentation software or scholarly journal databases, and adapted them to the online environment. However, this approach has resulted in a significant reliance on labor-intensive discussion, which poses at least three key problems for Capella. First, it is difficult to extend the discussion system to many learners at once, so course enrollment limits are kept low to assure appropriate learner-faculty ratios. Second, it is difficult to monitor discussions by using criteria beyond the frequency of postings or the postings' conformance to preset expectations. Third, it is difficult to judge the perceived value of the discussions to learners. These three problems have only become more pronounced as Capella has rapidly increased its enrollment.

The results of Capella's end-of-course evaluation surveys, which ask learners to report their degree of satisfaction with learner-faculty and learner-learner interaction, highlight the problems identified above. In spite of the emphasis that Capella has placed on discussion, evaluations indicated a degree of learner dissatisfaction with the interaction between learner and faculty. Responding to this dissatisfaction, in 2003 Capella initiated the FDFS, a program intended to improve the quantity and quality of faculty-learner feedback and of interaction in the weekly threaded discussions. Given that andragogic theory considers faculty feedback a key factor in learners' satisfaction with their learning experience, the FDFS was designed to evaluate instructors' contributions to the learning experience by assessing the quality of their feedback to learners in the courseroom. Specifically, the FDFS gathered data about current faculty interaction in the courseroom; developed data-supported, school-specific best practices for faculty; and created a faculty development program to implement those best practices.

The FDFS used both quantitative and qualitative measures to assess faculty feedback. The quantitative expectation was that faculty would post at least one useful, content-related message per learner each week, as well as one supportive message. Capella course monitors audited online course discussions, assessing the quality of instructor postings and categorizing them into six main types, according to a taxonomy developed through research conducted by Blignaut and Trollip (2003):

- Content-Related
  - **Informational:** Provides content-related information

- **Corrective:** Corrects a misconception or incorrect position
- **Socratic:** Elicits further thought and postings from the learner
- Noncontent-Related
  - **Administrative:** Furnishes information about course structure, logistics, and so forth
  - **Affective:** Provides the learner support
  - **Other:** Adds thoughts-of-the-day, quotations, and so on that are unrelated to the course

The FDFS included additional assessments by the monitors of the professional and personal tone used by instructors, instructors' presence in the courseroom, and the timeliness of instructors' responses to learner postings, as indicated by the number of different days in which instructor postings appeared in a given week. The executive directors of Capella's five schools used the FDFS monitors' weekly reports for faculty development and training.

In addition to this monitoring activity, end-of-course evaluations (EOCE) were used to ascertain learners' perceptions and actual experiences with their courses and instructors. On Capella's EOCE, overall learner satisfaction is measured by at least two items and can be inferred from open-ended comments. Instructor evaluation is measured by seven items and can also be inferred from open-ended comments. Analysis suggested that the results of the end-of-course evaluations did not always align with the analysis provided by the FDFS courseroom monitors. Therefore, a research project was undertaken to systematically analyze the relationship between the FDFS and learner satisfaction via end-of-course evaluations. The project asked three questions:

1. Does a relationship exist between instructor behaviors as measured by the FDFS and learner satisfaction as measured by the EOCE?
2. What instructor behaviors are most significantly related to student satisfaction?
3. What is the relationship between the FDFS monitors' findings and the qualitative and quantitative results of the EOCE?

The results of this study provide a case study of one university's attempt to combine online assessment, faculty development, and learner satisfaction to achieve its desired outcomes. The study sample included 193 course sections from Spring Quarter 2003 (April-June), which had both a minimum of 6 weeks of FDFS data and end-of-course evaluations. Course section size ranged from 3 to 23 learners, with an average enrollment of approximately 17 learners per section. End-of-course evaluations were returned at a rate that ranged from 1 to 22 per section, with an average of 9.36 responses per section. The most meaningful results were those derived from the aggregated, university-wide analyses. (School-based analyses were conducted but failed to yield significantly different results from the aggregate analyses.)

The study examined variables drawn from the Faculty Development Feedback System and from the EOCE. The FDFS assessed four key variables:

- **Instructor presence:** measured by the number of days per week that the instructor was in the courseroom
- **Content messages:** measured by the number of Socratic, corrective, and informative messages the instructor posted each week
- **Noncontent messages:** measured by the number of administrative, affective, and other messages posted each week (a single post in the course can include both content and noncontent messages)
- **Course indicator rating:** the monitor's binary rating of a number of weighted items and the presence or absence of a professional and personal tone in the instructors' responses to learners

The EOCE measured six key variables on a Likert scale running from 1 (strongly disagree) to 5 (strongly agree):

- The instructor encouraged learners to express their own ideas.
- The instructor showed respect for learners.
- The instructor showed commitment to learner progress.
- I [the learner] was frequently engaged in interactions with the instructor and other learners in this course.
- I [the learner] was challenged to think critically about subject matter of this course.
- As a result of what I [the learner] learned from this course, I believe my value as a professional increased.

Learners were also asked two other questions: "How would you rate the course overall?" (responses used a 1 to 5 point Likert scale where 1 = poor and 5 = excellent) and "About how many hours per week do you typically spend engaged in the course?"

Descriptive statistics were used to characterize the FDFS and EOCE results prior to the relationship testing. Scatterplots drawn for the relationships to be tested indicated linear relationships did not exist between variables. However, the exploratory nature of this formative research justified the relationship testing despite the lack of a linear relationship. Because both the FDFS and the EOCE have a noninterval, limited response range, Spearman-ranked correlations were run to measure the strength and direction of relationships between the FDFS and EOCE variables listed previously in this section. Additionally, a sample of comments in the EOCE were examined for content and consistency with overall course satisfaction ratings.

Findings and Results

The FDFS results, which essentially measured the quantity and quality of instructors' courseroom activity, indicated the following:

1. On average, instructors exceeded the faculty development guidelines for number of days in the courseroom.
2. On average, faculty met the expectation for one supportive (noncontent) message per learner per week.
3. On average, expectations on the number of content messages (Socratic, informative, and corrective) were not met.

The EOCE results showed that:

1. The average overall course rating was 4.36 on a scale of 1 to 5.
2. Average ratings on individual items were high, ranging from 4.0 to 4.93 on a scale of 1 to 5.
3. Learners spent an average of 15.79 hours per week on course work, with an average range of 8.08 to 34.67 hours per week.

Spearman correlation coefficients were used to measure the strength and direction of relationships between the FDFS and EOCE variables. Statistically significant, positive relationships existed between several variables at $p \leq .05$. However, as Table 1 shows, scores ranged from $r = 0.0142$ to $r = 0.317$, indicating relatively weak relationships. Although statistical significance was achieved for several relationships, the practical significance is limited because, at best, only 10% of the variance can be predicted.

Judging by comments submitted in end-of-course evaluations, learners appeared to be generally satisfied with their courses, but a lack of instructor feedback emerged as a theme across all sections and all schools. Most such comments related to the lack of feedback on assignments; many learners also indicated that instructors needed to be more involved, interactive, and responsive in the online course.

In sum, the analysis of the FDFS and EOCE appears to demonstrate that instructors who are present in the courseroom, interacting with learners through messages that support learner engagement and critical thinking, are more likely to have learners who actively participate in discussions. Moreover, these instructors are more likely to be rated as respectful of learners and committed to learning. Specifically, analysis of FDFS and EOCE reveals the following:

1. Learners indicated they are generally satisfied with their courses.
2. Affective messages had a significant and positive, although weak, relationship to learner participation and to learner perceptions of instructor respect for, and commitment to, learners and learning.

Table 1. Statistically significant correlations between FDFS and EOCE

End-of-Course Evaluation Item	Instructor Presence	Content (clustered)	Content			Non-content (clustered)	Noncontent			Course "indicator"
			S	I	C		AF	AD	O	
The instructor encouraged learners to express their own ideas.						*	*			
The instructor showed respect for learners.						*	*			
The instructor showed commitment to learner progress.		*				*	*			
I was frequently engaged in interactions with the instructor and other learners in this course.	*		*			*	*			
I was challenged to think critically about subject matter of this course.			*							
About how many hours per week do you spend typically engaged in this course?										
How would you rate the course overall?										*
As a result of what I learned from this course, I believe my value as a professional increased.										

Legend

Instructor presence: measured by number of days per week the instructor was in the courseroom

Content messages: measured by the number of Socratic, corrective, and informative messages posted each week.

(S) Socratic messages: elicit further thought and postings from the learner

(I) Informative messages: provide content-related information to the learner

(C) Corrective messages: correct a misconception or incorrect position

Noncontent messages: measured by the number of administrative, affective, and "other" messages posted each week.

(AF) Affective messages: provide psychological support for the learner

(AD) Administrative messages: provide technical or administrative information

(O) Other messages: provide content that did not fit in one of the other categories

The course "indicator" subjectively rates the number of weighted messages posted and presence or absence of professional conduct and personalized responses to learners.

Note: *Asterisks indicate areas where a statistically significant relationship (p = 0.05) existed.

3. Content-related messages had a statistically significant and positive, although weak, relationship to learner ratings of instructor commitment to learning.

4. Socratic messages had a statistically significant and positive, although weak, relationship to learner participation and critical thinking.

5. Learner course ratings appeared to correspond with instructor indicator ratings (subjectively based on messages and instructor tone).

6. Informative and corrective messages had no statistically significant relationship to learners' perceived increase in professional value.

7. Learners generally believed that instructors provided insufficient feedback to assignments and discussions and generally provided too little interaction and responses in the courseroom.

8. Specific types of messages did not appear to relate to overall learner course ratings, but the FDFS monitors' course indicators (subjectively based on messages and instructor tone) did seem to parallel learners' course satisfaction.

Study Conclusions

Learners appear more responsive in courses led by instructors who are supportive, encouraging, committed to learner success, and dedicated to prompting learners to improve their engagement with the subject matter, with the instructor, and with other learners. Socratic messages are related to learner engagement, but these messages do not seem to enhance the application of knowledge in ways that relate to learners' perceptions of improvements to their own professional value. An analysis of learner comments on the EOCE revealed that learners wanted more feedback on their assignments, a point not captured from the FDFS.

Capella found only a tenuous relationship between the FDFS and the EOCE, probably because the two tools used different indicators of performance to measure different aspects of the learning experience. Despite these differences, analysis of these two data sources did reveal that positive, although relatively weak, relationships existed between instructor behaviors (as assessed in the FDFS) and learner satisfaction (as assessed in the EOCE). Specific instructor behaviors that related positively to learner satisfaction included the number of days in the courseroom, the number of Socratic messages, and the number of affective messages to learners.

The results of this study were generally interpreted by Capella University to mean that the FDFS system had the potential to influence faculty development and learner satisfaction in three ways. First, the FDFS system provides a useful means to anticipate certain aspects of learner satisfaction. Second, the FDFS system measures instructors' courseroom behaviors. Third, the FDFS system provides faculty leaders with the information necessary to both develop those faculty who did not meet expectations and to acknowledge faculty who meet or exceed expectations. Capella confirmed that Socratic and affective messages related to learners' satisfaction with courseroom interaction, engagement, and critical thinking. Capella also confirmed that a key indicator of learner satisfaction was instructor feedback on assignments, a point that neither the FDFS nor the EOCE captured quantitatively. The study showed that the FDFS was not always used to its full extent, meaning that incomplete data limited its utility for faculty development and courseroom monitoring. (Data were incomplete because resource limitations precluded having faculty monitors in each course and section.) Finally, the relative lack of statistically significant relationships affected debates within Capella about the efficacy of the FDFS methods to capture data, the categories used to define message types, and the methodology used by monitors to assign a message to a certain category. Staff and faculty who had argued against the FDFS were led to further question its utility.

Although the results and conclusions of this study were mixed, the study did encourage the Provost's Office to continue using the FDFS within a limited scope. After some changes, the system is now considered a fairly reliable tool for quantitatively measuring instructors' courseroom activity. For instance, the subjective categorizing of messages as Socratic or affective has been eliminated. FDFS monitors now calculate the average number of postings per learner by counting the number of postings per unit, instructor days in the courseroom, and the number of active learners. Monitors also record the distribution of assignment and discussion participation grades. Additionally, faculty members now receive explicit guidelines as to the amount of time they should take to assess assignments and provide assignment feedback to learners. Monitors will be aware of these explicit guidelines when Capella expands its course management system in the near future.

This study indicated that no relationship exists between the use of Socratic discussion in online courses and learners' perceptions of the application of their new knowledge in their professional lives. The behaviors of faculty in the course—or at least those behaviors that resulted in high marks for Socratic discussion—were not related to learner perceptions of increased professional value. This indicates that learner needs predicted by adult learning theory—especially those needs related to immediate, practical application of new knowledge—were not being met through online discussions that emphasize Socratic interaction. In place of this Socratic method, it appears that learner satisfaction and realization of professional value may be more closely related to instructor feedback and interaction on learners' individual projects, application, and interaction with course content.

Future Trends

This study suggests that Capella University should continue to reexamine several assumptions about the widely accepted practice of highly interactive, faculty-facilitated, threaded discussions.

First, Capella must explore the study's implications for faculty expectations, roles, and development. Thus far in Capella's history, faculty have chiefly worked as facilitators of online discussions, but this study indicates that this role is not necessarily key to learner satisfaction. What role, then, should faculty play in online courses? On what basis should the university develop reasonable expectations regarding faculty performance? How would these expectations be articulated for faculty, and how would faculty members' fulfillment of those expectations be evaluated?

Second, Capella must explore the study's implications for instructional design, especially with respect to learner interaction with both faculty and content. Threaded discussions are completely dependent on text, the written word. Yet as John Seely Brown and Paul Duguid have argued, contemporary literacy requires the comprehension and manipulation of images or other nontextual symbols, often on computer screens, as well as traditional reading and writing skills:

> *The value of the Net doesn't simply lie in the way it allows groups of people to talk with one another. It also comes from the way that, unlike telephones or video links, the Net can provide common objects for participants to observe, manipulate, and discuss. It's not, then, simply a medium for conversation, nor is it just a delivery mechanism. It combines both, providing a medium for conversation* and *for circulating digital objects.* (1995, n.p.)

How can Capella and other institutions develop courses that enable both meaningful conversation and fruitful circulation of materials and that challenge learners to hone a full range of learning skills? Carol Twigg (2002) has advocated the redesign of courses to account for the fact that improvements in learning outcomes and retention rates seem to have more to do with learner interaction with content than learner interaction with full-time faculty. An institution's success in a digital environment may rest on its capability to develop courses that emphasize learner interaction with content.

Third, Capella must explore the study's implications for calibrating its learning model for its various degree levels. After all, faculty-learner, learner-learner, and learner-content interaction patterns differ widely at the bachelor's, master's, and doctoral levels. Capella began as a graduate institution, and the current learning model is highly dependent upon assumptions grounded in graduate (especially doctoral) education. However, because Capella plans to significantly increase its bachelor's degree enrollments, it must apply the learner-content interaction models proposed by Twigg and others to undergraduate students, especially in general education courses.

Conclusion

Issues and questions surrounding faculty interaction and feedback in online courses will continue to be explored and refined as Capella's thinking and knowledge about online teaching and learning evolve. Assessment and evaluation of the faculty's role in the online courses will continue to provide meaningful data and feedback as we define and redefine a model for faculty feedback that is robust, meets the needs of learners, and meets the needs of the institution for meaningful assessment.

References

Bischoff, A. (2000). The elements of effective online teaching. In K. W. White & B. H. Weight (Eds.), *The online teaching guide. A handbook of attitudes, strategies, and techniques for the virtual classroom* (pp. 57–72). Boston: Allyn and Bacon.

Blignaut, S., & Trollip, S. R. (2003). Developing a taxonomy of faculty participation in asynchronous learning environments—An exploratory investigation. *Computers & Education, 41*(2), 149–172.

Boyer, E. (1990). *Scholarship reconsidered—Priorities of the professoriate.* Princeton, NJ: The Carnegie Foundation for the Advancement of Learning.

Brookfield, S. D. (1986). *Understanding and facilitating adult learning.* San Francisco: Jossey-Bass.

Brown, J. S., & Duguid, P. (1995). *Universities in the digital age.* Retrieved May 25, 2004, from *http://www2.parc.com/ops/members/brown/papers/university.html*

Capella University. (2004). *Capella University's learning model.* Unpublished manuscript.

Cross, K. P. (1981). *Adults as learners.* San Francisco: Jossey-Bass.

Hase, S., & Kenyon, C. (2000). *From andragogy to heutagogy.* Retrieved January 14, 2003, from the UltiBASE Articles database.

Holmberg, B. (1995). *Theory and practice of distance education* (2nd ed.). New York: Routledge.

Knowles, M. S. (1980). *The modern practice of adult education: From pedagogy to andragogy* (2nd ed.). Chicago: Association Press/Follet.

Merriam, S. (Ed.). (1993). *An update on adult learning theory: New directions for adult and continuing education.* San Francisco: Jossey-Bass.

Muilenburg, L., & Berg, Z. L. (2000). *A framework for designing questions for online learning.* Retrieved May 25, 2004, from *http://www.emoderators.com/moderators/muilenburg.html*

Palloff, R., & Pratt, K. (2001). *Lessons from the cyberspace classroom: The realities of online teaching.* San Francisco: Jossey-Bass.

Palloff, R., & Pratt, K. (2003). *The virtual student: A profile and guide to working with online learners.* San Francisco: Jossey-Bass.

Rossman, M. (2000). Andragogy and distance education: Together in the new millennium. *New Horizons in Adult Education, 14*(1), 4–11.

Schon, D. (1987). *Educating the reflective practitioner.* San Francisco: Jossey-Bass.

Swan, K. (2002). Building learning communities in online courses: The importance of interaction. *Education, Communication & Information, 2*(1), 23, 27.

Twigg, C. (2002). *Rethinking the seven principles.* Retrieved June 28, 2004, from *http://www.center.rpi.edu/LForum/LM/Nov02.html*

Chapter IV

Authentic Online Assessment:
Three Case Studies in Teacher Education

Mike Keppell, The Hong Kong Institute of Education, Hong Kong

Eliza Au Kit Oi, The Hong Kong Institute of Education, Hong Kong

Ada Ma Wai Wing, The Hong Kong Institute of Education, Hong Kong

Abstract

An action research project conducted over a 12-month period focused on authentic technology-enhanced assessment. This chapter examines three case study experiences in the field of teacher education that attempted to align learning outcomes, activities, and assessment tasks in three teaching and learning modules. The modules focus on diverse content areas from creative arts (art education), information and applied technology (fashion design), and the Centre for Integrating Technology in Education (virtual learning communities).

Introduction

The Hong Kong Institute of Education (HKIEd) is a teacher education university. Within the institute there are 12 academic departments: Curriculum and Instruction, Educational Policy and Administration, Educational Psychology, Counseling and Learning Needs, Science, Social Sciences, Creative Arts, Mathematics, Information and Applied Technology, Early Childhood Education, Chinese, and English. The HKIEd:

> *Offers a range of programmes leading to the award of certificates, first degrees and postgraduate diplomas, which provide suitable preparation for a career in education and teaching in the preschool, school and vocational training sectors; and also offers a series of programmes which provide professional education and development for serving teachers in these sectors.* (Hong Kong Institute of Education, 2004b)

There are approximately 8,000 full-time and part-time students and approximately 700 nonacademic staff and 325 academic staff on campus. All modules are taught in the face-to-face mode, with some academic departments utilizing online learning to enhance teaching and learning. The HKIEd is one of the few universities in Hong Kong using the Blackboard ML Learning Management System at the Institutional level rather than just at the departmental level. These details are provided in order to illustrate the context for the learning-oriented assessment project.

The learning-oriented assessment project (LOAP) (HKIEd, 2004a) is a three year University Grants Committee (UGC)-funded project that involves collaboration among several tertiary institutions in Hong Kong. LOAP focuses on developing awareness and good practices in learning-oriented assessment in the context of higher education. The rationale for focusing on the learning aspects of assessment is fourfold: (a) Student learning is influenced by the assessments that they undertake; (b) good assessment practices offer the promise of creating the desired learning outcomes; (c) assessment has been identified both locally and internationally as a key area for tertiary educators' professional development; and (d) assessment is designated by the UGC as a focus area for the teaching and learning quality process review (TLQPR). Modeling and promoting good assessment practices will enhance the quality and culture of assessment, which has been identified as the solution to a major barrier to improving Hong Kong education. To investigate the value and benefits from learning-oriented assessment, six action-research teams were formed in order to examine core areas for improving assessment. These action-research teams comprised feedback for learning and assessment, field experience assessment, the know-want-learn (KWL) method of self-assessment, performance assessment, portfolio assessment, and technology-enhanced assessment (Hong Kong Institute of Education, 2004a).

The technology-enhanced assessment action research team consisted of four teacher-educators from four different departments: Early Childhood Education, Information and Applied Technology, Creative Arts, and the Centre for Integrating Technology in Education. Our focus over the 12-month period was to improve the use of learning-oriented assessment in four separate modules in teacher education. The focus of this chapter is on three of these modules, which were taught in the blended mode and employed some aspects of online learning. By initially examining teacher and student perceptions of technology-enhanced assessment, we hoped that we would refine our assessment, redesign our module to reflect this new assessment potential, and consequently improve teaching and learning within our three classes. A core question for our action research project focused on how technology-enhanced assessment could facilitate student learning. The project followed a process of planning, action, critical reflection, continual refining, and iteration (Stringer, 1999). The first aim of the project involved the documentation and capture of teacher conceptions of online assessment through group discussion, concept maps, audio interviews, and video interviews. Teacher conceptions of technology and assessment have a major influence on the design, teaching, and implementation of the modules as they reflect the underlying epistemological viewpoint of the individual teacher (Loughran, Mitchell, & Mitchell, 2003). By examining these teacher conceptions throughout the project, we hoped that the analysis of the concept maps and interviews would assist in the further refinement of the integrated assessment, teaching, and learning components for each module. A second aim of the project was to document student perceptions of technology-enhanced assessment through questionnaires, video interviews, and focus groups.

Eight research questions focused our attention throughout the action research project. These included the following:

1. What is technology-enhanced assessment? What is the role of technology in assessment?

2. What are the perceptions, attitudes, and practices in using technology-enhanced assessment within Hong Kong and teacher education?

3. What are the generic assessment principles applicable to all content areas? What assessment strategies are unique to specific content disciplines?

4. Does technology-enhanced assessment facilitate student learning? How does it affect the instructional and learning design of our subject?

5. What are the obstacles in using technology-enhanced assessment? How can these obstacles be addressed?

6. Can technology-enhanced assessment support the process of learning by peer assessment and self-assessment?

7. Can collaborative learning environments be facilitated with technology-enhanced assessment?

8. Does technology-enhanced assessment facilitate the development of critical thinking skills?

Part of our approach has been to clearly outline the action research by using a concept map. By clearly outlining our approach and refining the plan by making numerous iterations of the map throughout the project, our action research team was aware of the goals and the direction of the project. Figure 1 outlines this plan.

Figure 1. Concept map illustrating the action-research project on technology-enhanced assessment

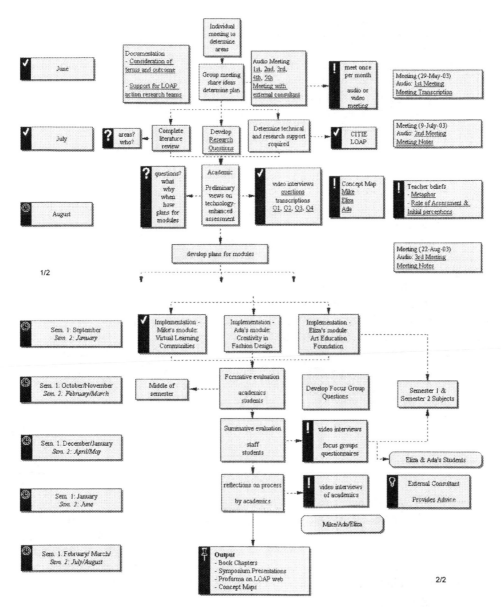

Background

Constructive Alignment

It is widely accepted that assessment must be designed to reflect course pedagogy, aims and objectives. Networked courses require the course designers to rethink the assessment strategy if it is to reflect the aims of the course and appropriately assess the skills developed during the course (Macdonald, Weller, & Mason, 2002, p. 9). As teacher-educators, we were acutely aware of the need to examine each target instructional module holistically. However, we were all surprised how focusing on the assessment resulted in a major redesign of how we taught the modules. In effect, focusing on changing the assessment to a learning-oriented approach required subsequent changes of module pedagogy, aims, and objectives. In other words, we were attempting to closely align the assessment with the teaching and learning activities so that there was constructive alignment. Biggs's (1999) model of constructive alignment represents a situation "where the learning outcomes, the teaching and learning activities and the assessment tasks are all working in unison to support student learning—the subject is then said to be constructively aligned" (Dunn, Morgan, O'Reilly, & Parry, 2004, p. 216). In essence, the Biggs instructional model suggests synergy among the curriculum, teaching methods, assessment procedures, interactions with students, and institutional climate. "Constructive alignment is a design for teaching most calculated to encourage deep engagement" of the learner with the content (Biggs, 1999, p. 31). This has been our aim throughout the action research project and has motivated us to (a) redesign our modules, (b) change our assessment to reflect this redesign, and (c) utilize online learning as a vehicle for our redesign and authentic assessment. Within this chapter the focus is on lessons learned in improving this authentic assessment (Herrington, Sparrow, & Herrington, 2000).

Authentic Assessment

The nature of authentic assessment attempts to assess learning that students may use in a real-world setting. The first case study focuses on the design of a virtual learning community. Preservice teachers need to be able to design learning environments to engage their students in realistic problem-solving contexts. Actually participating as a student in a virtual learning community (VLC) is the first step in learning about this environment. In addition students need experience in designing a VLC and obtaining feedback on the design. The second case study focuses on art education. Art teachers using digital cameras and video become more discerning evaluators of student work when they can accurately document and measure student proficiencies within this module. The third case study focuses on authentic assessment in fashion design. Home economics teachers need skills in evaluating good fashion design and being able to design in order for them to understand the added value of authentic assessment for their own students. The following model provides guidance in the development of authentic assessment. Initially we present the main features of the authentic assessment model, and in the Case Studies section we utilize this model to examine the three cases and their online application of authentic assessment. Herrington and Herrington (1998, pp. 309–310) describe seven characteristics of authentic assessment.

Context

- Requires fidelity of context to reflect the conditions under which the performance will occur, rather than contrived, artificial, or decontextualized conditions

Student's Role

- Requires the student to be an effective performer with acquired knowledge and to craft polished performances or products
- Requires significant student time and effort in collaboration with others

Authentic Activity

- Involves complex, ill-structured challenges that require judgment and a full array of tasks
- Requires the assessment to be seamlessly integrated with the activity

Indicators

- Provides multiple indicators of learning
- Achieves validity and reliability with appropriate criteria for scoring varied products

Online Learning

It comes as no surprise that online learning technology has significantly changed the landscape of teaching, learning, and assessment in the areas of electronic submissions of assignments, online collaborative assessment, and peer review of assessment tasks and items. Learning management systems such as Blackboard offer peer review of assessment by allowing students to submit work, which can be examined, analyzed, evaluated, and then returned to the student. In particular we focused our attention on some of these aspects of learning-oriented assessment in redesigning our modules. The three modules examined in this multi-case study focus on the areas of virtual learning community creation, visual art, and fashion design. Areas such as fashion design and visual design of graphics provide an avenue for peer review that can extend the collaboration, interaction, and dialogue within the online learning environment. Our online assessment focused on building online collaborative learning skills. There are two assessable components in producing the design of a virtual learning community in the form of a concept map. We can focus on assessing the *process* of collaboration and also on the collaborative *product* itself (Macdonald et al., 2002). As in all collaborative projects, there is a difficulty of recognizing and evaluating the individual contribution that needs to be addressed. Sometimes it may be best to avoid giving marks for the collaborative project and instead give marks for individual reflection on the collaborative work project (Resta, Awalt, & Menchaca, 2002).

In fact, "networking opens up possibilities for enhancing formative feedback to students through peer review, when scripts are posted electronically for comment and review" (Macdonald et al., 2002, p. 10). Other forms of online assessment include Web-based assignments, end of course assessment, reflective journals, e-portfolios, class projects, course reflections, live presentations using synchronous chat, e-readings, Web site developments, concept maps, and digital photographs. Other uses of the online learning environment involve the delivery of model exemplars, simulation, or performance environments and iterative assignment development, where students submit draft assignments for comment by peers, tutors, or lecturers before submitting their final assignment (Macdonald et al.). This process of "iterative assignment development" was utilized in the module "creating virtual learning communities." Palloff and Pratt (2003) also suggest that assessment should be learner centered, teacher directed, mutually beneficial, formative, context specific, ongoing, and firmly rooted in good practice. Many of these principles have been included in the redesign of the authentic assessment for our modules. All modules discussed in this chapter utilized continuous assessment throughout the modules.

Case Studies

The strategies have focused on redesigning the learning module and fostering learning-oriented assessment and engagement with the content area. In particular, we have attempted to examine what we did, how we changed the assessment, and what our success and issues with the initiative were.

Case Study 1: Creating Virtual Learning Communities for Primary Teaching and Learning

This module focused on creating virtual learning communities (VLCs) for primary schools with 21 in-service primary school teachers. The lecturer attempted to create two levels of community participation within the module. We attempted to create a community of practice for the class participants and the lecturer so that we could experience and participate in activities representative of a true virtual learning community. The teacher utilized a social-constructivist approach; teacher-as-coach is probably the closest metaphor to describe this role. A second level of community required the students to reflect on their primary teaching experience and attempt to develop a personalized prototype of a virtual learning community that could be implemented in their future teaching. Consequently we emphasized real-life community activities. Although this was a blended mode (i.e., online learning activities were blended with face-to-face teaching), module activities were undertaken as if they were a virtual community at a distance.

In this instance, students had two roles. One role included being a student in the class on virtual learning communities, in which they were guided in the VLC characteristics, design, student and teacher activities, and assessment and evaluation. In this role they learned about community in conjunction with the facilitator. This was a coteaching environment whereby the lecturer learned about the nature and context of teaching in Hong Kong primary schools throughout the class. Students also needed to take on the role as a teacher of primary students within the module. As the students acquired knowledge and became effective performers, they needed to draft a VLC rationale, create a VLC group concept map, develop a number of resources that they would use in the community for primary students, and then present the rationale, design, and resources to the other members of the class.

Students were asked to work in small groups for the development of the four representative assessment tasks and items. Six groups of three to four students developed the VLC on topics that they chose for primary students. The diverse topics addressed countries of the world, insects, senses, math, English writing, and verbal English. Groups of three students appeared to work best in developing the VLC. This seemed to optimize scheduling of their meetings, whether these meetings were face to face or online. The seven week module included three hours of face-to-face contact each week. Students were required to complete 72 hours of work within this period of time, including class contact. All activities selected for assessment were group based, and all activities within the class setting focused on group-based activities. Students needed to collaborate within their groups for the seven week class. The module emphasized a social-constructivist perspective, and students interacted extensively in their virtual group area within the Blackboard online assessment learning environment.

The module focused on an authentic activity in which small groups needed to design a prototype of a virtual community for learning or teaching relevant content and skills for primary education. The rationale for collaboration mechanisms used needed to be justified and the roles of learner and teacher explained. The general activities initiated by the lecturer were ill structured and required the students in their small group to negotiate, debate, and determine the best creative solutions for the development of the VLC for the proposed audience and content area. However, group assessment activities do not always turn out as expected. Sometimes members do not contribute equally, which causes some tension within the group. "A challenge in online collaborative learning teams is assuring that all members of the virtual learning team are actively engaged and contributing to the work of the team" (Resta et al., 2002, p. 682). The following provides an outline of the main assessment tasks and the guiding criteria for each assessment item.

1. A two to three page rationale for design, student interaction, and teacher interaction should be outlined for the proposed topic.

    • Why have you chosen this topic?

    • Why is it a good topic for creating a VLC?

    • What will the student learn in your community?

    • How will the teacher assist the student to learn in your community?

    • What important concepts in the readings are relevant to your community?

2. Create a concept map outlining the design framework for the virtual learning community.

    • Use the electronic notes function within the concept mapping software to annotate your design, that is, to provide additional information about the design.

    • Create hyperlinks to other concept maps if more detail is required.

    • Include links to photos, audio, video, and other Web sites if appropriate.

3. Create a prototype VLC. It should include:

    • Topic or focus (written for the students).

    • Resources (readings, Web sites, photos, video, audio).

    • Three to five questions for discussion by the students.

    • Dialogue between the design team group members on the three to five questions.

    • Choose among PowerPoint, Webpages, Flash, and other software to develop the resources.

    • The community must reside within the group section of Blackboard.

In addition, groups had to make a 30 minute presentation to the rest of the class on their topic and explain the rationale, show the concept map, and outline the predominant activities for the VLC.

The assessment and activities were closely aligned in the face-to-face and online classes. During each face-to-face class, one hour was devoted to working on the group projects. This meant that activities and the teaching and learning were seamlessly integrated. It was difficult to distinguish the content from the activities and the assessment. As a facilitator, the lecturer's role was to provide regular feedback to the students throughout the class. At several points the lecturer provided specific written feedback to each group and also general written feedback to all groups about the project work tasks. There were multiple indicators of learning, which focused on a conceptual paper, visual concept map, creative prototypes, oral presentations, and participation in a discussion forum. These provided a diversity of assessment tasks. On reflection, an assessment rubric for each assessable element, including a rubric for the discussion forum, would have improved the module (Palloff & Pratt, 2003). Student feedback was positive about the approach to the class and the assessment. (Italics in the remainder of this chapter present actual student evaluation results).

Figure 2. VLC concept map and group dialogue within the Blackboard learning management system

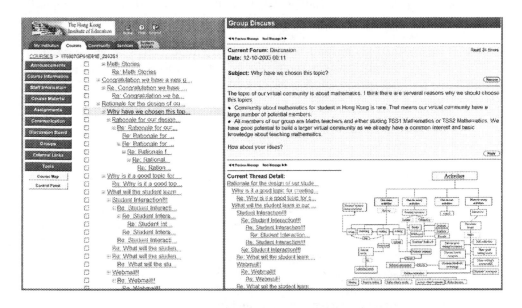

I think this course helps me to understand virtual community a lot. In the course, we have actually formed a virtual community. We have used a lot of features in virtual community to communicate. For example, we have used discussion board, file exchange system, the roster, and chat room. We have also experienced some modes of virtual communication in the course, like one-to-one, one-to-many, many-to-many, and so forth.

By the end of the group project I should be able to gain some experience in the planning and creating a virtual community which I can make use of in the future. In addition, the project helps to encourage us in thinking about more innovative ideas for creating an interesting and motivating atmosphere for students to learn.

It would be great if our school could support this kind of learning environment in various subjects. Using VLC may help students to develop many skills for life-long learning, such as searching skill, communication skill, and IT skill.

Case Study 2: Art Education Foundation

The Art Education Foundation learning module introduces the historical, social, cultural and psychological underpinnings of art education. It allows students to understand why some ideas in today's art education are valued, how the field of education relates to students' holistic learning, how it reflects their cultural context, and how it has been defined as a result of consideration of important social issues. The critical issue is how teacher-educators can address the complexity of theories to a group of first year preservice teachers. Having taught the learning module for the previous 2 years, the lecturer realized that direct teaching had a relatively small impact on students as the theories presented were often presented as a given. The body of knowledge was predetermined by the lecturer and became the curriculum that was delivered. The assessments were designed to determine whether the theories could be applied in practice. The art education module was thus redesigned to utilize authentic assessment strategies.

Use of Tasks

A combination of formative assessment tasks was used in the module. Regarding formative assessment tasks, preservice teachers were asked to use the discussion board in the online learning platform to share their metaphors and models for teaching and to respond to assigned readings, problem-based learning cases, and presentations. Regarding group assessment tasks, each group (five students) prepared two presentations on resolving the learning issues identified in the problem-based learning cases. An individual task involved each participant submitting an essay on the feasibility of integrating visual culture into a school-based curriculum.

> We felt less pressured, it's just like studying for interest, so I like this kind of formative assessment.
>
> I think whether we use similar assessment strategy depends heavily on what support we could get. But I will use the paper-based formative assessment if I don't have sufficient resources to do it online because I want my students to enjoy the advantages of formative assessment that we have mentioned before.

Learning Management System

First, the preservice teachers were asked to submit personal reflections and responses to the assigned readings, cases for problem-based learning on the discussion board of the online Blackboard learning management system (LMS). As the preservice teachers received responses from their peers, they could make changes in their initial writing as the learning module progressed. The reflections and responses of students formed part of the assessment in the module. Second, the preservice teachers worked in groups, using technology as a tool for investigation, documentation, and presentation of their investigation. They used Internet searches, Web surveys, digital cameras, and video in self-directed learning.

Figure 3. Student discussion about the authentic task (in Chinese) that focused on the visual arts curriculum

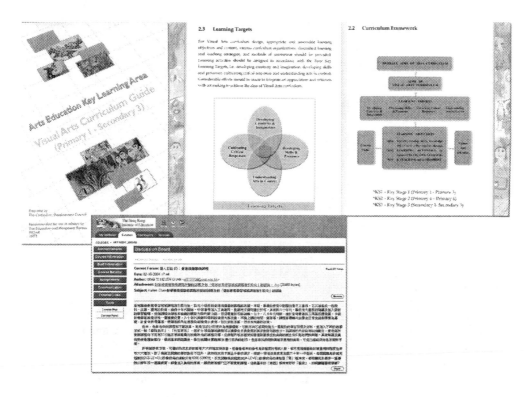

... *we could document our idea for the assignment whenever wherever, and we could always make changes to that before the submission deadline. Also we could read and comment on our classmates' assignment and response on the platform.*

When I was working on the personal reflective journal, I just typed out my thoughts. I did not have a feeling that it was an assignment given by a lecturer. Instead, I felt like having an online chat via ICQ (online chat) that made me feel more relaxed.

I think the difference of using technology in learning this module is that when we were preparing our presentation, we enjoyed the process very much. I would say only the report itself could not show how much we have learned in the whole process.

I think on the whole technology saved us a lot of time.

Real-Life Problems

The lecturer used two cases for problem-based learning. First, a feature story and digital images of a *cosplayer* (a person dressed up as a cartoon character-popular in some Asian cultures) from a newspaper magazine were used as triggers for raising issues about motivation in learning, identity, and peers. Second, video clips of teacher cases were used to identify conceptions and models of teaching. The preservice teachers worked in groups to identify the learning issues arising from the cases and investigated through interviews, Web surveys, and school visits. Because the problems posed were based on real-life situations, they helped familiarize preservice teachers with the different contexts and realistic situations possible in their future careers.

> *What I want to say is that I think those presentations are closely related to my living and are not too theoretical.*

Constructivist Learning

The assessment is student centered because learning starts with what the preservice teachers bring to the learning situation. They identified what they knew and what they needed to know through group negotiation. They decided what resources they would use and how to acquire the necessary information. They proposed solutions to the issues they identified and came up with more questions and issues. The assessment allows more student choice and construction in determining what is presented as evidence of learning. In other words, the assessment moves from "teacher structured" to "student structured" (Mueller, 2003).

> *Our group mainly used a digital camera.*
>
> *Yes, they used a Web survey to collect opinions on Cosplay and whether students want to add Cosplay into the curriculum.*
>
> *We had a variety of presentation methods and we presented in a more relaxed way.*

Collaborative Learning

Most of the assessment tasks were to be shared by all group members. Assessment is not always about finding solutions to known problems but about how the group collaborated in finding facts and information, brainstorming issues for learning, participating in discussion, critiquing, and sharing responses in the discussion board and presentations.

> *I think group work is important in tertiary education, and group assignments can train us on this aspect. We had a division of labour in group work, so we have to be very clear on what our individual scope of work is beforehand. As a result, we did a more in-depth information search within our scope and shared the processed knowledge among members. This made it much easier to learn [in a group] instead of learning by myself.*

> *Group one [suggested], as we have to compromise with members for objectives of the group work, I found that we came up with more specific objectives with the help of group discussions. . . . We understood the topic and our partners' work so well that we didn't have to list out our script for presentation.*

Case Study 3: Creativity in Fashion Design

Learning to learn is the theme of the current educational reform in the Hong Kong Special Administrative Region. Collaborative skills, communication skills, creativity, critical thinking skills, and skills in using information technology are thought to be the essential generic skills to be mastered by all learners (Education Commission, 2000). Learners should be well equipped with such transferable skills so that they can be responsive to the changing requirements of the workplace, which is dynamic and technology driven. Computer-supported collaborative learning (CSCL) is one of the many student-centered approaches that match with the philosophy of contemporary perspectives on learning and teaching, aiming to promote higher achievement, more positive interpersonal relationships, and greater psychological health and resulting in graduates being cooperative, caring, reflective, critical, and creative. In this regard, an initiative was undertaken to create CSCL opportunities and experiences and align these activities to the appropriate assessment design to promote student-centered learning and to foster transferable skills.

Assessment Design

In this study, students were assigned to a design project (fashion design with fabric and color illustrations), which involved the use of peer sharing and critique of the group design project by using the Blackboard online LMS. To ensure individual accountability, facilitate group processing, and make group dynamics transparent, learners were required to conduct an intragroup reflection on their design processes, analyze their progress, and give suggestions on methods and strategies to enhance the group's effectiveness through submission of an electronic weekly reflective journal. Developmental sketches of design works were posted on the Web for ongoing feedback and critique from peers and educators. Learners were also required to perform an intergroup assessment on the final performance demonstration of design work by giving feedback to the presenter. It was believed that the learners' social skills, creativity, collaboration, and critical reflective ability would be developed throughout this interactive and evaluative process.

Students' Feedback

Students perceived the assessment task as a useful tool to motivate them to develop a sense of ownership and to experience how to give quality feedback to others that would be of great value to their teaching career and professional development as teachers.

> *We can look at other groups work with the intergroup peer assessment that provides chances for us to experience how a teacher gives marks and constructive comments.*

> *It is not sufficient to have just one summative assessment, as we will not have chances to improve our work. Formative assessments, such as writing reflective journals and providing ongoing peer critique, can guide us to learn step by step and to learn from trial and error.*

Most students who had used the online assessment package indicated that the speed of the return of written comments for refinements plus the increased opportunity for self-reflection and review were identified as the great benefits of the system.

> *We can capture our learning process by reviewing and revisiting our work as well as comments from peers and teachers from time to time.*

> *We can obtain instant feedback from peers and teachers for improvement. I realize that my work has improved a lot because of other input and feedback.*

Learners' reflective capabilities and critical thinking skills were promoted through the assessment activities, and these skills will be highly treasured in their future careers. It was believed that creativity and collaborative skills could be fostered by social support in terms of cognitive diversity and distribution of expertise (Arias, Eden, Fisher, Gorman, & Scharff, 2000; Fischer, 1999; Kvan, Yip, & Vera, 1999). Most students remarked that the assessment tasks did foster their creativity and cultivate their positive attitudes toward collaboration and sharing, which could be confidently promoted to the school environment when they became the practicing educators.

Figure 4. First and second draft of a student's fashion design

We have received more than 10 feedbacks from our peers. Say, for example, if we take 5 of the feedbacks and make modifications, at least 5 different aspects of our design will have improved.

Peer critique makes us . . . review our design work. As a result, our final version looks very different from our first draft. The improvement is really remarkable!

Figure 4 illustrates how peer review can assist the design process.

Is it a one piece design? Sorry, I can't really figure it out. I cannot see the front in the last design. . . . The most special feature is the godet at the back . . . but I can see two "tails" at the back! I think if the sleeves look like an elephant's ears, it will be better.

Difficulties Encountered

Although most of the learners were positive about their use of technology, one group raised a relevant question about the usefulness of the online learning environment when students met regularly in the face-to-face classroom. Members of one group did not use the e-learning platform as their major communication channel because they preferred to exchange ideas in face-to-face situations:

> . . . we are full-time students and we can get in touch with other members very easily . . . the interaction on e-learning platform is not as direct as the face-to-face one in which we can see others' facial expression. Sometimes, we shall also communicate via telephone.

Other students also claimed that they would use ICQ (online chat) for communication, as ". . . it is speedy and convenient. We can activate the program all the time, not only when working on assignments, which facilitates idea exchange at all times." Staff members using online learning in the blended teaching and learning environment need to consider how tasks are designed to engage the students in the online environment. The blended environment represents a challenging environment that has potential benefits and drawbacks. Online learning allows the completion of tasks that cannot be completed in a face-to-face environment. Its future use by the students for their own professional development also needs to be emphasized. The use of technology means that students do not need to be collocated for meetings and discussions. They can engage in working or learning tasks at convenient times. Such rich experiences will equip learners to use technology as a learning enhancement tool and will open more possibilities for their lifelong learning.

Recommendations

As can be seen from the three target learning modules, the learning outcomes, teaching activities, and assessment have been aligned with authentic work tasks, authentic assessment problems, and evaluation rubrics. In analyzing all three cases using Herrington and Herrington's (1998) framework, we can see that there are a number of similarities in our attempt to create a dynamic and authentic assessment environment.

All three modules focus on real-life issues in their respective content areas. In the first case study, students needed to design a virtual learning community suitable for implementation in their future primary school. The learning outcomes, activities, and assessment focused on applying principles indicative of a virtual learning community to a real context. The second case study focused on art education. Video clips of teacher cases were used to identify conceptions and models of teaching. The preservice teachers worked in groups to identify the learning issues arising from the video situations and investigated these practical situations through interviews, Web surveys, and school visits. As the problems posed were based on real-life situations, they helped familiarize preservice teachers with the different contexts in their future careers. In the third case study, students assumed the role of fashion designers. In small groups, they designed a project (fashion design with fabric and color illustrations), which involved the use of peer sharing and critique of the group design project by using the online learning and assessment environment.

In all three cases, students needed to acquire knowledge through collaboration, discussion, and negotiation and develop a polished work output. In the first case study, students had to design a VLC with all features that could be implemented in a primary school in the next phase. In the second case study, each participant submitted an essay on the feasibility of integrating visual culture into a school-based curriculum. In the third case study, students created a fashion design with fabric and color illustrations and submitted this design for assessment after receiving peer feedback on the design. One learning module was seven weeks in duration, while the other two learning modules extended for 12 weeks. All three cases emphasized assessment activities throughout the duration of the module as opposed to single end-of-course assessments. All three cases used collaboration and small group activities within the online environment as the cornerstone of their assessment and emphasized the social-constructivist nature of learning.

The three cases focused on ill-structured and complex challenges. In the first and third cases, students were placed in the situation of learners-as-designers (which emphasizes multiple solutions to the solving of a design problem). In other words, no one correct or best solution for the design existed; instead, the group negotiated a solution that satisfied the evaluative criteria recommended by the lecturers. Likewise, the second case focused on ill-structured problems through cases and issues to examine. Participants identified what they knew and what they needed to know through group negotiation. They decided what resources they would use and how to acquire the necessary information. They proposed solutions to the issues they identified, coming up with more questions and issues.

All three cases seamlessly integrated the assessment with learning outcomes, activities, and the weekly class. The formative assessment tasks became a continuous activity throughout the learning modules, which allowed students to make numerous changes based on feedback from students and teachers in both the face-to-face setting and the online learning environment.

All modules provided a variety of tasks that were assessed, allowing the student to have multiple indicators of success. For instance, in the creation of the VLC, students had to complete a conceptual paper on the rationale, a concept map on the design, an oral presentation, and a variety of resources for the prototype. Although the learning in all modules was learner centered, "this does not mean that students can be given complex and authentic tasks with no support or coaching to guide their learning" (Herrington et al., 2000, p. 403). The role of the lecturer in fostering these interactions is critical.

Conclusion

Learners need real-world activities to foster skills in students. In teacher education, authentic assessment and constructive alignment are critical if we are to foster creativity and knowledge construction in our preschool, primary, and secondary students. Online learning can assist by providing additional opportunities for students to collaborate, discuss, provide peer feedback, and reflect on their own group work. The responsibility of teacher educators is to begin to foster new metaphors and models for our profession. We need to foster learners as designers, as evaluators, as researchers, and as authors to foster open-ended and generative tasks that emphasize collaboration and critical thinking skills. Assessment approaches that closely align with these metaphors will assure that learners are being assessed so that what is learned can be transferred to the real-world setting beyond the classroom.

References

Arias, E., Eden, H., Fisher, G., Gorman, A., & Scharff, E. (2000). *Transcending the individual human mind—Creating shared understanding through collaborative design.* Retrieved July, 2003, from *http://www.cs.colorado.edu/~gerhard/papers/tochi2000.pdf*

Biggs, J. (1999). *Teaching for quality learning at university.* Suffolk, UK: Society for Research into Higher Education & Open University Press.

Dunn, L., Morgan, C., O'Reilly, M., & Parry, S. (2004). *The student assessment handbook: New directions in traditional and online assessment.* London: RoutledgeFarmer, Taylor & Francis Group.

Education Commission. (2000). *Learning for life, learning through life—Reform proposals for the education system in Hong Kong.* Hong Kong: China Government Printing Office.

Fischer, G. (1999). *Social creativity: Bringing different points of view together.* KBS Special Issues "C&C '99".

Herrington, J., & Herrington, A. (1998). Authentic assessment and multimedia: How university students respond to a model of authentic assessment. *Higher Education Research & Development, 17*(3), 305-322.

Herrington, J., Sparrow, H., & Herrington, T. (2000). Instructional design guidelines for authentic activity in online learning units. *Proceedings of the World Conference on Educational Multimedia, Hypermedia and Telecommunications,* Montreal, Canada (Vol. 1, pp. 435-440).

Hong Kong Institute of Education. (2004a). *Learning oriented assessment project.* Retrieved August, 2004, *from http://www.ied.edu.hk/loap/index.html*

Hong Kong Institute of Education. (2004b). *Strategic plan for rollover year 2004/05.*

Kvan, T., Yip, W. H., & Vera, A. (1999). Supporting design studio learning: An investigation into design communication in computer-supported collaboration. In C. Hoadley & J. Roschelle (Eds.), *Computer Support for Collaborative Learning (CSCL) Conference* (pp. 328-332). Mahwah, NJ: Lawerence Erlbaum Associates.

Loughran, J., Mitchell, I., & Mitchell, J. (2003). Attempting to document teachers' professional knowledge. *International Journal of Qualitative Studies in Education, 16*(6), 853-873.

Macdonald, J., Weller, M., & Mason, R. (2002). Meeting the assessment demands of networked courses. *International Journal on E-learning, 1*(1), 9-18.

Mueller, J. (2003). *What is authentic assessment?* Retrieved July, 2004, from *http://jonathan.mueller.faculty.noctrl.edu/toolbox*

Palloff, R. M., & Pratt, K. (2003). *The virtual student: A profile and guide to working with online learners.* San Francisco: Jossey-Bass.

Resta, P., Awalt, C., & Menchaca, M. (2002). Self and peer assessment in an online collaborative learning environment. *Proceedings of the World Conference on E-Learning in Corporate, Government, Health & Higher Education,* Monteal, Canada (Vol. 1, pp. 682-689).

Stringer, E. T. (1999). *Action research* (2nd ed.). Thousand Oaks, CA: Sage.

Chapter V

Electronic Tools for Online Assessments:
An Illustrative Case Study from Teacher Education

Jon Margerum-Leys, Eastern Michigan University, USA

Kristin M. Bass, University of California, Berkeley, USA

Abstract

The tools used in assessment allow instructors to communicate performance information to students. Each tool has particular things that it does well or poorly, encouraging particular kinds of assessment and discouraging others. This chapter explores the use of three particular software tools-Rubistar, an assessment database, and a document comparison feature—within a teacher education course. We comment on the tools' affordances, role in the assessment process, and ability to help instructors model effective practices for teacher education students. We also discuss two measurement issues, construct validity and consequences of use, that pertain to tool use in this environment.

Introduction

Assessment serves a vital and unique function in online teacher education. The measures used should not only provide teacher education students with information about their progress in a particular course, but also model practices they can employ in their own classrooms. Providing feedback to students is particularly important in the online environment, given the inherently limited opportunities for informal interactions. Tools are needed that facilitate the interactions between the teacher and students and maximize the clarity and quality of the information students receive regarding their performance.

In this case study, we explore the use of three software tools in the assessment of an opinion paper assignment in the context of an online educational technology class. The first is Rubistar, a Web-based rubric generation, storage, and evaluation product. The second is a FileMaker database designed to streamline the process of using rubrics, make communicating with students easier, and yield more comprehensive data on student performance. Finally, the use of Microsoft Word's electronic document comparison feature allows Jon to quickly see and evaluate student progress as a document moves from draft to final form.

For this chapter, we intentionally selected a traditional assignment to provide a backdrop that we believe will be well understood by an academic audience. All three of the tools described in this chapter are commonly found in university settings and are usable by instructors with moderate technological expertise. Each of the three tools can and has been used in the assessment of student work produced in both online and face-to-face settings. In this chapter, we situate the use of the tools in an online undergraduate teacher education course, commenting on ways in which such use capitalizes on the affordances and minimizes the barriers inherent to their application in online education.

Following the descriptions of the tools is a discussion of the measurement issues (e.g., construct validity and consequences of use) embedded in their use within an online setting. This chapter is organized as an illustrative case study. Stopping short of describing our methods as *best practices,* we term them *warranted practices,* carefully elucidating the reasoning behind our decisions. Throughout the chapter, we strike a balance among three areas of interest: (a) a description of how the tools are used in this setting, (b) a discussion of the measurement issues raised by using these tools in this way, and (c) observations regarding modification of the use of the tools to fit other online settings.

Background

Online universities are becoming more mainstream (Guri-Rosenblit, 1999; Peat & Franklin, 2002), and traditional universities are offering a wider variety of courses online (Maloney, 1999). With this expansion in offerings, more college faculty will be expected to teach in online environments. As they do so, challenges in managing and assessing student work will come to the fore (Stallings, 2002). Tools for making the assessment process more manageable are available, but many faculty members are unaware of the tools that are available to them and the techniques for their use. When faculty members do use advanced tools and techniques for assessing student work, they can give more feedback to students and aggregate student data in ways that allow demonstration of connections to national standards (Wright, Stallworth, & Ray, 2002). Effective and efficient assessment is key to understanding student progress (National Research Council, 2001) and is especially important in the asynchronous, non face-to-face world of the online course (Schrum, 1999).

Types of Online Assessment

Some of the most common forms of online assessment are tools that allow automatic grading and distribution of scores on objective tests (Atkins, Juchnowski, & Cashion, 2004; Siew, 2003; Zimmerman & Lear, 2003). CourseInfo is one such program that facilitates the development and administration of tests with multiple choice, true/false, and matching questions (Zimmerman & Lear, 2003). Other work has considered the assessment of longer, more complex performances, such as message board communications, individual papers, and group projects. These measures have taken the form of rubrics, Web-based evaluation templates, and peer and instructor feedback during online chats (Bauer, 2002; Freeman & McKenzie, 2002; Gray, 2002; MacDonald & Twining, 2002; Nicolay, 2002; Zimmerman & Lear, 2003). Our work is aligned with these latter efforts to assess student work in more complex ways.

Our approach also takes advantage of free and/or widely available commercial tools to assess online learning. Gray (2002), for instance, describes the value of word processing programs' "insert comments" and "track changes" features for providing feedback on written work. Familiarity, flexibility, and functionality are chief selling points in our selection of assessment tools. Like Gray, we advocate tools that are easy to use, can be applied to a variety of assignments, and are accessible from most computer desktops.

Evaluation of Online Assessments

Reports of online assessment techniques (e.g., Anderson, Bauer, & Speck, 2002) typically describe how to bring an assessment online but say very little about how and why the assessments effectively measure learning. Online assessment, like all other forms, should be firmly and explicitly built upon the foundations of educational assessment and the central issues in their planning and evaluation (Joint Committee on Standards for Educational and Psychological Testing, 1999; National Research Council, 2001). Like all other assessments, online measures should be valid, reliable, and fair (Australian National Training Authority, 2002). The criteria, however, have yet to be applied to public reviews of online evaluations.

The tools we describe are not so much assessments in and of themselves as much as they are means of organizing course assignments and responses to students. We therefore cannot evaluate these tools in terms of their psychometric properties but must separate the qualities of the online tools from those of the assessments they help create. For instance, we cannot say whether the Rubistar rubric generation tool exhibits validity but would instead evaluate the validity of a rubric created within Rubistar. Consequently, we analyze how the tools offload aspects of assessment design and data management to allow users to better consider issues of assessment quality.

In particular, we discuss how the tools can spotlight two aspects of assessment validity. First, construct validity is the gold standard for all types of assessment (Cronbach, 1988) and demands the precise definition of the aspects of achievement to be measured, along with the evidence for that achievement. Second, determining the consequences of an assessment justifies a test's use in a particular setting (Messick, 1989a, 1989b). For instance, assessments administered formatively during a course should help students improve their performance on later assignments (Assessment Reform Group, 2002; Bell & Cowie, 2001a, 2001b; Black & Wiliam, 1998). If there is no evidence of this, the task and/or the feedback to students would need to be altered. In our case study, we discuss the affordances and limitations of three tools for evaluating the construct validity or consequences of online teacher education assessments.

Setting and Context

Eastern Michigan University (EMU) is one of America's largest teacher education institutions. Each year, EMU graduates over 1,000 teachers, administrators, school counselors, and other education professionals. Introduction to Educational Media and Technology (EDMT 330)-the course in which the assignment described here is situated-is a required course for nearly all undergraduate preservice teachers. Sections of the course are taught by five educational technology faculty members as well as by assorted lecturers. Although variations exist in how the course is taught by each instructor, all instructors assign a portfolio of student work, and all portfolios are assessed using standards set by the International Society for Technology in Education (ISTE). The course is offered in both online and face-to-face versions. High student demand for the online version has resulted in an increasing number of sections.

Since 2001, Jon has taught approximately eight sections per year of EDMT 330 as part of a four-courses-per-term teaching load. He teaches approximately half of these sections face-to-face and half online. Class size ranges from 20 to 25 students. To host online courses, EMU contracts with eCollege. Course shells within eCollege provide space for course materials, a means of handling student work, calendar and gradebook functions, and tools for hosting threaded discussions and electronic chats.

The assignment we used as a setting in this chapter was a traditional, 4 to 6 page opinion paper. Students are asked to form an opinion on the question "What is and should be the role of technology in education?" To answer this question, students were to bring together support from course readings, course activities, and their own experiences. The paper assignment was described at the beginning of the course. A draft was due at approximately the six week point in a 15 week semester. Feedback on drafts was given one week later, and the final draft was due near the end of the term.

In the sections that follow, we describe three tools used in the assessment of this assignment. Along the way, we comment on how the tool was used in the assessment process. Following these three descriptions, we devote sections to the measurement issues raised by the features of each tool and general recommendations for the assessment of student work in an online setting.

Tool Selection

Part of Jon's underlying philosophy of teacher education is that courses should pay attention to teaching transparently, explaining instructional decisions as they are made and keeping a metalevel awareness when possible. His own practice should be a model of what he would want his students to do in the classroom when they become teachers. There are exceptions; for example, some of the activities in the course would be developmentally inappropriate for very young students. But for the most part, Jon tries to model effective teaching in ways that can be carried into the classroom, including choosing assessment tools that are available to his students.

The particular tools discussed in this chapter will be available to Jon's students when they enter the teaching profession. In addition, all the tools shown work equally well regardless of the type of computer used. If Jon models the use of these tools in his own teaching, his students will have ideas about the availability of the tools and positive and negative impressions about practice that uses the tools. Jon deliberately shies away from proprietary tools. For instance, the online environment we describe in this chapter provides a gradebook. Jon deliberately does not use it. When the students reach the classroom as teachers themselves, this tool will not be available to them, reducing its value to Jon as a teacher education model.

Tools Used

Each of the subsections that follow introduces a software tool that Jon used in the assessment process. The tools are introduced in the order in which they appeared to students: (a) a rubric generation tool to help frame the assignment, (b) a database tool to manage formative feedback, and (c) a document comparison tool to assist in the analysis of progress from draft to finished form.

Rubistar for Rubric Generation

Scoring rubrics are convenient tools for characterizing student learning (Arter & McTighe, 2001; Luft, 1999; Shafer, Swanson, Bené, & Newberry, 2001). Rubrics are defined as scoring systems for judging the quality of an assignment. Essential to a rubric is the notion of levels of performance that distinguish and communicate various qualities of thinking and reasoning (Arter & McTighe, 2001). Clarifying these levels helps teachers clarify the purpose of an assignment and gives students explicit criteria to consider as they draft and revise their work (Luft, 1999). This is especially important in online education where written communication, as the main means of interaction, must be as clear and detailed as possible. The challenge, therefore, is to produce rubrics that systematically identify and describe evaluation criteria.

Rubistar, a product of the High Plains Regional Technology in Education Consortium, is one such solution. The program is a Web-based rubric generation, storage, and evaluation product that can be accessed at http://rubistar.4teachers.org/. Illustrations in this chapter were created by using the version current in June 2004. Rubistar allows teachers and other education professionals to quickly access preexisting rubric templates, modifying the templates to fit their own contexts. Completed rubrics can be stored on the Rubistar Web site and accessed by students and other teachers. Rubrics can also be downloaded to the creator's computer for further revision or publication in another format (e.g., inclusion in a syllabus). Limited item analysis is also available on the site. Although designed for K-12 teachers, Rubistar is easily adaptable for higher education uses.

The process of creating a rubric begins with choosing a template. Figure 1 shows a partial listing of the rubric templates available. An exact match for the assignment is unimportant, because templates are infinitely customizable.

Figure 1. Beginning the creation process by choosing a rubric type

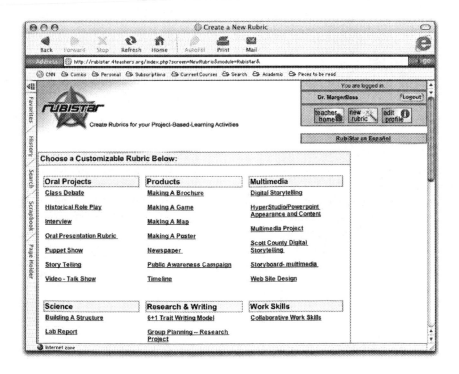

Figure 2. Categories vary with the type of rubric. Shown are categories for the research report type.

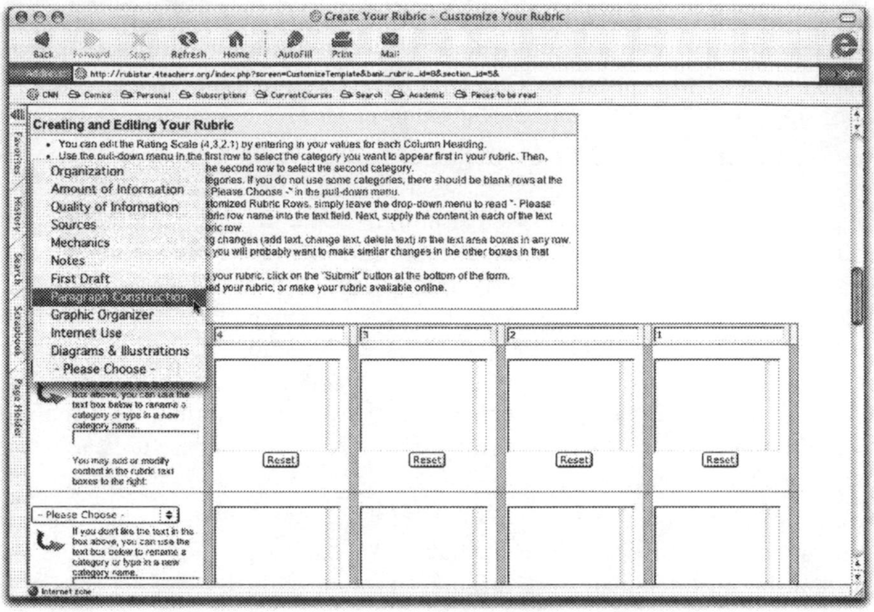

Figure 3. Each category has a set of sample prompts. These can be edited at will.

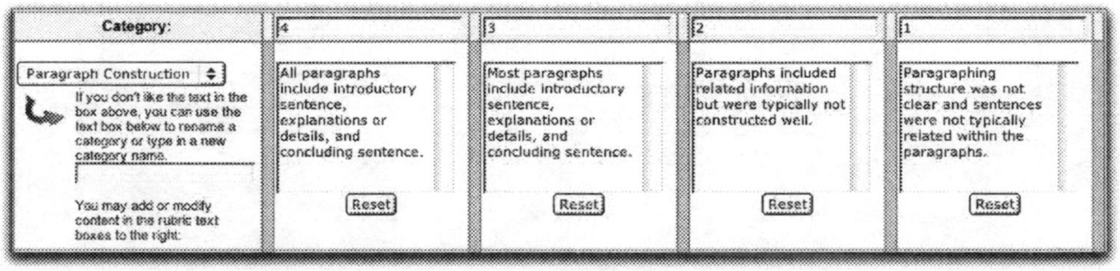

Choosing an assignment type brings up the main feature of the Web site, the rubric creation grid. Figures 2 and 3 show the core of the rubric creation process as it takes place in Rubistar. Each assignment template has its own set of associated categories, as seen in Figure 2. New categories can be created from within the program, and existing categories can be renamed to suit particular needs for an assignment. After a category is selected, Rubistar generates an opening set of prompts, shown in Figure 3. These too can be modified as needed.

After categories have been selected and prompts written, Rubistar generates a completed rubric (see Figure 4). This rubric can be downloaded in Excel spreadsheet format for further refinement or saved in HTML form for posting on a Web site. In the case of the assignment described in this chapter, the rubric appears on the assignment's Web page.

Figure 4. Completed rubric, ready for viewing online or copying into a syllabus

Research Report : Synthesis Paper

CATEGORY	Very Good	Good	Needs Improvement	Notes
Specific support for your position	All arguments are supported with convincing evidence that directly addresses the position. When an author is cited or quoted, it is always for a specific purpose.	Some arguments are missing evidence, OR are not supported with specific references to the text. Quotations are included, but their relevance is not made clear to the reader.	Evidence is either missing or irrelevant to the position	Support for your position must begin with having a position to support. If you don't clearly state a position, you won't get credit in the support category.
Error-free mechanics	A couple of typos, or minor grammar errors in the entire paper.	A couple of errors per page, but nothing that interferes with understanding the writing.	Errors are so frequent or so major that they interfere with reading the paper (e.g., run-on sentences and paragraphs, sentence fragments,	Missing page numbers count as a mechanical error: Please include page numbers
Polished Writing	Ideas flow naturally. All transitions are clear, clean, and coherent.	Ideas flow naturally within arguments, but the transitions from one argument to the next are stilted and incoherent.	Ideas are choppy within and between arguments. There are no transitions between paragraphs.	This category differs from the category below. Polished writing refers to the quality of the writing itself. Easy to follow logic has to do with the quality of the structure of the argument being made.
Easy to follow logic	Arguments are presented in a clear and compelling fashion. It is easy to follow the chain of reasoning between the stated positions, the arguments for the position, and the evidence to support each argument.	The chain of reasoning is present but subtle or illogical in some places. The logic for some arguments is stronger than for others.	Chain of reasoning is difficult to detect quickly, OR is present but illogical. Reasoning is generally weak/circular.	

Notice that in Figure 4 we have created a three column rubric, with the fourth column for descriptive notes. In assessing students' work quickly and consistently, it is important to be able to justify the difference between "Very Good" and "Good." Using three columns as opposed to four or five makes the assessment process more manageable.

The value of Rubistar is threefold. First, the preloaded categories and prompts are well thought out. They provide a valuable starting place when creating a rubric. Often, the template will suggest areas for assessment that might not have occurred to the teacher. Second, Rubistar automates the process of formatting the rubric, allowing Jon to concentrate on the content rather than the form. From the standpoint of online education, Rubistar is particularly valuable. Rubrics are created as HTML tables, a form that is ideal for the online environment. Students may access the rubric online, independent of their course space. Alternatively, teachers may copy and paste the HTML for the rubric to their course space, saving the usual step of converting a desktop document to a Web-friendly format.

Database Tool for Giving Formative Feedback

Although Rubistar can be used with little or no technical training, the use of FileMaker is moderately technologically challenging. We include it in this chapter for two reasons. First, it is an essential tool in the case that we are describing. The assessment process would be very different if this particular tool-or one very much like it-were not used. Automated conversion of rubric category marks to numbers, and collections of comments into an easy-to-manage set of e-mail messages cannot be done without some sort of database tool. Second, we believe that the time required to learn to use the tool would be well invested by a variety of online instructors. Our recommendations are generalizable to other online instructors, even though for most, some assistance would be required in order to make the most effective use of the tool.

A *database* is a tool designed to organize and manage large amounts of information. Data are organized by fields and records. Each *record* is a set of information, and each *field* is an aspect of the information. Take, for example, a paper phone book, which is a simple database. Information about each person is a record. The record is divided into fields-first name, last name, address, and phone number. All the records have the same fields ordered in the same way, so it is easy for the reader to grasp the organizational structure of the phone book and to use it to retrieve information. Electronic databases take this model and expand it, allowing the database creator to organize information around multiple axes and to work with subsections of the data as needed.

The particular database software used in this example is FileMaker Pro; similar results could be accomplished using Microsoft Access or any other modern relational database tool.

In our example, a database is used to keep track of student information. Some of this is contact information: name, student number, e-mail address, and phone. Much of the information, though, is assessment information. For each major assignment, students are given a rubric. Each section of the rubric becomes a field in the database, along with fields for comments and for calculating section and final scores.

Rubric-based grading is time consuming and does not fit neatly into a numbers-based gradebook system. Each student product must be individually examined along multiple axes. Determinations of quality may need to be converted to numbers in order to determine a category score. Various categories may be weighted differently, complicating the process of calculating a final score. Additionally, in an online environment communication of detailed information to a large number of students has its own challenges. Use of a database system addresses these issues.

Figure 5 shows one screen of Jon's assessment database. The student's name is listed, followed by buttons to record whether the assignment was turned in on time and the instructor's judgment as to the quality of the work. At the bottom of the page is a text box in which the instructor can give detailed feedback to the student.

The categories and marks for each category ("Very Good," "Good," and "Needs Improvement") are drawn directly from the completed rubric. Clicking on the prompt buttons causes the database to enter a score in the corresponding category. Total and

Figure 5. Sample screen showing how the rubric from the previous section is scored and the data is managed

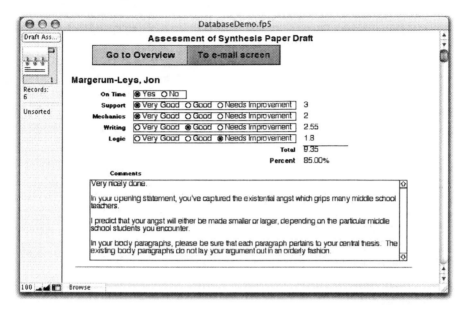

Figure 6. Field definition area showing some of the 26 fields in the sample database

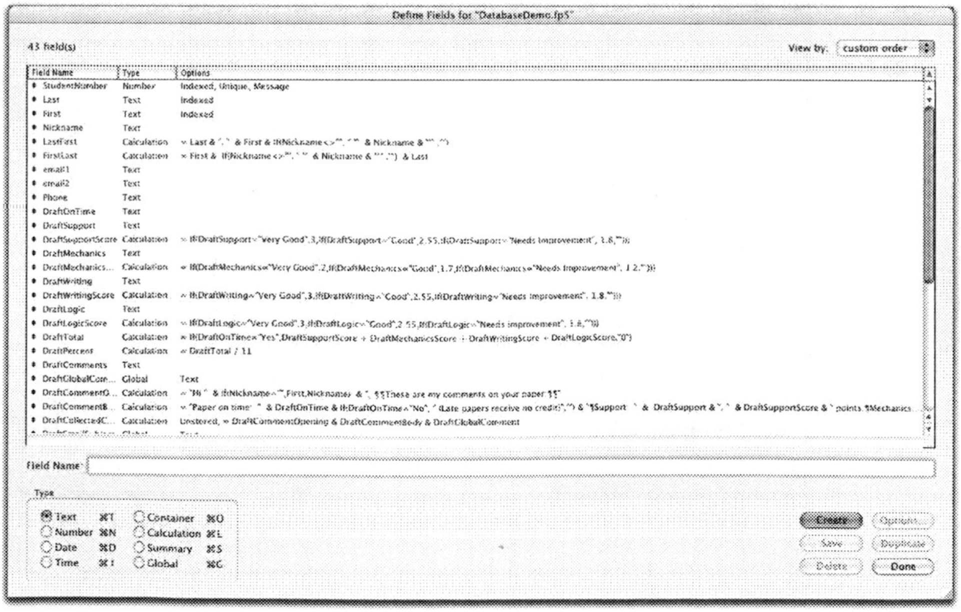

percent figures are updated automatically. After the assessment information has been entered, having all the information converted to an e-mail message and sent out to the student is a two-click trip, as will be described shortly.

Each box and number on screen represents a field in the database. In the next section, we show the underpinnings of the fields that make up the system.

Figure 6 shows the fields used to set up the view shown above. Some fields, such as *first* and *last,* are straightforward: They are fields for first and last names. Other fields, such as *draft total,* are more complicated to set up correctly. For readers not accustomed to working within a database system, Figure 6 may appear daunting. However, as database tasks go, this one is relatively simple.

One of the strengths of this system is its ability to assemble a coherent set of e-mail messages by using the information generated by the streamlined input system shown in Figure 5. In Figure 7, the instructor checks the e-mail address and the text of the message to be sent. An overall comment for all students can be added along with the subject line. Clicking on a button causes the database to assemble an individualized opening and body into a set of full messages that are then sent by using the instructor's e-mail program. Each student in the course receives a customized message with his or her individual assessment.

In assessing final drafts of progressive assignments, it is important to be able to track both the students' previous work and the instructor's feedback and previous assess-

Figure 7. E-mail construction system showing the collected assessment score and comments ready to mail to students

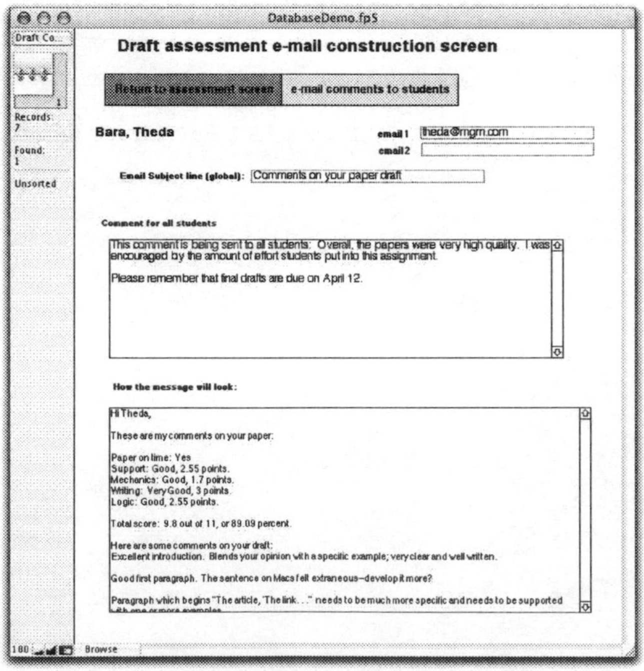

Figure 8. Screen for scoring the final draft of a paper. Note the information carried over from the first draft assessment.

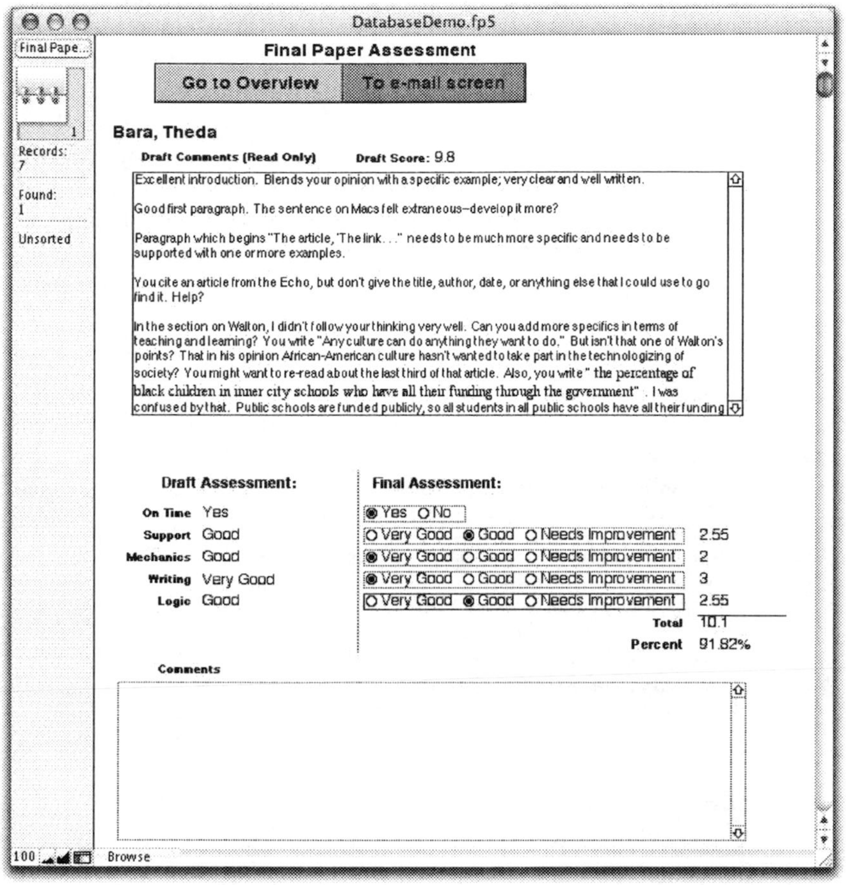

ment. The section of this chapter on document comparison shows how an instructor can see the progression in student work. Figure 8 shows how Jon uses the database to see his first draft comments and category marks while being able to assess the current draft.

Notice in the bottom part of Figure 8 that the draft assessment is now shown as words instead of buttons, while the final assessment categories appear as a set of buttons for easy data entry. One of the primary values of a database is its ability to represent information in multiple ways. The underlying data remains the same, but in different contexts it is helpful to have a variety of views of the information available.

In the course of a normal semester, Jon sends over 700 e-mail messages to his online students. Using the database system described here, he is able to manage communication of assessment information to students in a way that is efficient for him yet individualized for his students.

Document Comparison for Tracking Progress

Effective writing requires the ability to make improvements to drafts. As teacher educators, one of our charges is to help our students become more effective in their written communications. Feedback on drafts should help students to move their work from rough to more final form. But does it? Are students able to respond to feedback? And how is an instructor to know what changes a student makes from draft to final form? Traditionally, some professors have required students to attach their drafts when handing in their final papers. But in order for a professor to accurately compare the two versions of the paper, he or she would have to reread both in their entirety. With instructors' teaching loads, which commonly are upward of 70 students, such careful reading of double sets of papers would be a huge commitment.

Document comparison allows an assessor to quickly see differences between versions of a paper. Combined with a system that carefully tracks feedback, this feature can give an instructor an extremely accurate picture of how the student has responded to feedback. It has two areas of value. First, instructors can evaluate their own feedback. If as a group students do not respond to instructor feedback as the instructor might have predicted, he or she can adjust the type of feedback given. Second, having a means to see progress from draft to final makes it much more efficient and objectively defensible to evaluate students on this progress as well as on whether they respond to observed areas of needed improvement.

Figure 9. Managing documents for comparison purposes requires a systematic filing system.

Figure 10. Invoking the document comparison command

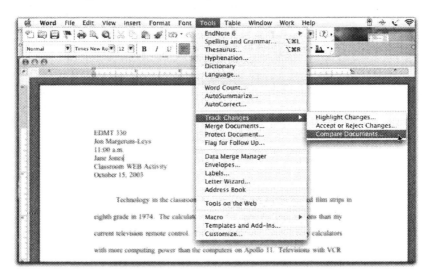

For document comparison to be feasible, it is important to have a systematic means of storing drafts and final products. In Figure 9, the folder containing students' final papers shows the system Jon uses. Students send their files to Jon through the online course environment. The assignment directions instruct students to name their papers LastNameFirstName.doc. After all the assignments are turned in, moving them to his computer is simple. Fortunately, word processing documents are quite small. The set of 70 documents shown would easily fit on a floppy disk.

Figure 11. Choosing a document to compare

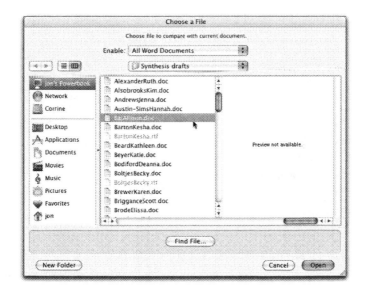

Figure 10 shows the final draft of an assignment open on Jon's computer screen. The document comparison command is invoked by pulling down the Tools menu and choosing Track Changes —> Compare Documents. Figure 11 shows the resulting dialog box. *Note:* The latest version of Microsoft Word lists the document comparison tool separately from the track changes tool, but the functionality remains the same.

No special action is required on the part of the students. Nothing is unique about the documents that are being compared, other than that they are Microsoft Word documents. This feature works on any Word document, regardless of whether it was created on or is being viewed with a Windows or Macintosh computer.

Figure 12 shows the final version of the document open and the computer comparing it with the draft turned in by the student. All changes are shown in a contrasting color, and a line in the margin indicates a section that has been changed. Even in the longest document, scrolling through and observing the work that has been done in bringing a draft to final form is an easy matter.

By using Word's built-in document comparison, Jon is able to efficiently assess the progress the student has made from draft to final form; he has some sense of the

Figure 12. Document comparison in action

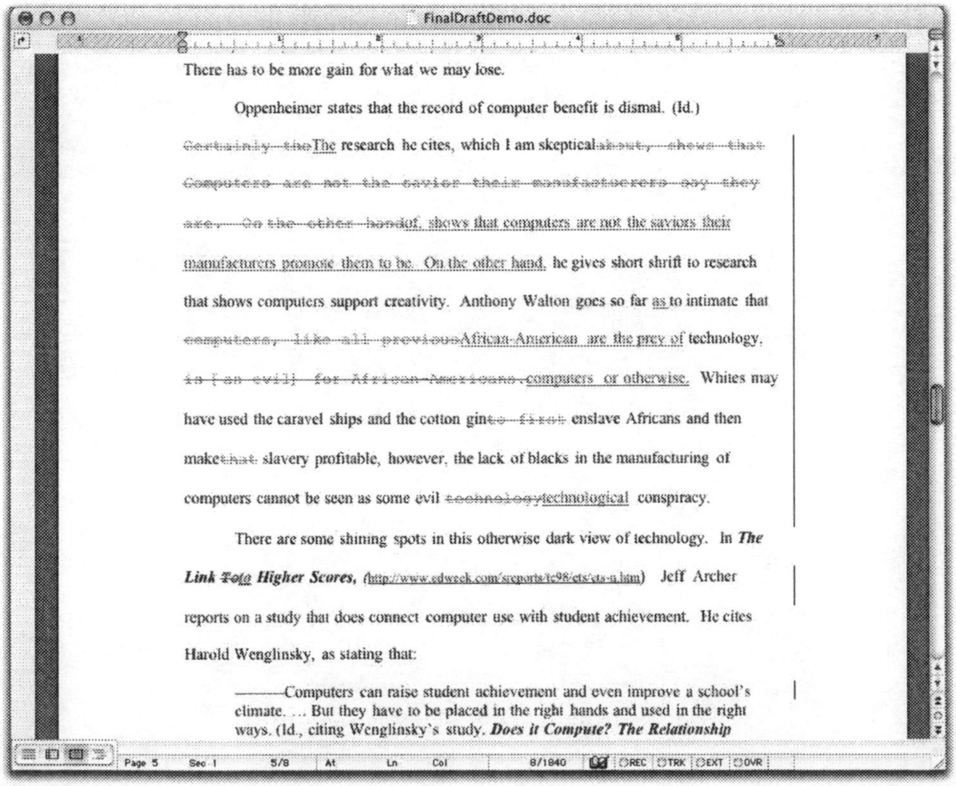

process that the student has gone through. Combined with a database system that allows him to track feedback given to each student, he can be more consistent and can improve his ability to examine student work and give feedback.

Measurement Issues Raised

As noted in the introduction to this chapter, each of these assessment tools addresses particular aspects of assessment development and evaluation. In this section we discuss two such issues-construct validity and consequences.

Construct Validity

The three tools address two determinants of construct validity. First, establishing construct validity begins with precise definitions of the knowledge and skills the assessment should measure. Rubistar is uniquely capable of helping instructors define what they will be measuring and will be presented as the sole example of a tool that facilitates construct planning. Second, item analyses can evaluate the quality of the information an assessment provides about student understanding, which is itself a reflection of the clarity and appropriateness of the construct being measured. All three tools can be used for item analysis and will be discussed in turn.

Construct Definitions

Rubistar allows teachers to consider multiple aspects of performance that they want to assess and identify the specific evidence they will seek for different levels of proficiency. One of Rubistar's main strengths is its ability to break down common classroom assignments into a series of assessable components or criteria. It provides templates and sample rubrics to suggest criteria and evidence while giving teachers the freedom to adapt those criteria to their own assignments.

Rubistar has certain limitations in its support for assessment development. One shortcoming is that it focuses on analytic rubrics, which break performances down into several components. There will also be times when teachers will want to use holistic rubrics that consider the overall quality of student work (Arter & McTighe, 2001; Luft, 1999). Rubistar says little about that beyond adding up points in the rubric for a total score. Furthermore, Rubistar does not provide any quality controls or information on how to evaluate rubrics. Common criteria include content coverage, clarity, usability, and technical quality (Arter & McTighe, 2001), none of which are addressed in Rubistar's templates or design instructions.

Item Analysis

The range of responses is one way to check the validity of an assessment. If an assessment elicits uniform responses, it would suggest that the task could not properly discriminate between students based on their understanding or skill (i.e., construct underrepresentation) (Wilson, 2004). Furthermore, erratic score changes over time may indicate a lack of effort or motivation to complete an assignment, which is another threat to construct validity.

All the tools have at least basic opportunities for item analysis and revision. Rubistar and the database, for instance, allow users to review the score distributions. The distribution data is a first pass to determine if the assessments warrant additional analyses; it cannot make claims about construct validity by itself. If all students fall into one or two levels or scores on a particular criterion, for instance, that criterion is not very informative and will probably need to be revised. Likewise, if scores do not change from a rough draft of an assignment to its final form, that situation could be a red flag that students may not have had the time or motivation to make revisions, meaning that the scores are more reflective of social factors rather than cognitive skills. The track changes function allows instructors to pinpoint the nature of those revisions and speculate on the causes of score changes. Overall, the item analysis functions afforded by these online assessment tools should be seen as a first line of defense for measurement claims and a quick way to identify potential problems with the assessment. Other validation procedures, such as comparing scores to another task to establish convergent validity, can be conducted if the assessment does not appear to have any immediate discrepancies.

Consequences

Another way to evaluate assessment quality is by its impact on students (Messick, 1989a, 1989b). The effectiveness of formative assessments is moderated by the quality of feedback provided in the early stages of a project or paper (Assessment Reform Group, 2002; Black & Wiliam, 1998). The document comparison function helps teachers determine whether their feedback is actually improving student performance. If a teacher gives feedback on criteria A, B, and C, and the student only improves in areas A and B, then the teacher may need to clarify the comments for criteria C.

Although document comparison offers a quick, simple means to identify changes, it has several caveats. One repeats a point raised in the previous analysis of construct validity—the tools do not claim to help teachers solve the assessment problems they might encounter. Another caveat is that the document comparison feature is a fairly rudimentary check of student work. It does not permit any detailed analyses of the qualitative or quantitative differences in two papers, nor can it consolidate information across students to track improvement on a class level. Document comparison must be combined with a database of feedback and changes in order to realize its full potential as an assessment tool. This extra step makes it somewhat more labor intensive to use document comparison as a formal means to track large groups of students over time and suggests that the feature is most easily employed as a relatively informal check of student progress.

Conclusions and Recommendations

The assessment tools we have presented meet certain needs while making others more evident. Rubistar, the database, and document comparison all aggregate and analyze student work, freeing teachers to interpret results and adapt their assessment and/or instruction. The software could be modified to assist teachers with these tasks, but that is not within our control as teacher educators. Rather, it becomes incumbent upon us to consider the ways to use tools that already exist.

Within teacher education, we envision an online instructional program that uses assessment tools within the context of more general issues of measurement design and evaluation. Rubistar, for instance, could fit within lessons about "backwards design" (Wiggins & McTighe, 1998), whereby assessment developers establish end goals for what they would like students to learn, and generate tasks and scoring systems intended to track the achievement of these goals. Rubistar can be presented as a tool that can assist in this process by organizing and suggesting evaluation criteria. Likewise, because all the tools speak to issues of assessment validity, they could illustrate issues in assessment quality. The tools could fit in an instructional sequence about threats to assessment validity (e.g., construct underrepresentation), methods for identifying problems, and possible solutions. Overall, the modus operandi for teaching with these tools is to establish them within the larger field of assessment and evaluation and supplement their introduction with discussions of what teachers should know and do before and after they use the tools.

An alternative instructional approach harkens back to the beginning of this chapter, where we introduced the idea of *instructional transparency,* or modeling the types of practices that we would like to see teachers use in their own classrooms. The instructor's act of using these tools during a course, explaining why and how they are used, and demonstrating how to respond to assessment results shows teacher education students how assessments directly influence classroom practice. In this manner the tools go beyond simply facilitating certain assessment practices to becoming active agents of teacher learning and instructional reform (Ball & Cohen, 1996).

The future of online assessment in teacher education depends upon identifying and realizing the potential of familiar computer programs for classroom assessment. Innovations in online instruction will not only come from new technologies but also from discovering new applications of current software. Our case study illustrates how current free or widely available tools can be easily and efficiently used in the service of teaching, learning, and assessment.

References

Anderson, R. S., Bauer, J. F., & Speck, B. W. (Eds.). (2002). Assessment strategies for the online class: From theory to practice [Special Issue]. *New Directions for Teaching and Learning, 91*(Fall).

Arter, J., & McTighe, J. (2001). *Scoring rubrics in the classroom: Using performance criteria for assessing and improving student performance.* Thousand Oaks, CA: Corwin Press.

Assessment Reform Group. (2002). *Assessment for learning: Ten principles.* Retrieved March 28, 2002, from *http://www.assessment-reform-group.org.uk/CIE3.pdf*

Atkins, P., Juchnowski, M., & Cashion, J. (2004). *Online assessment: Let's do it.* Retrieved June 16, 2004, from *http://www.tafe.swin.edu.au/indsci/assess/doit.htm*

Australian National Training Authority. (2002). Assessment and online teaching. Retrieved June 16, 2004, from *http://flexiblelearning.net.au/guides.assessment.pdf*

Ball, D. L., & Cohen, D. K. (1996). Reform by the book: What is-or might be-the role of curriculum materials in teacher learning and instructional reform? *Educational Researcher, 25*(9), 6-8, 14.

Bauer, J. F. (2002). Assessing student work from chatrooms and bulletin boards. *New Directions in Teaching and Learning, 91*(Fall), 31-36.

Bell, B., & Cowie, B. (2001a). The characteristics of formative assessment in science education. *Science Education, 85,* 536-553.

Bell, B., & Cowie, B. (2001b). *Formative assessment and science education.* Dordrecht, The Netherlands: Kluwer.

Black, P., & Wiliam, D. (1998). Assessment and classroom learning. *Assessment in Education, 5,* 7-74.

Cronbach, L. J. (1988). Five perspectives on the validity argument. In H. Wainer & H. I. Braun (Eds.), *Test validity* (pp. 3-17). Hillsdale, NJ: Erlbaum.

Freeman, M., & McKenzie, J. (2002). SPARK, a confidential Web-based template for self and peer assessment of student teamwork: Benefits of evaluating across different subjects. *British Journal of Educational Technology, 33,* 551-569.

Gray, R. (2002). Assessing students' written projects. *New Directions in Teaching and Learning, 91*(Fall), 37-42.

Guri-Rosenblit, S. (1999). The agendas of distance teaching universities: Moving from the margins to the center stage of higher education. *Higher Education, 37*(3), 281-293.

Joint Committee on Standards for Educational and Psychological Testing. (1999). *Standards for educational and psychological testing.* Washington, DC: American Educational Research Association.

Luft, J. A. (1999). Rubrics: Design and use in science teacher education. *Journal of Science Teacher Education, 10,* 107-121.

MacDonald, J., & Twining, P. (2002). Assessing activity-based learning for a networked course. *British Journal of Educational Technology, 33,* 603-618.

Maloney, W. A. (1999). Brick and mortar campuses go online. *Academe, 85*(5), 18-24.

Messick, S. (1989a). Meaning and values in test validation: The science and ethics of assessment. *Educational Researcher, 18*(2), 5-11.

Messick, S. (1989b). Validity. In R. Linn (Ed.), *Educational measurement* (3rd ed., pp. 13-103). New York: Macmillan.

National Research Council. (2001). Knowing what students know: The science and design of educational assessment. In J. Pellegrino, N. Chudowsky, & R. Glaser (Eds.), *Board on testing and assessment, center for education, division of behavioral and social sciences and education.* Washington, DC: National Academy Press.

Nicolay, J. A. (2002). Group assessment in the online learning environment. *New Directions in Teaching and Learning, 91*(Fall), 43-52.

Peat, M., & Franklin, S. (2002). Supporting student learning using computer-based formative assessment models. *British Journal of Educational Technology, 33,* 515-523.

Schrum, L. (1999). Trends in distance learning. In R. M. Branch & M. A. Fitzgerald (Eds.), *Educational media and technology yearbook: Vol. 24* (pp. 11-16). Englewood, CO: Libraries Unlimited.

Shafer, W. D., Swanson, G., Bené, N., & Newberry, G. (2001). Effects of teacher knowledge of rubrics on student achievement in four content areas. *Applied Measurement in Education, 14,* 151-170.

Siew, P.-F. (2003). Flexible online assessment and feedback for teaching linear algebra. *International Journal of Mathematical Education in Science and Technology, 34,* 43-51.

Stallings, D. (2002). Measuring success in the virtual university. *Journal of Academic Librarianship, 28*(1–2), 47-53.

Wiggins, G., & McTighe, J. (1998). *Understanding by design.* Alexandria, VA: Association for Supervision and Curriculum Development.

Wilson, M. (2004). *Constructing measures: An item response modeling approach.* Mahwah, NJ: Erlbaum.

Wright, V. H., Stallworth, B. J., & Ray, B. (2002). Challenges of electronic portfolios: Student perceptions and experiences. *Journal of Technology and Teacher Education, 10*(1), 49-61.

Zimmerman, J. B., & Lear, J. (2003). Online assessment in the twenty-first century. *National Social Science Journal, 18*(2), 151-156.

Chapter VI

Online Assessment of Foreign Language Proficiency:
Meeting Development, Design, and Delivery Challenges

Paula M. Winke, Michigan State University, USA

Abstract

In this chapter, the challenges involved in creating online Arabic and Russian proficiency tests by using a commercial test product are discussed. Guidelines used for item and test development are presented, along with specific challenges test developers faced in designing computerized, semiadaptable tests. Also discussed are the issues involved in delivering the tests securely over the Internet to examinees, who took them on computers in college and university language labs across the United States and abroad. The chapter concludes with a list of five important lessons that could help others who are contemplating a similar test development project.

Introduction

Standardized tests of foreign language proficiency for languages that are less commonly taught in the United States—that is, languages other than Spanish, French, German, or English (Walker & McGinnis, 1995)—are needed more than ever to meet the growing demand for accurate information concerning students' foreign language proficiency in these languages. One common challenge for professionals teaching less commonly taught languages (LCTLs) is the lack of available tests that measure students' progress and proficiency or help with the placement of new students into the appropriate levels of instruction. (See Hughes, 1989, or Bachman & Palmer, 1996, for more information about different kinds of foreign and second language tests.) Because college and university departments and programs that need such language tests are typically small and have low numbers of potential test-takers, few resources are allocated for the development of nationally available standardized tests. In addition, currently available paper and pencil tests for the LCTLs in the United States are often difficult to locate, are inconvenient, and are expensive to administer and score due to the small volume of use. One solution is to create Web-based proficiency tests for these languages. Such tests are more easily available, allow for use by a large variety of programs and institutions, and provide the option of automatic and immediate scoring of test items.

However, Web-based testing of these languages poses a few problems: (a) LCTLs in the United States include languages with logographic (e.g., Chinese) or non-Roman (e.g., Arabic and Russian) alphabets that can be difficult to enter into Web formats; (b) reliable resources for creating authentic test items are scarce; (c) individuals who know the languages well enough to create items may not be at the same location and may not be trained as test developers; and (d) the development of a Web-delivery system for such tests can be time-consuming and costly (Chalhoub-Deville & Deville, 1999; Dunkel, 1999b), especially when compared to the small audience for the tests.

In this chapter, the challenges involved in creating two online LCTL proficiency tests, one for Arabic and one for Russian, at the Center for Applied Linguistics are discussed. Each test has two sections, listening and reading, that can be taken separately or back-to-back in either order. The basic template for these two semiadaptable[1] tests is provided, and insights are offered into how other foreign language online test developers, especially LCTL test developers, could start a similar project.

Background

The Center for Applied Linguistics (CAL) is a not-for-profit institution in Washington, DC, committed to improving communication through a better understanding of language and culture. CAL's Language Testing Division has maintained the paper and pencil Arabic Proficiency Test (APT), developed by Dr. Raji M. Rammuny and Dr. Mahmoud E. Sieny at the University of Michigan, since it became operational in 1993. The APT is administered to about 200 students per year.

Project Goals

In 1999, in response to widespread use of networked computer labs at institutions of higher education and advances in computer-assisted and computer-adaptive testing for foreign languages (Brown, 1997; Chalhoub-Deville & Deville, 1999; Chapelle, 2001), CAL proposed to the United States Department of Education the adaptation of the APT to a Web-based, semiadaptive format. The primary goal was to facilitate administration of the test. A second project goal was to replicate the creation of the Web-based Arabic test to create a new Russian proficiency test. Because there are few blueprints for second language test developers who want to create computer-adaptive tests (Dunkel, 1999a), CAL also proposed to develop a general framework for this project—the mandate, test guidelines, and item specifications—so that other institutions interested in creating their own Web-based tests would have a template for doing so. (See Davidson & Lynch, 2002, for more information on general foreign language test mandates and specifications and Eignor, 1999, for foreign language computer-adaptive test specifications in particular.) In 2000, CAL's Language Testing Division received a grant from the United States Department of Education to develop online, semiadaptive listening and reading proficiency tests in Arabic and Russian.

Project Teams

Before test development could begin, four teams were identified to work on the project. The first team consisted of the CAL staff members who would manage the project. The second team, whose role was to review the framework and the item specifications after they were drafted by CAL staff, consisted of one representative each from the American Council on the Teaching of Foreign Languages (ACTFL) and the governmental Interagency Language Roundtable (ILR) and six members of the National Council of Organizations of Less Commonly Taught Languages (NCOLCTL).

The third team, all native speakers of Arabic, worked specifically on the Arabic test. The team consisted of Arabic item writers; an external board that reviewed the items created by the writers; and a group of graduate students who evaluated the effectiveness of the items, commented on the items' interest levels, and provided technical language assistance to CAL staff when needed.

The fourth team worked on the Russian test. The Russian team mirrored the Arabic team in composition and tasks. However, because the Russian item development team needed to create considerably more items than the Arabic team (because the Russian test did not incorporate items from a previously existing assessment), there were two more Russian item writers than Arabic item writers.

Other native speaking consultants were called upon to help re-record audio files for some of the listening items whose original audio files were of poor digital quality.

Meeting Development Challenges

Creating Online Listening and Reading Items

Because reliable resources and materials for LCTL instruction and testing in the United States are scarce (Janus, 2000), the test developers decided to use the Web as a materials source for creating authentic listening and reading test items. All Arabic and Russian item writers attended item development sessions at CAL, where they discussed with CAL staff the procedures for developing items based on the ACTFL Proficiency Guidelines for listening and reading (Byrnes & Canale, 1987) and based on the language-specific guidelines for Arabic and Russian (American Council on the Teaching of Foreign Languages, 1988, 1989). The American Council on the Teaching of Foreign Languages (ACTFL) guidelines describe four main levels of proficiency: novice, intermediate, advanced, and superior, which are the target levels of proficiency to be assessed by the Arabic and Russian Web tests.

The item writers for this project were professors and experts in their language fields, but CAL staff were concerned that some of them might not be technically prepared to develop authentic items for insertion into an online examination. To address this issue, all item writers were given the following suggestions:

1. Download audio files from Russian and Arabic news Web sites according to copyright guidelines. Standard audio files can be edited by using the Windows accessories program Sound Recorder. More sophisticated digital audio editing can be done at CAL with the program Sound Forge from Sony Media ($400; available online at http://mediasoftware.sonypictures.com/products/soundforgefamily.asp).

2. Make recordings from Web-based radio stations by using Total Recorder from High Criteria, Inc. ($11.95; available online at http://www.highcriteria.com). Lists of Arabic and Russian online radio station guides can be found at CAL's Web site (2004).

3. Use the print screen (Print Scrn) button on a PC to create a screen shot of any Internet Web page. Create a graphic JPEG file of the relevant parts with the standard Windows accessories program Paint.

4. Go to CAL's Web site (2004) for tips on how to view Arabic or Russian text through an Internet browser, and see Madhany (2003) for tips on how to set Windows to read and write in Arabic.

Arabic and Russian teams developed, reviewed, and revised approximately 125 items for each language's reading and listening test sections, about 500 items total. Items were developed across the full range of ACTFL proficiency levels for listening and reading, from novice to superior.

Choosing a Commercial Online Assessment Product

Instead of building a new program to administer online foreign language proficiency tests, CAL staff members decided to purchase existing commercial software for Web-based assessment (Chalhoub-Deville, 2002). Table 1 lists currently available test packages, though this list is by no means exhaustive. Test products are listed in alphabetical order, along with the company name and URL. Not listed are the item types available with each test package (e.g., multiple choice, essay, matching, and fill in the blank), because each package has many item types available. Included are adaptability functions (item-by-item or testlet level[2] adaptability; see Wainer et al., 2000, pp. 245-254 for an elaboration on testlets), options for security, and availability of a hosting service. (With a hosting service, the company, usually for a fee, hosts your Web-based tests, the media associated with them, and the scores, all of which are accessed via the Web.) Price information is also included. Prices are often dependent on the complexity of the test program (i.e., adaptability levels), the type of organization purchasing the product (tax exempt or not), and the number of administrators and potential examinees involved.

For the Arabic and Russian Web tests CAL purchased the software product Perception, for Web and a Microsoft SQL Server. This test package and server system was chosen because Perception for Web had all the features needed for these particular tests — graphic and audio file capabilities, high security, multiple choice and essay items, and adaptability at the testlet level[3]—at an affordable price.

Perception for Web requires examinees to have a designated login name and password to log on. CAL staff can restrict the time and date for the test period, the amount of

Table 1. Currently available off-the-shelf online testing packages

Product, Company, & Web Site	Adaptability	Security	Hosting	Price
1) i-assess, EQL International Ltd., http://www.iassess.com	No	Student login ID & password restriction is integrated	No	Contact i-assess for pricing
2) Perception for Web, Questionmark, http://www.quest	Item-by-item or testlet branching	Password & logins, option to use free secure browser (locked, proctor can be required) for PCs available	Available	Contact Questionmark for pricing
3) Test Generator Enterprise, Fain & Company, http://www.testshop.com	Not available yet	Passord & logins, other features such as a locked browser or dual login requirement available	Available	Contact Fain & Company for pricing
4) Test Pilot Enterprise, ClearLearning, McGraw-Hill Higher Education, http://www.clearlearning.com	Item-by-item or testlet branching	Login ID & password restrictions available	Available	$750 to $20,000 depending on number of participants
5) Quiz Factory 2, LearningWare Inc., http://www.learningware.com	No	No	No	$6,995 to install player on an unlimited basis, 3 creators
6) WebMCQ, WebMCQ Pty Ltd., http://www.webmcq.com	No	General access codes to individual logins and passwords are available	Free, part of the system	Contact WebMCQ for pricing
7) WebQuiz XP, SmartLite Software, http://www.smartlite.it	No	No	No	$499.95, custom services extra

time to be spent on the test, and the number of times the test can be attempted. The program comes with a secure browser, which is free for examinees; tests can also be set so that the examinees cannot exit the test until they have completed all items, nor can they copy, paste, or print.

Secure browsers are readily available with many online testing packages. Unfortunately, Perception for Web's secure browser only works with PCs. However, if tests are not restricted to be administered with a secure browser, tests developed with Perception for Web can be taken on either a PC or a Macintosh. Because the Arabic and Russian Web tests are relatively high-stakes tests, a secure browser is needed (along with an on-site proctor who checks student IDs and monitors the test session), so CAL restricted the Arabic and Russian Web tests to PC administration only.

Meeting Design Challenges

Specifying Item Types

Two different item types are used in the online Arabic and Russian proficiency tests: standard multiple choice (Haladyna, 2004) and essay response. Although Perception for Web offers a variety of item formats, including the use of video and the incorporation of JavaScript-based drag and drop items, CAL staff members restricted the item types to be used on the Arabic and Russian tests for four reasons. First, developing numerous item types would have taken more time, money, and server space than allotted to this project. Second, for high-stakes testing, it would take too much time and space to give examinees directions for several item types. Third, the test developers decided, in this case, it would be better to focus resources on the content of the items rather than on bells and whistles that would not necessarily improve the assessment of examinees' language proficiency. Finally, video files would have been too large to be sent efficiently to examinees at remote computers.

This case study illustrates the dilemma often faced by computer-adaptive test developers (Grabe, 2000). Bells and whistles are attractive. Some argue that innovative item types may improve measurement by reducing the amount of guessing by examinees and by expanding the content coverage of a test (Parshall, Spray, Kalohn, & Davey, 2002), but practical issues, in this case, outweighed the benefits of multiple item types and video.

Specifying Item Layouts

For the Arabic and Russian Web tests, each item is presented first with an orientation, that is, a context in which the examinee might come across the reading text or listening passage. Next, the listening file (a linked MP3 listening file) or the reading text (a JPEG graphic) is given. Then the question is presented and either the multiple choice

Figure 1. Novice-level, multiple-choice Arabic reading item

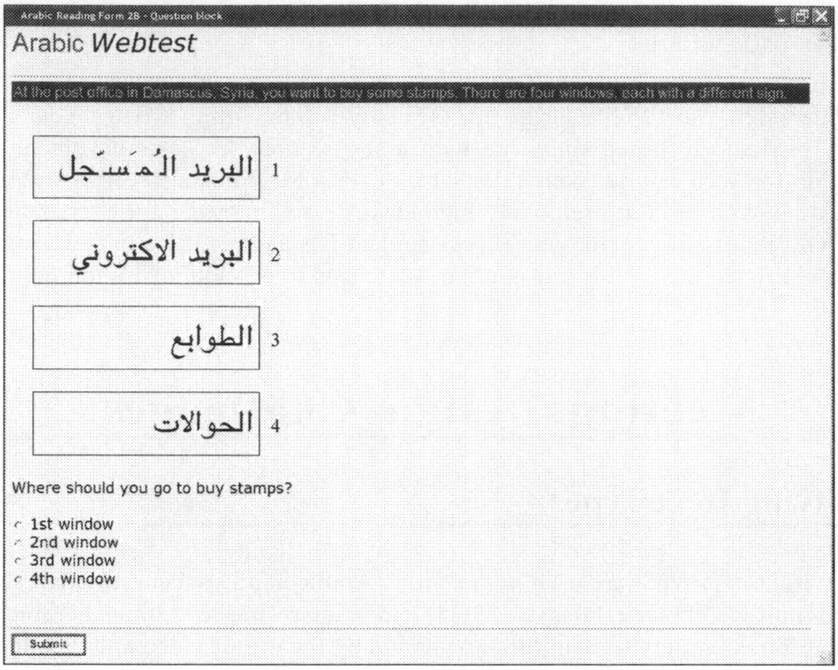

Arabic Reading Form 2B - Question block

Arabic *Webtest*

At the post office in Damascus, Syria, you want to buy some stamps. There are four windows, each with a different sign.

البريد الُمَسّجل 1

البريد الاكتروني 2

الطوابع 3

الحوالات 4

Where should you go to buy stamps?

- 1st window
- 2nd window
- 3rd window
- 4th window

Submit

Figure 2. Superior-level, essay-response Russian listening item

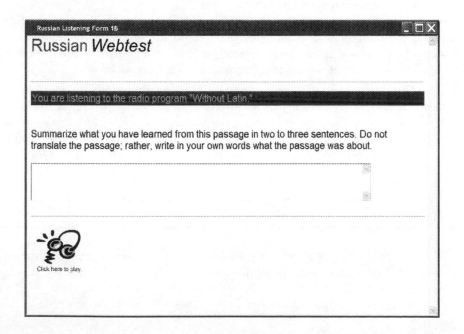

Russian Listening Form 1B

Russian *Webtest*

You are listening to the radio program "Without Latin."

Summarize what you have learned from this passage in two to three sentences. Do not translate the passage; rather, write in your own words what the passage was about.

Click here to play.

options are listed or a text box is presented in which test takers type their response in English. The essay items are the most difficult items on the test; they are at the superior level on the ACTFL scale. Essay questions are not scored automatically: The scoring of a Web test is fully automatic only for students at lower levels of proficiency, that is, those who do not reach the superior-level items and who are tested only with multiple choice questions. Examples of an Arabic novice-level, multiple choice reading item and a Russian superior-level, essay response listening item are presented in Figures 1 and 2.

All Arabic and Russian reading texts are presented as JPEGs because Perception for Web does not support non-Roman fonts. Using JPEGs allows the incorporation of authentic items exactly as they appear on the Web or in print, with their different fonts, colors, and photos. The inability of Perception for Web to support non-Roman fonts also means that all essay responses must be in English. This is a limitation, but CAL staff believe that not all the test takers would know how to type in Arabic or Russian. In addition, having the responses in English facilitates the scoring of the essay items. English speakers at CAL are trained to use the scoring rubrics and assign scores based on content, not on spelling or punctuation. A downside to this method is that at the highest levels of proficiency, students are forced to use English to demonstrate their comprehension of Arabic or Russian. Students who are native speakers of English may be at an advantage over native speakers of other languages who take these tests, especially at the higher levels of proficiency.

Determining Item Difficulties

To calibrate the items developed for this project, the items were first field tested at more than 25 different institutions. Students of Arabic and Russian from all levels participated in the field testing, which was organized by CAL and the proctors at each institution who administered and monitored the test taking sessions. At CAL, a Rasch analysis using Winsteps was performed for each test to calibrate the items and to determine each item's difficulty level. (For more information about Rasch analyses, see Athanasou, 2001; Bond & Fox, 2001; El-Korashy, 1995; and McNamara, 1990.) The difficulty levels corresponded significantly with the items' predetermined ACTFL levels at approximately the 0.70 level for each test (Spearman's *rho*, 2-tailed correlations, $p < .01$). After the item difficulties were determined, the items were separated into four levels of item difficulty according to a modified bookmarking procedure based on Mitzel, Lewis, Patz, and Green (2001).

In preparation for the item analyses, CAL staff first formatted the examinee responses for the statistical analyses. Although many off the shelf test packages come with built in statistical features, the statistical features provided are generally not intended for analyzing data in connection with large scale, standardized test development projects. Getting results from field test forms that were administered selectively across institutions and classes and that contained a set of repeated items taken by each examinee (the anchor items) was beyond the scope of Perception for Web's reporting program. (See Ward & Murray-Ward, 1994, for more information on item banking and anchor items.) Thus, scores received by individuals from each institution on the different field test forms were downloaded into Excel spreadsheets. The data were then merged appropriately for the Rasch analyses.

Rudner (1998) warned that compiling test forms, making testing arrangements, collecting data, and preparing data for processing are particularly important steps in creating item banks. He stated that "depending on the frequency of students taking multiple subtests from different levels and forms, this . . . can be a major undertaking" (p. 4). Even with the progress in technology and the advanced reporting features that come with online test packages, this is still the case.

Meeting Delivery Challenges

Creating Item Banks and the Test Path

For a Web test, two separate item banks are necessary: one for the preliminary placer test and one for the testlets. In Figure 3, the placer test is shown as having 20 items pooled from all levels of the test, from the easiest items to the most difficult.

Figure 4 shows the testlet item bank. The superior-level items in this pool are either essay or multiple-choice, whereas in the placer test, the superior-level items are only multiple-choice.

In Figures 3 and 4, the item difficulty levels, which were used to separate the items for placement into the item banks, do not align strictly according to ACTFL levels; correspondence was highly significant at the 0.70 level, but not 100%. Therefore, the graphic displays of the ACTFL levels corresponding with the difficulty levels in Figures 3 and 4 are an idealistic representation.

Figure 3. Item databank for the placer test

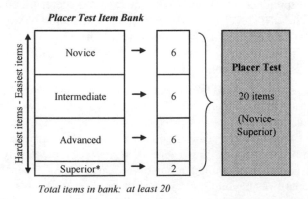

Total items in bank: at least 20

*All Superior-level items (the hardest items) in the placer test item bank are multiple-choice.

Figure 4. Item databank for the testlets

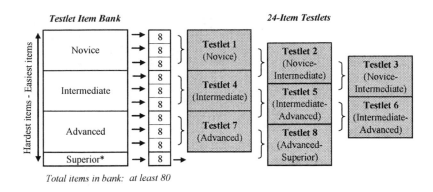

Total items in bank: at least 80

*Superior-level items (the hardest items) in the testlet item bank are either multiple-choice or essay.

When an examinee logs in for a test, he or she is first presented with the placer test that has 20 items ranging from the easiest (ideally novice level) to the hardest (ideally superior level). The outcome of the placer test directs the examinee to an appropriate testlet with items centralized around his or her ability level. If the examinee does as well as expected on the first testlet (e.g., receives a score between 33% and 66%), the examinee's test ends, and he or she receives a score report. However, if the examinee does not do as well as expected, he or she will take a second testlet at a lower or higher level of difficulty, depending on the first testlet's outcome. In this case, the score report is issued after the second testlet. This test path is represented in Figure 5.

According to this semiadaptive template, depending on whether an examinee takes one or two testlets, a test has either 44 or 68 items. Students at lower proficiency levels are expected to take less time because their items are shorter, while students at the advanced or superior level need more time. The time, however, is also influenced by the number of testlets (one or two) the examinee takes. There is no time limit on the Arabic or Russian tests. In general, the semiadaptability of a test makes it shorter than a standard fix-form test, which typically has more items at all difficulty levels for each test taker (Young, Shermis, Brutten, & Perkins, 1996).

Adapting to Changing Test Technology

The Arabic and Russian Web test project was budgeted to take three years. However, several problems arose. The original budget was written in 1999, but changes in technology costs between 2000, when the project began, and 2004, when it was finished, affected the project design and influenced the test development process. Originally, $6,000 was budgeted for the Web-based assessment program, Perception for Web. By the end of 2001, the cost for most programs was over $10,000, and prices have continued to climb since then.

Figure 5. The test taker's path

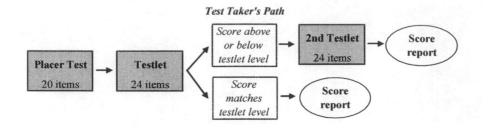

In 2000, the audio files to be used in the tests were created in standard AU (audio file; the file extension is .au) formats. However, during the first round of pilot testing, many university computers did not have audio players that could open these files. Therefore, the audio format was switched in 2001 to WAV (Windows waveform), which was more accessible to examinees in computer labs at colleges and universities. Over time, as the field testing expanded and more examinees logged in simultaneously, it was found that these files were hard for remote computers to download due to the relatively small bandwidth and server capacity available at CAL.

In 2003, CAL upgraded to a newer version of Perception for Web (version 3.4). This newer version allowed for the insertion of MP3 (MPEG audio layer 3) files, which are considerably smaller than WAV or AU files, so CAL staff converted all the audio files to MP3s. Staff members on the project were fortunate to have a license with Question*mark* that provided free product upgrades as long as CAL's Language Testing Division continued to pay the annual support fees.

Living with Program Constraints

Not wanting institutions' technical limitations to prevent them from having access to the tests, the test development project needed to adapt according to the constraints on computers and server systems at typical institutions across the United States. Thus, for example, when it was discovered that some of the possible test users—universities that wanted to use the Arabic test for placement—had internal server blocks (firewalls) and browser specifications set up against incoming JavaScript on the public computers used in testing, CAL staff eliminated all JavaScript utilities in the tests to prevent losing this significant population of potential test takers.

This was unfortunate for two reasons. First, Perception for Web has a test tracking bar that can be included in a test. The bar can be used by an examinee to flag items to review later before submitting the answers and maps where the examinee is in the test, how many test questions have been answered, and how many remain. CAL staff had to eliminate the test tracking features because they run with JavaScript. Instead, the items were numbered manually (e.g., 12 out of 24).

Secondly, CAL staff was using JavaScript to restrict the number of times an examinee could listen to an audio file. Perception for Web has no built-in feature for this. With

JavaScript, CAL staff had examinees access a listening file through a link that would disappear when clicked, thus taking away the option to hear the passage more than once. Forced to eliminate JavaScript, CAL staff created two items for every one listening item: an unscored audio-file-empty item and an exact duplicate with the audio file embedded and set to play automatically. On a listening Web test, these two items are always presented as a set. This solution is not as good as using JavaScript, but it works and allows the tests to be accessible to more examinees.

Concluding Lessons for the Future

In this chapter, I discussed the challenges involved in creating online Arabic and Russian proficiency tests using a commercial product. I provided suggestions for developing online test items and for purchasing an off-the-shelf test package. In addition, I described the challenges CAL staff faced in designing and delivering tests securely over the Internet.

Staff members in CAL's Language Testing Division hope to use the knowledge they gained in refining their approaches to developing online tests for developing Web-based proficiency tests in other LCTLs. The five major lessons CAL staff learned that could help test developers begin a similar online test development project are summarized in the following list:

1. Be prepared to spend considerable time with foreign language item developers, who sometimes have limited experience with computers or with test development. They will need help in creating items using materials currently available on the Web. They will not only need to know which Web sites to visit but also be provided with the tools to download and edit materials from the Web. They also need to know how to record where they found the materials they have chosen in order to request copyright permissions.

2. Be prepared for software and other materials to cost much more than originally budgeted. Unforeseen expenses tend to arise, such as having to pay for audio files to be converted or needing to buy more memory for your server space as you add new multimedia to your items. Something that costs $1,000 today may cost $2,000 tomorrow.

3. When using an off-the-shelf testing product, make sure it can grow and change with your project and with current trends in technology. Get a renewable site license that will provide upgrades and newer versions of the software with annual support payments.

4. Consider having the test project hosted by the test company's server system for a monthly or annual fee (or on a per test basis) rather than buying and maintaining your own server, especially if you are a small institution. One of the major problems in online testing, especially when large multimedia files are involved, is getting the items or the entire test delivered in a fast and efficient manner. The

efficiency depends on remote computer download speeds, Internet traffic, the size of the multimedia, and the bandwidth and competing incoming and outgoing data at the host server's door. It depends very little on the online test program you are using.

5.   Be prepared for constraints caused by limitations on your end or on the test takers' end. Some features of commercial test packages, such as security measures, reduce the number of platforms or browsers on which the tests are administrable. Other features, such as JavaScript-supported timers and counters, novel item formats, or test tracking bars, may not be usable due to delivery problems. Sometimes the programming language of these features will reduce the number of potential test takers because examinees' computers do not allow the features; they may be blocked by firewalls or public computer lab download restrictions.

Despite the challenges involved in creating online, standardized tests of foreign language proficiency, especially for the LCTLs in the United States, the benefits are worth it. The challenges to the tests' development can be met by being prepared: Establish item and test development guidelines ahead of time, be savvy when it comes to purchasing commercial test products, and research what others have done to learn from their mistakes and successes.

Acknowledgments

A special thanks to Dr. Dorry M. Kenyon, director of the Arabic and Russian Web test project and the Language Testing Division at CAL, for his guidance and instruction.

References

American Council on the Teaching of Foreign Languages. (1988). ACTFL Russian proficiency guidelines. *Foreign Language Annals, 21*(2), 177-197.

American Council on the Teaching of Foreign Languages. (1989). ACTFL Arabic proficiency guidelines. *Foreign Language Annals, 22*(4), 373-392.

Athanasou, J. A. (2001). Analysis of responses to vocational interest items: A study of Australian high school students. *Journal of Career Assessment, 9*(1), 61-79.

Bachman, L. F., & Palmer, A. S. (1996). *Language testing in practice.* UK: Oxford University Press.

Bond, T. G., & Fox, C. M. (2001). *Applying the Rasch model: Fundamental measurement in the human sciences.* Mahwah, NJ: Erlbaum.

Brown, J. D. (1997). Computers in language testing: Present research and some future directions. *Language Learning and Technology, 1*(1), 44-59.

Byrnes, H., & Canale, M. (Eds.). (1987). *Defining and developing proficiency: Guidelines, implementations and concepts.* Lincolnwood, IL: National Textbook.

Center for Applied Linguistics. (2004). *Arabic and Russian Web test project.* Retrieved September 4, 2004, from *http://www.cal.org/projects/webtest/*

Chalhoub-Deville, M. (2002). Technology in standardized language assessments. In R. B. Kaplan (Ed.), *The Oxford handbook of applied linguistics* (pp. 471-486). New York: Oxford University Press.

Chalhoub-Deville, M., & Deville, C. (1999). Computer adaptive testing in second language contexts. *Annual Review of Applied Linguistics, 19,* 273-299.

Chapelle, C. A. (2001). *Computer applications in second language acquisition.* UK: Cambridge University Press.

Davidson, F., & Lynch, B. K. (2002). *Testcraft: A teacher's guide to writing and using language test specifications.* New Haven, CT: Yale University Press.

Dunkel, P. A. (1999a). Considerations in developing or using second/foreign language proficiency computer-adaptive tests. *Language Learning and Technology, 2*(2), 77-93.

Dunkel, P. A. (1999b). Research and development of computer-adaptive test of listening comprehension in the less commonly taught language Hausa. In M. Chalhoub-Deville (Ed.), *Issues in computer-adaptive testing of reading proficiency: Vol. 10* (pp. 91-121). UK: Cambridge University Press.

Eignor, D. (1999). Selected technical issues in the creation of computer-adaptive tests of second language reading proficiency. In M. Chalhoub-Deville (Ed.), *Issues in computer-adaptive testing of reading proficiency: Vol. 10* (pp. 167-181). UK: Cambridge University Press.

El-Korashy, A.-F. (1995). Applying the Rasch model to the selection of items for a mental ability test. *Educational and Psychological Measurement, 55*(5), 753-763.

Grabe, W. (2000). Reading research and its implications for reading assessment. In A. J. Kunnan (Ed.), *Fairness and validation in language assessment: Vol. 9* (pp. 226–262). UK: Cambridge University Press.

Haladyna, T. M. (2004). *Developing and validating multiple choice test items* (3rd ed.). Mahwah, NJ: Erlbaum.

Hughes, A. (1989). *Testing for language teachers.* UK: Cambridge University Press.

Janus, L. (2000). An overview of less commonly taught languages in the United States. *NASSP Bulletin, 84*(612), 25-29.

Madhany, al-H. N. (2003). *Arabicizing Windows: Enabling Windows applications to read and write Arabic.* Retrieved April 10, 2004, from *http://www.nclrc.org/inst-arabic3.pdf*

McNamara, T. F. (1990). Item response theory and the validation of an ESP test for health professionals. *Language Testing, 7*(1), 52-75.

Mitzel, H. C., Lewis, D. M., Patz, R. J., & Green, D. R. (2001). The bookmark procedure: Psychological perspectives. In G. J. Cizek (Ed.), *Setting performance standards: Concepts, methods, and perspectives* (pp. 249–281). Mahwah, NJ: Erlbaum.

Parshall, C. G., Spray, J. A., Kalohn, J. C., & Davey, T. (2002). *Practical considerations in computer-based testing* (pp. 71-91). New York: Springer.

Rudner, L. (1998). *Item banking*. Washington, DC: ERIC Clearinghouse on Assessment and Evaluation. (ERIC Document Reproduction Service No. ED423310)

Wainer, H., Dorans, N. J., Green, B. F., Mislevy, R. J., Steinberg, L., & Thissen, D. (2000). Future challenges. In H. Wainer (Ed.), *Computerized adaptive testing: A primer* (2nd ed., pp. 231-270). Mahwah, NJ: Erlbaum.

Walker, G., & McGinnis, S. (1995). *Learning less commonly taught languages: An agreement on the bases for the training of teachers* (The Ohio State University Foreign Language Publications Series No. FLP01). Bryn Mawr, PA: National Council of Organizations of Less Commonly Taught Languages. (ERIC Document No. ED438729)

Ward, A. W., & Murray-Ward, M. (1994). Guidelines for the development of item banks: An NCME instructional module. *Educational Measurement: Issues and Practice, 13*(1), 34-39.

Young, R., Shermis, M. D., Brutten, S. R., & Perkins, K. (1996). From conventional to computer-adaptive testing of ESL reading comprehension. *System, 24*(1), 23-40.

Endnotes

[1]   An adaptable test is "one in which the examinee's responses to earlier items in the test influence which subsequent items must be answered in the same test" (Young, Shermis, Brutten, & Perkins, 1996, p. 23). Some tests are adaptable at the item level (fully adaptable tests), while others are adaptable after a group of items are administered (semiadaptable tests). In item-level adaptable tests, if an examinee gets an item right, the next item is more difficult; if the examinee gets an item wrong, the next item is easier (Young et al., 1996). In semiadaptable tests, the score an examinee receives on a group of items determines the difficulty level of the next group of items he or she will receive.

[2]   For our purposes, a testlet is a group or "prearranged cluster" of items (Wainer et al., 2000, p. 238) that may be presented to an examinee based on his or her ability level (as predetermined by a placer test, for example). His or her outcome on the testlet determines the following path that the examinee will take. Assessments that are adaptable with testlets are semiadaptable tests.

[3]   Item-level adaptable tests demand an extremely large item pool in order to function; therefore, thousands of examinees must be available to field test and validate the items (Chalhoub-Deville & Deville, 1999, p. 276). Resources are not available for the LCTLs to produce and validate item banks with thousands of items. Therefore, we believe semiadaptable tests with testlets (prearranged clusters or groups of items)

are more appropriate for LCTL tests of this kind. They need fewer items and can be validated adequately on the smaller number of LCTL students available for field testing.

Chapter VII

Using Web-Enabled Technology in a Performance-Based Accreditation Environment

John C. Wise, Penn State University, USA

Dhaneshwar Lall, Penn State University, USA

Peter J. Shull, Penn State University, USA

Dhushy Sathianathan, Penn State University, USA

Sang Ha Lee, Penn State University, USA

Abstract

This chapter describes two online systems that support the transition from instructor-based to student-outcome-based education in an engineering technology context. The first system facilitates communication among faculty while establishing a baseline of current curricular practice. This data can be used to identify appropriate measurement points for various student performance outcomes. The second system is designed to collect and display student performance data related to particular educational outcomes in preparation for program accreditation. Data are collected from both students and faculty. The system is scalable, so it can be adapted to various levels of need. This data are being used to assess individual or group performance across several distributed campuses.

Introduction

Recent changes in accreditation requirements for colleges of engineering have brought a need for performance-based assessment of student outcomes. This chapter describes two online systems designed to maximize stakeholder (in this case, higher education faculty) participation in the change process and design of assessments. The first system collects outcome-based data from faculty on a course-by-course basis in order to establish baseline data for a particular program. A second system is used to continuously track the performance of students and course effectiveness vis-à-vis the program outcomes and objectives. Readers will become familiar with a systemic application of online data collection linking 12 outlying campuses for analysis of student preparation and performance in common programs across the campuses. Although the technology presented herein is not new, its application as a tool to facilitate understanding of the systemic nature of the engineering technology curriculum is novel.

The objectives of this chapter are (a) to introduce the reader to two complementary online evaluation and assessment systems designed for both collecting data and enhancing collaboration among faculty in a higher education setting and (b) to report on the authors' experiences in implementing and using these performance-based assessment systems.

Background

Definition of Terms

- **ABET Criteria:** The accreditation board for engineering and technology (ABET) establishes standards for college programs desiring accreditation. The latest criteria emphasize specifying objective program outcomes and an assessment process that measures student performance against these outcomes and provides feedback for improving the educational program.

- **Program Educational Objectives:** Statements that describe the expected accomplishments of graduates during the first few years after graduation.

- **Program Outcomes:** Statements that describe what students are expected to *know* and be able to *do* by the time of graduation, the attainment of which indicates that the student is equipped to achieve the program educational objectives. (ABET-designated outcomes must be included.)

- **Continuous Quality Improvement (CQI):** A process in which performance data are routinely collected and used to make decisions to improve system performance.

- **Suboutcomes (course-level):** As program outcomes tend to be general statements, suboutcomes are written to define the specific knowledge and abilities that are included in the program outcomes. Suboutcomes are linked with (or "mapped to") particular courses.

- **Assessment:** Assessment is the collection and analysis of data related to the performance outcomes. Tools for assessment *(assessment instruments)* include tests, homework, demonstrations, presentations, lab reports, and so forth. Anything that demonstrates a student's ability to meet a desired outcome is a viable assessment instrument.

- **Evaluation:** Strictly speaking, evaluation takes place when the data gathered and analyzed through assessment are used to make statements and decisions regarding the educational program.

- **"Closing the Loop":** A phrase referring to using assessment data and evaluation decisions to continuously improve the educational system. Classroom performance data, for example, need to feed back to the classroom instructor so that he or she can make improvements at that level. Course performance data need to inform decisions made by course supervisors and others. ABET requires evidence that this process, which is essentially a continuous quality improvement cycle, is in place and functioning.

- **Embedded Assessment:** Embedded assessment means using assessments that are already in the curriculum rather than imposing extracurricular instruments and measurement requirements. Classroom instructors are asked to identify appropriate measures for each suboutcome that are already in place in their classrooms, then provide performance data based on these activities. The use of existing assessments reduces the impact of outcome-based data collection on both students and faculty; voluntary participation in data collection should therefore be enhanced.

- **Authentic Assessment:** An attempt to measure learner performance on realistic tasks in realistic settings.

- **Outcome-Based Assessment:** As implied, this term refers to assessment based on student performance learning outcomes. If the outcome requires the student to construct a circuit, for example, the assessment will measure whether the student can construct a circuit. The type of assessment tool selected is highly dependent upon the desired outcome.

- **Performance-Based Evidence:** As noted in the preceding definition, if the desired *outcome* is for the student to construct a circuit, the *evidence* would be a circuit built by the student.

Context

Beginning in the year 2000, ABET established new criteria for the accreditation of engineering programs, entitled "Engineering Criteria 2000," or "EC 2000." Programs will no longer be measured by the number of math credits offered or the amount of available laboratory space. Instead, each program is now required to develop a list of program outcomes that are based on student performance. After these outcomes are established, a system for assessing their attainment needs to be activated. The new requirements established for engineering technology programs, designated "TC2K," are similar (Accreditation Board for Engineering and Technology, 2004). This chapter reports on the process of designing, testing, and implementing two separate but related online tools to facilitate college assessment in the engineering technology context.

TC2K represents a major philosophical change for engineering technology program accreditation from a *resource-based* approach to an *outcomes-based* approach. Previous ABET standards focused on a program's past performance, resources, and inputs. TC2K requires programs to develop a continuous improvement plan and system for self-analysis and improvement. The new approach allows a considerable amount of flexibility for programs, because each college program is free to define its own objectives and outcomes and then demonstrate that they are being achieved. Nontraditional approaches to teaching and learning engineering technology are encouraged, and programs are motivated toward continuous self-improvement. Table 1 shows the former approach compared with the new approach (the information comes from the Accreditation Board for Engineering and Technology, 2002).

Penn State University has 17 engineering technology programs distributed over 12 campuses across the Commonwealth of Pennsylvania. Responsibility for the curriculum is designated at the system, program, course, and campus levels. Coordination is critical to ensure that the education received by students taking the same course at different locations is essentially equivalent, particularly because there is some

Table 1. ABET prior and current approaches compared

Prior Criteria	TC2K
Resources and inputs for programs	Competencies of graduates
Snapshot-in-time approach	Continuity of program
Program presents data; ABET team draws conclusions	Program presents results of continuous self-assessment
Accredit based on past performance	Accredit based on effectiveness of quality assurance system
Uses measures that can change rapidly	Uses measures with momentum
Program must have a working continuous improvement plan	Continuous improvement plan is the heart of the system

transfer of students, notably between the commonwealth colleges and the University Park campus.

Administratively, the system is supervised by the head of Engineering Technology Commonwealth Education (ETCE). The head organizes curricular committees that ensure program integrity across the system. Each course is overseen by a course chair, who is responsible for system-wide course continuity across all campuses. Finally, each campus has a program chair. The program chair works at the local level to make certain that the program is functioning correctly. ABET accreditation occurs at the program level. Each program at each campus must satisfy ABET requirements. The student enrollment at each campus by itself is often too small to generate the numbers necessary for certain statistical data analyses. Collecting data system-wide will help to alleviate this problem. The distributed nature of the constituent campuses is tailor-made for an information technology solution.

Outcomes-Based Assessment

Education in general has been moving from a teacher-centered to a more learner-centered approach (Huba & Freed, 2000; Pine & Boy, 1977). Simply stated, the emphasis is no longer on what is *taught;* rather, it is on what is *learned*. In a teacher-centered environment, covering two book chapters in 1 week may be a measure of success. In a learner-centered environment, what matters is what the students learned during that same week. Active learning, project-based learning, collaborative learning, problem-based learning, and cooperative learning are all examples of learner-centered teaching techniques that have been promoted in recent years in *The Journal of Engineering Education* and other publications (see Adams & Hamm, 1994; Bonwell & Eison, 1991; Marlowe & Page, 1998; Sanders, Walvoord, & Stanforth, 1995).

Table 2. ABET's base program outcomes

An engineering technology program must demonstrate that graduates have
a) An appropriate mastery of the knowledge, techniques, skills and modern tools of their disciplines
b) An ability to apply current knowledge and adapt to emerging applications of mathematics, science, engineering, and technology
c) An ability to conduct, analyze, and interpret experiments and apply experimental results to improve processes
d) An ability to apply creativity in the design of systems, components, or processes appropriate to program objectives
e) An ability to function effectively on teams
f) An ability to identify, analyze, and solve technical problems
g) An ability to communicate effectively
h) A recognition of the need for and an ability to engage in lifelong learning
i) An ability to understand professional, ethical, and social responsibilities
j) A respect for diversity and a knowledge of contemporary professional, societal, and global issues
k) A commitment to quality, timeliness, and continuous improvement

ABET provides a starting point by publishing 11 *program outcomes* that must be addressed (see Table 2; information retrieved from Accreditation Board for Engineering and Technology, 2004). Programs can add to the program outcome list—and should—based on their individual needs. *Program Educational Objectives* (PEOs) are defined by stakeholders (i.e., faculty, employers, graduates, and industry partners) and reflect accomplishments typical of graduates within the first two or three years following graduation. These PEOs are regularly reviewed by the stakeholders to verify their continued applicability. Changes in "typical accomplishments" will be reflected in updated PEOs, which in turn will affect the program outcomes. This activity is beyond the scope of the system being described in this report but is important for context.

As stated previously, program outcomes are broad statements that apply at the point of graduation. When the list of outcomes has been agreed to, they are mapped to the different courses in the curriculum. In order to be measurable, they need to be further defined through course-level outcomes, which our group termed "suboutcomes." Effective outcomes-based assessment requires that these suboutcomes be based on a consensus among the faculty as to what a student needs to be able to *know* and *do* at graduation. These outcomes need to be written from a student-centered point of view and reflect specific performances under specific conditions (Mager, 1984; Wankat & Oreovicz, 1993). The general format agreed upon looks something like this statement:

> *Given [certain conditions], the student will [do something that demonstrates ability or understanding] to [a certain level of quality].*

The development and use of suboutcomes is similar to a certification process. If, for example, one wished to certify someone as an automobile operator, it makes sense to start by making a list of things he or she would need to do to demonstrate knowledge and ability. Imagine a checklist of these items. It may include a basic understanding of traffic rules, the mechanics of the automobile, and the ability to operate primary controls (e.g., gas pedal and steering wheel) and secondary controls (e.g., windshield wipers). Any group of driving instructors and other experts may disagree as to which specific suboutcomes are the most important, but a consensus list can be developed and adopted. When a student successfully demonstrates achievement of each of the items on the list, the student will be certified as a driver and given a license. In a similar way, when a student in an engineering technology program demonstrates achievement of each of the program's outcomes, the student will be certified by the granting of a diploma.

In summary, outcomes-based assessment looks at what the student can actually do as a result of the education he or she has received instead of simply looking at the courses and grades on his or her transcript (Schalock, 1995). The two online tools described in the following sections were designed to help faculty familiarize themselves with ABET requirements, develop a systemic understanding of their curriculum, develop measurable outcomes, and identify appropriate assessment measures. Online forms were developed and linked to dynamic databases that allow review of the data by all system users, including students, faculty, and administrators.

System 1: Establishing a Baseline

A surefire way for a major program change to fail is to identify a few dedicated members of the faculty and charge them with the complete design. Sequestered from reality, any solution they devise is sure to face determined opposition from affected faculty peers, who often become distracted and may have even forgotten that a change was underway (see Rogers, 1995). After considering the need to involve the greatest number of stakeholders in the process, a technology-based solution was developed in order to avoid this pitfall.

An online instrument was designed that would collect data directly from each and every teaching faculty member on a weekly basis. This data consisted of only three items: (a) the learning goal for the week, (b) the learning objectives that supported the goal, and (c) a performance summary, termed, "How did it go?" The primary concern during design and pilot testing the online instrument was that it be simple to use and provide benefit to the faculty beyond the idea that it would eventually help with certification.

Training on basic instructional design principles, specifically the writing of learning objectives and goals, was conducted prior to implementing use of the online instrument. Faculty were introduced to the idea of student-centered learning outcomes and how they could be measured. Again, emphasis was placed on the benefits for the *faculty* in clearly articulating their expectations of student performance to each other and to the students. Following this training, the faculty had the knowledge needed to complete the three items in the online instrument. In doing so, they would be

Figure 1. Sample course master page

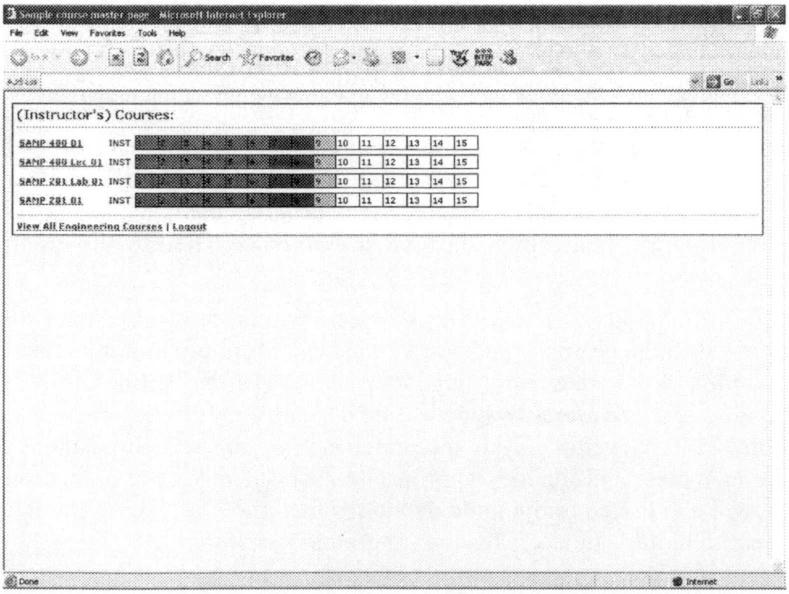

Figure 2. Sample course data page

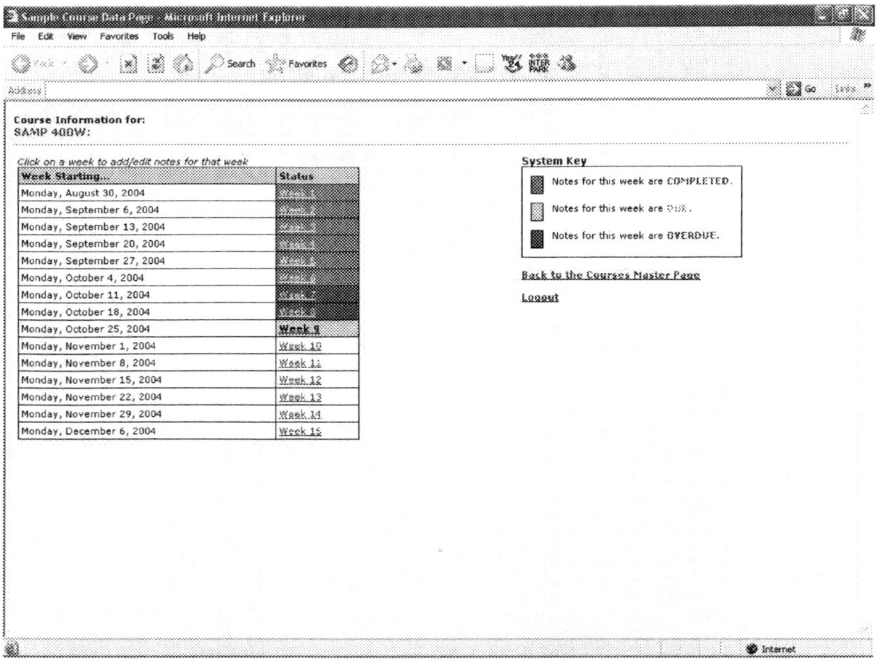

reinforcing the training they received on the writing and use of educational objectives, reflecting on their work, and simultaneously building a record of the curriculum *as it was actually being taught*. The following paragraphs provide some examples of the variety of data submitted by the faculty.

Users enter their Penn State ID and password in order to access the system. When the login is complete, a list of current courses being taught by the faculty is displayed on the course master page (see Figure 1). This information is generated automatically through an interface with the engineering data warehouse, which is the college's primary repository for course information. This display is updated whenever the page is accessed and will, of course, remain current when the semester or term changes.

All screens in the system are color-coded to indicate current status. The list of courses has a cell for each course and each week of the semester. If a cell is colored green, it means that data has been entered for that week. If yellow, data is due to be entered. If red, the data is overdue. After a faculty member has logged in, any of his or her entries are available for viewing. This can be restricted, of course, but we are trying to keep the system open to foster communication among faculty. This also means that administrators are able to log on and quickly see which faculty members are keeping up with their entries.

After the faculty member selects a particular course, the course information page is displayed (see Figure 2). Similar color-coding is used for this page. In order to enter data, the user clicks on the appropriate week.

Figure 3. Sample data entry page

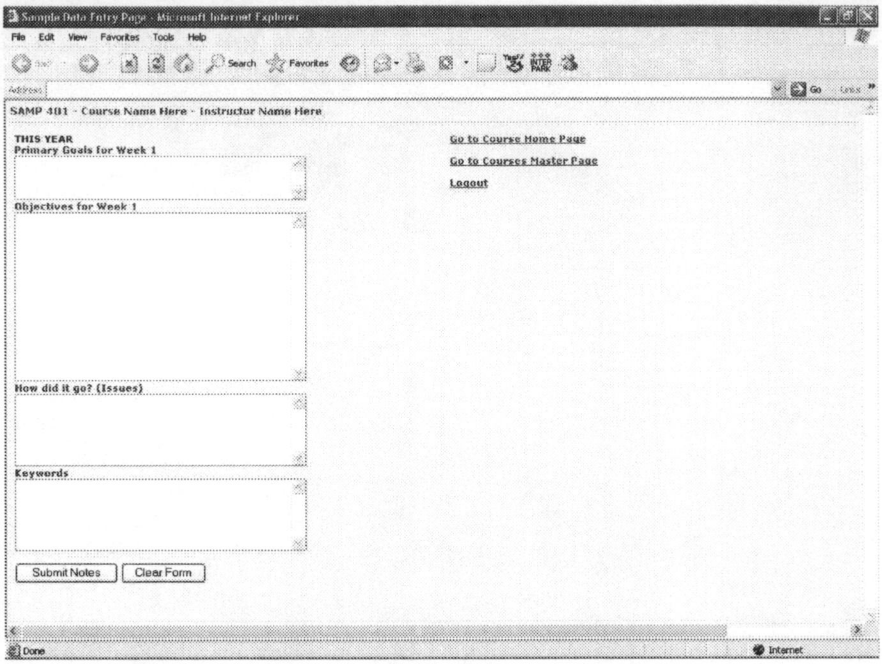

Figure 4. Sample data review page (Note: Copyright 2004 by ASEE. Reprinted with permission.)

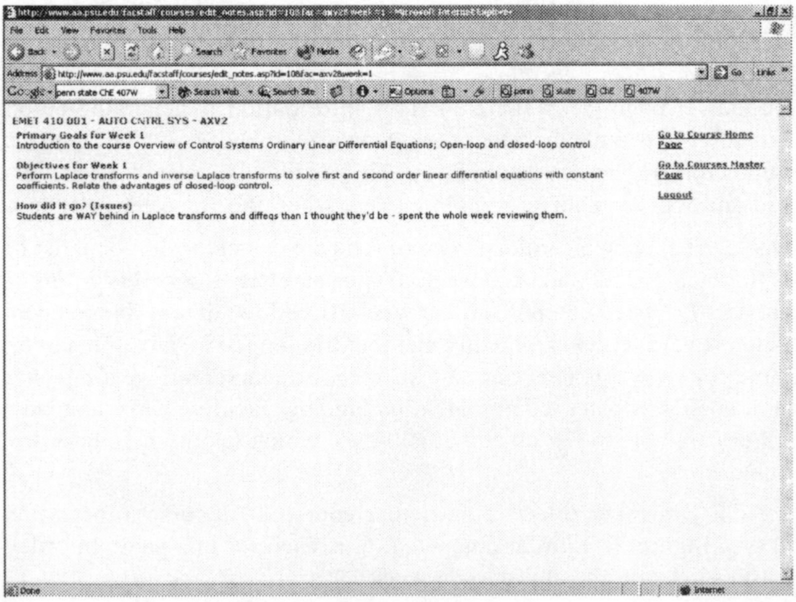

In keeping with our design goal of simplicity, the data entry page (see Figure 3) is rather spartan in appearance. Three fields are available to the user: (a) primary goals for the week, (b) objectives for the week, and (c) a catch-all item to record issues and thoughts, labeled, "How did it go?" This last field was intended to foster thought and reflection and give the faculty member a place to make notes to him or herself. For example, it often happens that a particular class may not go as well as planned due to a problem with lab equipment or a poor example in the text. A faculty member may promise to be sure to correct the problem the next time the class is taught, but seldom is the event recorded and action taken. Requiring faculty to reflect and record this information increases the chance that faculty will make corrections before the class is taught again. The record will be available for the faculty member to review prior to teaching the same class the next year. If a different faculty member is teaching next year, the new teacher can still benefit from this data.

After the data have been entered, any user may review it (see Figure 4; taken with permission from Wisc & Shull, 2004). As the data are collected over the years, archived data elements will also be displayed. In this example, all the entries for the course EMET 410 will be displayed at the same time. This allows comparison of course information between years and instructors. New instructors, for example, will be able to refer to previous years' goals and objectives when planning their own classes.

At the end of the first semester, users had a week-by-week summary of the goals and objectives for each course in the program, recorded contemporaneously by the faculty member actually providing the instruction. These data can be used to generate the program outcomes and objectives required by ABET and map them to the appropriate course in which they are being addressed. This should increase buy-in of the overall ABET system on the part of the faculty, because they were all involved in identifying the goals of their shared program rather than receiving the goals "from above" (Rossett, 1987). If a committee works separately from the system to craft course outcomes, the data gathered from this instrument can be used to verify or modify those outcomes. It is also extremely useful to have an idea of where in a course or a program different topics and skills are actually being addressed instead of asking a committee to identify where these things should be happening.

After providing baseline data for the program outcomes (a 2 year evolution in most cases), this system can be downgraded into a customizable faculty tool for archiving course performance data. It will, however, be available again if the need arises to once again collect current performance data program-wide.

Faculty response following the first semester of the online performance instrument was positive. Participation was high, but it should be noted that the college administration was firmly behind the initiative. Over 75% of the possible entries were actually made. Most faculty members felt that the online tool enabled them to understand their own courses better and to see how their courses fit into the larger curriculum. They expressed no concern over the openness of the system, and several reported looking at their faculty peers' entries. The faculty decided to continue using the tool in future semesters and suggested several improvements:

1. Reworked goals and objectives will be built into subsequent versions of the instrument, allowing users to select the appropriate goal or objective from a drop-down menu instead of having to retype goals each week.

2. Pop-up definitions and examples of good goals and objectives will be provided for reference in order to move toward greater standardization of form.

3. Faculty will be given the option of making entries weekly or based on class periods.

4. Output will be improved to allow for a complete listing of all goals and objectives so that they can be mapped within the curriculum and connected to ABET requirements where appropriate.

Establishing a Baseline: Conclusion

It appears that use of this online tool is helping faculty to become familiar with the terms used in outcome-based learning. Building the faculty's knowledge of outcome-based educational goals and objectives is an important first step in moving towards the adoption of an ABET-style continuous improvement system (see Rogers, 1995). In the first follow-up meeting, faculty initiated a discussion of student abilities in prerequisite and subsequent courses based on student weaknesses observed and recorded through use of this online instrument. This is a strong indicator that faculty are beginning to think in terms of performance outcomes.

Good program assessment requires quality data from multiple independent sources. The first step in assessment is to determine a baseline in order that the effect of any future curricular changes can be demonstrated. This online tool was effective in giving all faculty practice in writing learner-centered goals and objectives, improving their understanding of the outcome-based approach necessary for successful ABET accreditation.

System 2: A Sustainable System

In designing a system for collecting performance-based evidence in support of the engineering technology programs, the authors kept several factors in mind. First, the system must have a minimal supplemental time and effort impact on faculty and students. In order to do this, the system should make extensive use of existing assessment measures that are already embedded within the curriculum (Phillips, 1997). Secondly, the system must be scalable. In the initial stages, maximum data will be needed to establish the operating limits for the educational system. After the limits have been identified, the system should be able to be tailored to a more minimal level, enabling more focused data collection. For example, if data indicates that outcome 5 is not being met by a number of students at a particular campus, the system can be set to maximize data collection related to outcome 5 without impacting courses unrelated to this outcome.

Figure 5. Student performance evidence reporting

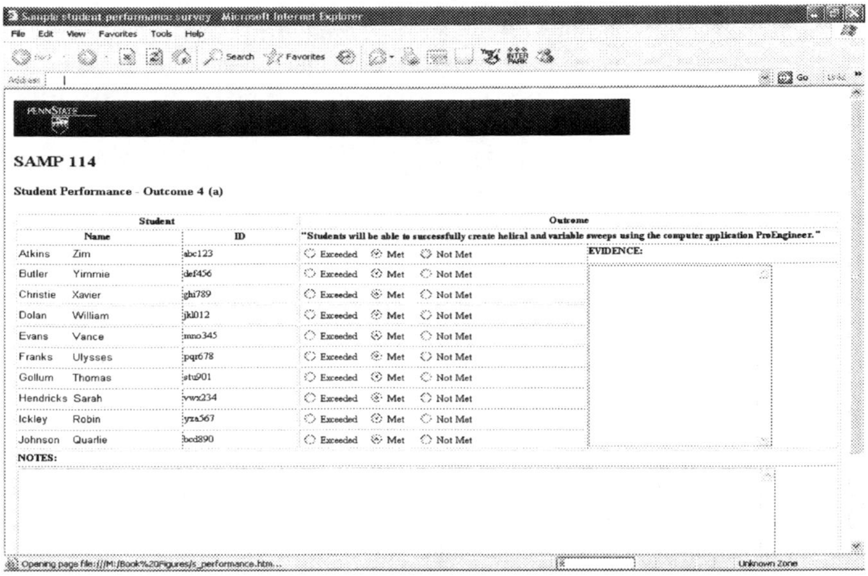

Although each campus in the system will address some assessment issues particular to their setting, it is also desirable to collect some data system-wide. Particularly, programs would like to have evidence of the achievement of educational outcomes at the program level and information regarding student and faculty satisfaction with each targeted course. Gathering this information at the system level will let users slice it more ways, such as at the campus level, the course level, the curricular level, or the system level. This will allow users to add data from other campuses when needed to increase the statistical power or to make comparisons when appropriate among programs and campuses.

Although many potential measurement points exist, the assessment team has concentrated on three measures that have meaning when considered in any context from the course level to the system-wide level. The system includes performance-based evidence reporting (Student Performance Survey), faculty perception of course effectiveness (Faculty Perception Survey), and student perception of their own ability (Student Perception Survey). All these online instruments are solidly based on the program outcomes and suboutcomes developed by the faculty. The data from the three instruments can be combined to provide information as to the functioning of the curriculum.

Performance-based evidence reporting is carried out via an online interface that asks faculty to rate each student's work against the suboutcomes addressed in their courses. The student list and the list of outcomes are automatically generated. The faculty member assigns a rating to each student based on whether the student has met, exceeded, or not met each outcome (see Figure 5). The faculty member is also requested to provide the evidence used to make this judgment. For example, did the students complete a lab assignment, in-class presentation, or project that demonstrated an ability to satisfy the outcome? Each program will decide the extent to which hard copies of student evidence will need to be retained for ABET review. The system asks for only the evidence to be identified.

Finally, the system allows faculty to make notes related to each performance outcome. These notes will be accessible in future semesters and to other users of the system. Instructors can address difficulties in the course or make suggestions for the improvement of the outcomes. This information is entered on the online form and saved with the student ratings. This mitigates an inclination by faculty to rate everyone higher or lower than they may deserve, because the administration may, at any time, request to see the actual record of student performance. This is superior to an externally imposed measure of student performance because it uses what already exists, lessening the overwhelming feeling that can accompany a large-scale change such as that being brought about by ABET. Because the online system is accessible across all campuses, a faculty member at campus B may also review the evidence types selected by a faculty member at campus A. Communication among faculty is again fostered, with a focus on student outcomes.

Although the perceptions of students and faculty are addressed through simple surveys, the responses obtained can be matched and analyzed in light of relevant demographic information such as gender, GPA, and SAT scores—the only limitation is the amount of information already stored by the college in a relational database, the previously mentioned engineering data warehouse. This is a *clear advantage* of using online instruments over the more traditional paper and pencil versions. A disadvantage

Figure 6. Sample faculty perception survey

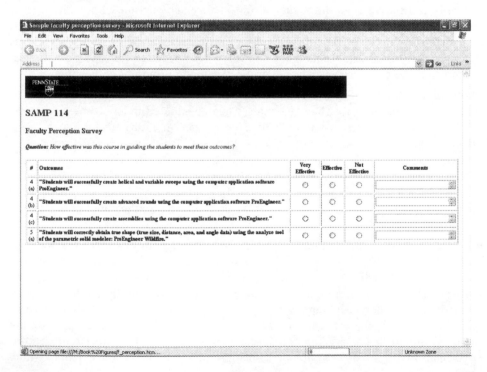

is that the responses are necessarily *confidential* rather than *anonymous*. This could affect our eventual return rate within the online system.

Both the student and the faculty perception surveys focus on the performance outcomes rather than what may be the more traditional questions that are asked at the end of a semester. Once again, the list of performance outcomes is generated from a linked table. Faculty members are asked to rate the effectiveness of the course in helping the students achieve the listed outcomes. A space is also available for entering comments related to each of the outcomes (see Figure 6). This lets the faculty make notes regarding specific observations, such as the inability to meet an outcome due to certain reasons, or perhaps the opinion that the outcome should not be addressed in his or her course at all!

Faculty perception of outcome achievement is collected at the end of each semester. The faculty member is asked to rate the course as either very effective, effective, or not effective in helping the students to achieve the specified outcomes. Although the student performance survey focuses on the individual student, the faculty perception survey focuses on the effectiveness of the course experience.

Student perception of outcome achievement is also collected at the end of each semester. A list of the course outcomes is generated, and the students are given the opportunity to rate themselves using the scale, "I can do this well," "I can do this," or "I can't do this." The student is also asked to rate the effectiveness of the course experience in helping him or her to complete each targeted outcome. This survey differs from typical instruments in its focus on the course outcomes. Comparisons can be made between the student perception of ability and the instructor's rating of that student's performance and between the student's and the instructor's rating of course effectiveness.

The system is scalable in that after a steady state is reached, the data collection can be reduced to some minimum required to identify changes. When necessary, however, the system can be quickly ramped up to maximum data collection levels for short times to identify the source of student performance shortcomings. This capability is critical to faculty acceptance, as the inconvenience of regular data entry can be presented as a temporary condition. Once established, the system will quietly collect performance-based data related to student outcomes while being responsive to changing needs regarding the depth of data.

The maximum data collection would involve all courses providing evidence and ratings for all outcomes. Minimal data collection may focus on particular outcomes, particular courses, or particular programs. The system can be adjusted to collect data on (a) *all* courses and *all* outcomes from *all* instructors and *all* students, (b) *some* courses and *some* outcomes from *some* instructors and *some* students, or (c) any combination of these. For the first iteration, users will most likely wish to collect maximum data in order to identify all the measures being used to assess outcome achievement. When the system is stable, data can be collected based on random or matrix sampling or it can be focused on particular problem areas.

The online data will be available on all levels, from faculty to the chair of the technology program. Each administrative and faculty level will be able to view different aspects as necessary. Faculty will be able to review previous semesters as formative feedback.

Figure 7. Possible data representation

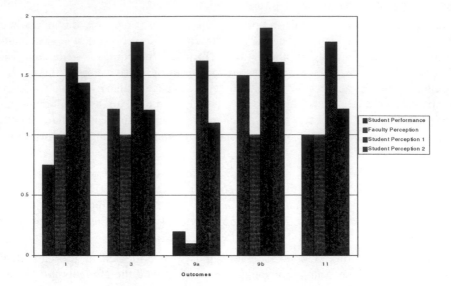

Course coordinators will be able to compare performance within courses at different campuses. Program heads will be able to view student performance related to their program outcomes. Although the possibilities are not in fact endless, nevertheless, quite a few are available for data analysis and program evaluation.

It is important to remember that this system does not claim to satisfy all the requirements for ABET accreditation. The online system will prove to be valuable in the collection of basic data that is directly linked to program outcomes. Following one iteration, programs will have a complete list of the assessment instruments being used by faculty across institutions to measure the achievement of outcomes. Decisions can be made as to the effectiveness and efficiency of these measures. Faculty will have the ability to review assessments used at other campuses and those used in prerequisite courses. The following sections describe possible uses of the data obtained through this system.

The individual faculty member will be able to review course data, comparing actual student performance to perceived student ability and faculty perception of course effectiveness. Figure 7 is a possible representation. This example includes simulated data from student performance, faculty perception, and two student perception questions. In this example, the faculty can see that the student performance on outcome 1 is much lower than the students' perception of their ability to do outcome 1. This indicates a discrepancy to be examined by the faculty. The data can also be displayed at the individual student level or expanded to include all instances of outcome 1 (perhaps the problem is with the outcome) or all instances of this particular course, including data from all other campuses. Again, the primary difference between this type of data and the more traditional after-course surveys is the emphasis on student performance on the outcomes.

The campus program coordinators will be able to view data from all courses within their programs, both at their campus and throughout the system. If an unusual finding shows up at their campus, they can easily compare the data with other campuses. All the outcomes connected with their program can be displayed along with student performance and evidence used.

Some possibilities for data use at the student and administrative levels are not directly related to ABET requirements and will not be introduced here. Suffice it to say that the potential of this system can be extended beyond the individual program level and used to help students assess their own performance progress.

Closing the Loop

Informing Program Improvements

This system is a good match for Penn State's engineering technology programs, because many individual courses at different campuses have insufficient enrollment for meaningful data analysis at the individual campus level. When appropriate, this system will allow aggregation of data across campuses and comparisons that are currently unavailable.

There is no point in collecting a large amount of data if it will not be put to good use. This system is intended to be lean and not to require a great investment of additional faculty and student time. This limits the use of the data to more or less behave as an indicator of program functioning. If all students are achieving all outcomes on their way to graduation, the data obtained using this system will do nothing but confirm the fact. If some students are having trouble with many of the outcomes, this system will identify this trend, perhaps earlier than traditional grading schemes. If many students are struggling to meet certain outcomes, this system should raise a red flag in time for faculty to take action. Unfortunately, the system will make no recommendations for corrections and improvements; it will only identify aberrations for further investigation by program personnel. In order to close the loop, users of this system will need to recognize when data indicates that something is not working and take action to gather more specific information (via student focus groups, surveys, classroom observations, etc.).

Future Trends

Online systems such as the ones described in this chapter will make it possible for greater participation by faculty stakeholders in the development and delivery of curricula as a coherent instructional and learning system. This democratization will take the place of faculty committees that are more subject to destructive phenomena such as group-think. A curriculum and faculty that go through this process will be open to all users and thus more flexible and responsive to faculty and student needs. Faculty also will likely develop a greater sense of ownership and responsibility for the overall curriculum rather than only their specific courses.

Conclusion

The online assessment system described in this chapter is capable of collecting data on student performance relative to a continuously updated list of learning outcomes. The amount of data collected can be modified based on the needs of the group. After a picture of system performance has been obtained, data collection can be scaled back to the minimum until an aberration is observed, at which time the system may rapidly be ramped up to a maximal setting. No new assessments are required; faculty simply report on student performance on existing assignments related to the course outcomes.

Online assessments offer several advantages for a situation such as ours in which common programs are distributed across several locations. Common program and course performance outcomes can be assessed contemporaneously and the data aggregated to allow more in depth analysis of curricular performance. The different levels of interest, from faculty member to head, can access data important to the types of decisions they need to make. Each faculty member can see how his or her contribution fits into the larger curriculum, increasing dialogue, collegiality, and articulation.

These two systems are examples of how online assessment can move beyond opinion surveys and anecdotal data to recording curriculum-embedded student performance data, the most elusive yet valuable type of assessment data.

Care was taken in each of the two online systems to consider sustainability. The most complete data gathering system will fail if the users find it too onerous and do not support it. Both systems are scalable, allowing for decreased data collection at times rather than presenting themselves as data-devouring juggernauts that will never be satiated.

These online systems are also examples of the democratization possible through technology. Without these systems, it would be necessary to establish committees to draft outcomes and objectives and present them to the rest of the faculty. With these systems, every teaching faculty member is responsible for identifying outcomes and objectives within their courses and, going even farther, to isolate the most appropriate assessment of each outcome. None of this would be feasible without the use of online technology.

References

Accreditation Board of Engineering and Technology. (2002). *EAC orientation for deans and team chairs*. Retrieved May 20, 2004, from *http://www.abet.org/images/DeansDay/ASEE_Institutional_Session.pdf*

Accreditation Board of Engineering and Technology. (2004). *Criteria for accrediting engineering technology programs*. Retrieved May 15, 2004, from *http://www.abet.org/images/Criteria/T001%2004-05%20TAC%20Criteria%201-19-04.pdf*

Adams, D. M., & Hamm, M. (1994). *New designs for teaching and learning: Promoting active learning in tomorrow's schools*. San Francisco: Jossey-Bass.

Bonwell, C. C., & Eison, J. A. (1991). *Active learning: Creating excitement in the classroom*. Washington, DC: George Washington University, School of Education and Human Development.

Huba, M. E., & Freed, J. E. (2000). *Learner-centered assessment on college campuses: Shifting the focus from teaching to learning*. Boston: Allyn and Bacon.

Mager, R. F. (1984). *Preparing instructional objectives* (Rev. 2nd ed.). Belmont, CCA: D.S. Lake.

Marlowe, B. A., & Page, M. L. (1998). *Creating and sustaining the constructivist classroom*. Thousand Oaks, CA: Corwin Press.

Phillips, J. J. (1997). *Handbook of training evaluation and measurement methods* (3rd ed.). Houston, TX: Gulf Publishing.

Pine, G. J., & Boy, A. V. (1977). *Learner centered teaching: A humanistic view*. Denver, CO: Love.

Rogers, E. M. (1995). *Diffusion of innovations* (4th ed.). New York: Free Press.

Rossett, A. (1987). *Training needs assessment*. Englewood Cliffs, NJ: Educational Technology.

Sanders, H. M., Walvoord, B. E. F., Stanforth, S. C., & University of Cincinnati. (1995). *Making large classes interactive* [Motion picture]. Available from the University of Cincinnati, Raymond Walters College Media Services Center.

Schalock, R. L. (1995). *Outcome-based evaluation*. New York: Plenum Press.

Wankat, P. C., & Oreovicz, F. S. (1993). *Teaching engineering*. New York: McGraw-Hill.

Wise, J. C., & Shull, P. J. (2004). Establishing baseline goals and objectives for the development of educational outcomes using an online instrument. *Proceedings of the American Society for Engineering Education (ASEE) Annual Conference and Exposition, USA*.

Chapter VIII

Moving Beyond Objective Testing in Online Assessment

Helen S. Ashton, Heriot-Watt University, UK

Cliff E. Beevers, Heriot-Watt University, UK

Colin D. Milligan, Heriot-Watt University, UK

David K. Schofield, Heriot-Watt University, UK

Ruth C. Thomas, Heriot-Watt University, UK

Martin A. Youngson, Heriot-Watt University, UK

Abstract

Computer-aided assessment (CAA) is traditionally seen as an efficient approach to testing large numbers of students by utilizing objective questions with the emphasis firmly on measurement. This chapter describes the development of a system that also seeks to contribute to improving student learning by enhancing the quality, sophistication, and authenticity of the assessments delivered. The system supports students and tutors through the learning process by providing diagnostic and directed feedback to learners and a clear measurement of their true ability to the teacher. The chapter also looks at current work focused on developing assessment systems that can assess higher order skills and begin to blur the boundary between learning and assessment.

Introduction

Online assessment has captured the imagination of many as the panacea for testing large numbers of students in a reliable, consistent fashion in which marks are immediately available for analysis and publication. Typically, this type of online assessment takes the form of objective testing, utilizing multiple choice and multiple response questions, offering scalability and time saving solutions with large groups of students. However, this focus has diverted attention away from many of the key benefits that online assessment offers to learning.

The experience of the authors in online assessment has been radically different in that from the outset, the focus has been on supporting student learning. This focus has led to using online assessment in diagnostic, formative, and summative modes; supporting independent learning; encouraging reflection; and involving both student and teacher in the process.

This chapter describes the experiences of the authors through a range of projects over the last two decades in which CAA has been used to support learning and deliver assessment to students in both tertiary and secondary education in the UK. In the long term, online assessment can play a positive role in enhancing the quality of learning by (a) providing diagnostic and directed feedback to learners, (b) supporting students and teachers through the learning process, (c) increasing the interactivity of the learning experience, (d) enhancing the quality and authenticity of the assessment delivered, (e) helping to identify misconceptions, and (f) helping teachers and lecturers grade the students they teach.

This chapter presents a case study of a series of CAA projects that, from their inception, have been different from the norm.

Background

Using a computer to aid the assessment of student performance has been an option for several decades. Various groups pioneered the delivery of CAA in higher education in the UK and internationally since the mid-1980s, as reviewed elsewhere (Ashton, Beevers, & Bull, 2004). Within the UK, early projects and tools include the Computer-Aided Learning in Mathematics (CALM) Project at Heriot-Watt University (Beevers, Foster, & McGuire, 1989; Beevers, McGuire, Stirling, & Wild, 1995; Beevers, Youngson, McGuire, Wild, & Fiddes, 1999), Ceilidh CourseMaster computer science programming software at Nottingham University (Benford, Burke, Foxley, Gutteridge, & Zin, 1993), and various language tools, such as LUISA (Leeds University Italian Software). Since those early days, the tools of CAA have advanced dramatically. Systems are now capable of supplying a range of question types well beyond the multiplechoice format, incorporating images, multimedia, and animation. In many universities CAA is used for both formative and summative assessment in a variety of disciplines (Bull & McKenna, 2003).

In discussing the assessment of learning it is valuable to consider the types of learning that can be assessed and, particularly, which types currently lend themselves to CAA. Practitioners and developers frequently debate the effective pedagogical use of CAA. Themes include a) the potential to support and enhance learning through structured and directive formative assessment and feedback and b) the capabilities of CAA to test different types of skills effectively and reliably. It is generally accepted that Bloom, Englehart, Furst, Hill, and Krathwohl (1956) provide a sensible taxonomy of educational objectives that apply to most academic subjects, and this taxonomy has been updated to reflect changes in educational practice (Anderson et al., 2001). In mainstream practice, CAA can be applied to test the so-called lower order skills (knowledge, comprehension, and application), and attempts are already appearing to provide automatic testing for the higher order skills or extended competencies of analysis, synthesis, and evaluation (Beevers & Paterson, 2003; Bull & Hesketh, in press).

Developments from CALM to PASS-IT

This case study encompasses a number of projects since 1985, as outlined in the following table.

Table 1.

1985-92	*CALM* Network-delivered weekly tutorial material with formative assessment component to support first-year undergraduate calculus course, then CD-based courseware to support pre-university mathematics (Scottish Higher).
1992-96	*Mathwise* National U.K. initiative to develop computer-based learning materials and assessment support for the teaching of the mathematics part of the syllabus for the European engineer.
1995-98	*Interactive Past Papers* CD-based assessment provision for mathematics at Scottish sixth-year studies (SYS), A-level, Scottish Higher, general certificate of secondary education (GCSE) and Scottish standard grade levels.
1997-2001	*CUE* (Paterson, 2002) Development of an online assessment engine.
2000-present	*SCHOLAR* (Livingston & Condie, 2004) E-learning initiative to develop materials and online assessments to support subjects across the school and university interface.
2002-present	PASS-IT (Project on ASsessment in Scotland using Information Technology) Research into the issues surrounding the online delivery of minimum competency assessments into Scottish schools in a range of subjects and levels.

Through all this work, the focus has been on the following main issues: (a) nonobjective questions (construction of answers, automatic marking), (b) immediate feedback and support, (c) the provision for staged answers, and (d) support for postassessment feedback and reflection.

CALM started in the Department of Mathematics at Heriot-Watt University in Edinburgh in 1985. Heriot-Watt is a technological university with large groups of engineering, science, and business undergraduates. These subjects all require significant mathematical skills, and the delivery of numerical and mathematical tests is where attention was first focused. Initially, a series of weekly computerized tutorials was established to support the teaching of a first course on calculus to large groups of science and engineering undergraduates. The resources in the computerized tutorial replaced the traditional pen and paper approach, which at the time was struggling to provide suitable support for the large number of students attending the course. Each week throughout a 25 week course, mathematical topics were covered to the recipe: (a) summary screens of the theory delivered in lectures, (b) worked examples illustrating technique, (c) motivating examples to inspire deeper study, and (d) a test section to allow students to follow their own progress and enable teachers to reflect on class performance.

The motivating examples were designed to engage the students in problems such as calculating the escape speeds from a variety of planets, determining the optimal angle for the trajectory of a water jet in a game called Firefighter, and taking the largest plank around a corner in a tunnel from an exercise known affectionately as Escape from Colditz. However, from the outset the students chose to spend 3/4 of their time practicing within the test section itself. The randomization of parameters within questions had been an important early feature designed to keep the questions fresh for reuse.

Beyond Objective Questions

From the beginning of the CALM project, it was considered important to allow students to input answers as mathematical expressions rather than select an option from a multiple choice format. This allowed students to construct their own answers and express them in a format they felt was appropriate. This led to the CALM project's dealing with the issue of marking mathematically equivalent expressions as correct, even if they were in a different format than that stored in the computer (for example, a student could input a correct answer of $2x$ as $+2x$ or $x+x$, etc.). The CALM method of comparison for marking correct answers was groundbreaking at the time, though other groups have subsequently followed this approach (Cook, Hornby, & Scott, 2001; Ramsden, 2004).

This use of student-constructed mathematical expressions involved students using a

string format to express their answers. For example, $\frac{1}{2x}$ would be expressed as $1/(2x)$.

Figure 1. Screen shot showing the use of the input tool to enter mathematical expressions

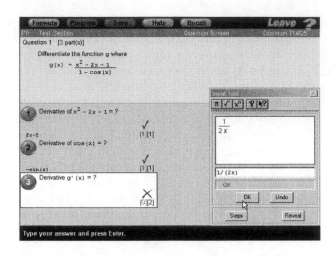

Although students may initially find this confusing, most quickly become comfortable with the format.

However, to aid students in entering mathematical expressions, the development of an input tool became an important element through the Mathwise project, culminating in the input tool incorporated into the Interactive Past Papers CD (Beevers, Fiddes, McGuire, Wild & Youngson, 1997; see Figure 1). The input tool dynamically transformed the string format and displayed it on the screen in a more familiar format so the students could be sure that the computer was properly interpreting their answers.

Following an educational evaluation of the Mathwise project, groups of students piloted the use of computer tests to measure lower order skills (Beevers et al., 1995) in a university first year course on algebra and calculus at Heriot-Watt University. In the evaluation of this pilot study, students highlighted the need for confirmation of the computer interpretation of their mathematical string expression, which led to the construction of the input tool.

More recently, PASS-IT began investigating the issues surrounding the delivery of online summative assessments into Scottish schools. As with Mathwise, the assessments were designed to measure lower order skills; however, the online delivery mechanisms have placed restrictions on the practical implementation of an input tool. As a result, the current method is to render a student's submitted answer in a mathematically familiar form, and the student may then modify the answer as appropriate.

As part of PASS-IT, investigations have started to realize the use of new measurement mechanisms to extend the range of questions that can be asked. Using multimedia applications embedded into the assessment engine opens up a multitude of possibilities for allowing students to record answers to questions that were previously available only for paper-based assessment. For example, by integrating Macromedia

Flash applications into the assessment engine, students are able to draw a line on a graph, and in music tests students can now manipulate musical notes on a stave or annotate a music score. The assessment engine is able to mark the students' answers.

Partial Credit

Another issue identified by the evaluation of the Mathwise pilot study was the students' concern about partial credit. In traditional paper-based assessment, teachers can award partial credit for rough working and the application of the correct concepts (follow-through), even when the final answer is incorrect. In most online assessments, the practicalities of capturing the students' work proves too great an obstacle, resulting in an *all or nothing* situation-students may make significant progress toward an answer, but become stuck, or make an arithmetical slip and be awarded no marks for their efforts (their final answer not being mathematically equivalent).

One solution to this issue was the introduction of optional steps. Initially this idea was implemented as part of the formative assessment in Mathwise and Interactive Past Papers, where rapid feedback was given to both right and wrong answers. Good students could reinforce their learning through success, and weaker students had the choice of steps toward an answer. More recently, the notion of optional steps has been researched as a mechanism for the provision of partial credit in summative assessments (McGuire, Youngson, Korabinski, & McMillan, 2002).

Supporting Students' Learning

The main reason the authors became involved in CAA was to support students' learning. The students welcomed the rapid feedback offered by CALM, and one of them spoke for many when he reported, "It is like having a human tutor in front of you all the time." However, they recognized the importance of involving the teacher in this process.

The CALM assessment system collected a vast amount of information about the assessments the students were taking. The ability to review this data allowed a teacher to provide additional feedback to the students and to identify common areas of weakness that needed to be addressed. To aid this process, a crude but effective reporting tool was developed that gathered up the student test records at the end of each week ready for human scrutiny. The lecturer then had to go through the data manually to see how each individual was progressing. This effort was time consuming though worthwhile, as it meant that comments could be sent back to the students at the start of the next week. A reporting system was created, which allowed the lecturer to view the class records and then visit the file of any individual student, see that person's marks, and review his or her answers to any of the questions. The lecturer could report back to students by the creation of text messages, which were stored on the file server that displayed the next time the student logged on to the system. This method became a powerful way of communicating with the large numbers of students using the system; it provides an early example of a database results system with reporting capability. It should be noted that this approach predated the widespread provision of e-mail.

The modern day version of this reporting system plays an important role in the PASS-IT project. Reporting tools have been developed for students, teachers, and researchers, enabling immediate access to assessment data. The PASS-IT assessment engine records every action a student makes in an assessment, such as navigation to a question, every submitted answer, and the choice to view steps. If a user wishes to review or collate data over many students, assessments, or attempts at a single assessment, this process quickly becomes unmanageable without a reporting system to collate, filter, and present this data as meaningful information.

From a teacher's perspective, the benefits of reviewing student answers and progress are supported. The ability to obtain an instant visual representation of the progress of an individual or class can provide useful information. Figure 2 shows just such a representation, where the student began by attempting the majority of the questions within the assessment. Then the student made repeated attempts at an individual

Figure 2. Graphical representation of assessment performance

Attempt	Duration	Q1	Q2	Q3	Q4	Q5	Q6	Q7	Q8	Q9	Q10	Q11	Q12	Q13	Total Mark	Student Responses
1	00:33:46	2	4	3	0	3	2	4	3.5	2	0	1	3	0	27.5	
2	00:33:46	1	4	2.09	5	3	2	4	3.5	1.5	1	0			27.09	
3	00:39:48	2	4	0	0	3	2	2.5	3.5	2	3	4	4		30	
4	00:23:02	2	4	2.09	0	3	2	2.5	0	0	0	0	3		18.59	
5	00:01:28	2													2	
6	00:02:53	0	4												4	
7	00:01:46	0		3											3	
8	00:02:32	0			5										5	
9	00:01:47	0				3									3	
10	00:01:53	0					2								2	
11	00:01:51	0					0								0	
12	00:01:33	0					1								1	
13	00:00:56	0					2								2	
14	00:01:26	0					0								0	
15	00:00:39	0					2								2	
16	00:00:25	0					0								0	
17	00:01:39	0					2								2	
18	00:04:42	0					0	2.5							2.5	
19	00:02:33	0							3.5						3.5	
20	00:01:16	0							1.5						1.5	
21	00:01:15	0							2						2	
22	00:01:21	0							0						0	
23	00:02:17	0							1.5						1.5	
24	00:03:04	0							5						5	
25	00:00:49	0								2					2	
26	00:02:29	0								0	1				1	
27	00:01:29	0									1				1	
28	00:02:28	0									0				0	
29	00:01:36	0									0				0	

Figure 3. Tabulated report of student responses and performance

Question No. 1. You scored 3 out of 3 marks.

Part	Steps Used	Correct	Your Answer	Expected Answer	Attempts
1		✓	1	1	3
2		✓	Chromatid	Chromatid	2
3		✓	Crossing over	crossing over	1

Question No. 2. You scored 1 out of 2 marks.

Part	Steps Used	Correct	Your Answer	Expected Answer	Attempts
1		✗	Substitution	Gene inversion	3
2		✓	Duplication	Gene duplication	1

Question No. 3. You scored 4 out of 6 marks.

Part	Steps Used	Correct	Your Answer	Expected Answer	Attempts
1		✓	RRHH	RRHH or HHRR	2
2		✓	rh	rh or hr	1

question (each instance of a question contained random parameters), revealing the student's strategy. This information is also of value to a student for reflection, allowing both student and teacher to investigate areas of weakness.

The ability to review the details of submitted answers to particular questions and question parts also provides insight into possible misconceptions. Figure 3 shows a report that allows students to review their answers in light of their performance (question marks, ticks, and crosses) and the expected model answer. In the example shown, the student has incorrectly identified the type of gene mutation. A more detailed discussion of the current features and benefits of the reporting system can be found in a recent report by Ashton, Beevers, Schofield, and Youngson (2004).

Current and Future Directions

Over the course of its development, the testing engine employed at Heriot-Watt University has evolved into a pedagogically robust and technologically advanced system. This has been achieved, in part, by working closely with teachers, and the system has been used to provide tests to thousands of learners. Moving forward, how else can it be used to improve the assessments delivered?

Some years ago, Bennett (1998) suggested that online assessment had not yet achieved its full potential. He stated, "Like many innovations in their early stages, today's computerized tests automate an existing process without reconceptualizing it to realize dramatic improvements that the innovation could allow". Bennett identified three stages in the growth of online assessment: first, automation of existing tests;

second, a move to incorporate new formats and more complex question types (as has been reported here); and third, the use of complex simulations, virtual reality, and the seamless embedding of assessment within learning (which forms the basis of our current development work).

The reconceptualization process must involve a number of changes. One crucial area for change is the closer integration of assessment into the overall learning process. Anderson et al. (2001) point out that the importance of aligning overall assessment strategy, individual assessment methods, and the criteria used in judging the quality and standards of learning with the teaching and curriculum objectives and intended learning outcomes is being increasingly recognized. Similarly, Harding and Craven (2001) argue that the rise of computer-based classroom activities must be mirrored by an increase in assessment being delivered in this way to ensure that the assessment is meaningful.

Alignment of assessment and learning outcomes is often not well addressed in current practice. For example, Elshout-Mohr, Oöstdam, and Overmaat (2002) have argued that constructivist learning techniques, in which active and self-directed learners acquire knowledge and skills by undertaking authentic complex tasks, cannot be easily aligned with traditional assessment techniques. Ultimately, skills that have been learned during a student's education will be applied in the real world. Consequently, authentic assessment that is aligned to the requirements of the specific environment in which the student will apply knowledge is important if a student's true potential is to be measured. In school science teaching, for instance, the testing of knowledge of scientific concepts rather than the ability to analyze, evaluate, and reflect on this knowledge is seen as a weakness in the current curriculum design (Black, Harrison, Osbourne, & Duschl, 2004). Online assessment can also suffer from being somewhat artificial in nature; what is tested is often what can easily be tested, not the actual learning outcomes. With its overreliance on objective testing, online assessment is seen by many as useful for assessing lower order skills, such as the recall of knowledge, while being ill equipped to assess higher order skills, such as the ability to apply knowledge in new situations or to evaluate and synthesize information.

The present work within SCROLLA (the Scottish Centre for Research into Online Learning and Assessment) centers on addressing the issues of the assessment of higher order skills and, in particular, extending the functionality of the current system by integrating simulations to cope with them. Simulations can be used to provide activities that support education where learning outcomes require more than the acquisition of knowledge. They bring both reality and interactivity to the learning experience, allowing learners to manipulate a system directly and to observe the effect of the change, thus providing a form of feedback that facilitates exploration, enabling learners to build their own understanding. To date, simulation use in auto-mated assessment has been limited. Bespoke assessment systems involving either hardware or software simulators do exist (see Lapointe & Robert, 2000), and in some cases, human assessors evaluate the student's performance on a simulator (see Cleave-Hogg, Morgan, & Guest, 2000). The TRIADS assessment system (MacKenzie, 1999) has a variety of question styles, some of which are equivalent to simple simulations.

The work of SCROLLA takes the use of simulations to the next stage by working on a system that can make use of preexisting simulations (Thomas & Milligan, 2004) or other applications in the assessment process. This is not just a case of allowing the simulation to exist within the system (which has been possible for a number of years) but of ensuring that the assessment system and the simulation software communicate at a much deeper level to improve authoring capabilities and enable more complex assessments that can be managed, assessed, and reported in an appropriate manner. This extends the work on new question types initiated as part of the PASS-IT project described previously in this chapter.

The integrated simulations can be used in three ways: as part of the assessment question, to provide answer mechanism/new response forms, and to provide feedback to the learner. This multifunctionality allows students to be assessed in the same environment in which they learn and integrates the assessment activity more fully into the educational process. The forms of assessment can be diagnostic or formative, providing guidance and help as the student carries out a task or a summative assessment of an entire process, providing a measure of competency upon fulfilling a task. Instead of asking questions of the form "How would you . . . ?" it would be possible to follow students as they undertook a process and to monitor the choices involved. Thus, assessment can be closely aligned to learning outcomes, even when those outcomes involve higher order skills. This work is summarised in two recent reports (Thomas & Milligan, 2003; Thomas et al., 2004).

Conclusion

In a wider sense, what SCROLLA aims for in the current work is a blurring of the boundary between learning and assessment. With closer integration of the assessment and learning processes, the balance from summative toward formative assessment will follow, thereby enhancing the student learning experience (Black & William, 1998, Nicol & Macfarlane-Dick, 2004).

Thinking of an ideal assessment system leads to the following features:

- **Authenticity:** Instead of being assessed at the end of a unit of study, students are assessed *as* they learn, *in the environment* in which they learn.

- **Individualized Feedback:** The system may be able to detect alternative conceptions and provide appropriate coaching and scaffolding.

- **Opportunities for Reflection:** The students can re-examine their performance, perhaps replaying an activity or examining assessment reports. Such a facility could be mediated through e-Portfolio tools, where the students are encouraged to integrate their learning and identify gaps in their knowledge.

- **Dialogue:** The students can communicate asynchronously or synchronously with their tutor and peers and also interact with knowledge bases that could be interrogated by using natural language.

In creating such a system, some key research issues can be identified:

- How would such a system fit with existing models of learning?
- How can higher order skills best be measured?
- How can a more valid measure of performance be created?
- How can the teacher and computer best work in partnership?

Looking further into the future, it is hoped that the boundaries between assessment and learning will blur completely, as predicted by Bennett (1998). Assessment functionality will play a central role in future online learning environments in contrast to the current situation, where assessment functionality is often rudimentary, encouraging poor assessment practice.

References

Anderson, L. W., Krathwohl, D. R., Airasian, P. W., Cruikshank, K. A., Mayer, R. E., Pintrich, P. R., et al. (Eds.). (2001). *A taxonomy for learning, teaching and assessing: A revision of Bloom's taxonomy of educational objectives*. New York: Longman.

Ashton, H. S., Beevers, C. E., & Bull, J. (2004). Piloting e-assessment in Scottish schools-Building on past experience. *International Journal on eLearning, 3*(2), 74-84.

Ashton, H. S., Beevers, C. E., Schofield, D. K., & Youngson, M. A. (2004). Informative reports—Experiences from the Pass-It Project. *Proceedings of the Eighth International CAA Conference,* Loughborough, UK (pp. 3-15). Retrieved May 16, 2005, from *http://s-d.lboro.ac.uk/caanew/pastConferences/2004/proceedings/ashton.pdf*

Beevers, C. E., Fiddes, D. J., McGuire, G. R., Wild, D. G., & Youngson, M. A. (1997). *Interactive past papers for A level/higher mathematics*. Glasgow, UK: Lander Educational Software.

Beevers, C. E., Foster, M., & McGuire, G. R. (1989). Integrating formative evaluation into a learner centred revision course. *British Journal of Education Technology, 20,* 115-119.

Beevers, C. E., McGuire, G. R., Stirling, G., & Wild, D. G. (1995). Mathematical ability assessed by computer. *Computers and Education, 25,* 123-132.

Beevers, C. E., & Paterson, J. S. (2003). Automatic assessment of problem solving skills in mathematics. *Active Learning in Higher Education, 4*(2), 127-145.

Beevers, C. E., Youngson, M. A., McGuire, G. R., Wild, D. G., & Fiddes, D. (1999). Issues of partial credit in mathematical assessment by computer. *Association for Learning Technology Journal, 7*(1), 26-32.

Benford, S. D., Burke, E. K., Foxley, E., Gutteridge, N. H., & Zin, A. M. (1993). Early experiences of computer-aided assessment and administration when teaching computer programming. *Association for Learning Technology Journal, 1*(2), 55-70.

Bennett, R. E. (1998). *Reinventing assessment: Speculations on the future of large scale educational testing.* Retrieved September 28, 2004, from *ftp://ftp.ets.org/pub/res/reinvent.pdf*

Black, P., Harrison, C., Osborne, J., & Duschl, R. (2004). *Assessment of science learning 14-19.* Retrieved September 28, 2004, from *http://www.royalsoc.ac.uk/education/assessment/Kings_report.pdf*

Black, P., & William, D. (1998). Assessment and classroom learning. *Assessment in Education: Principles, Policy & Practice, 5*(1), 7-74.

Bloom, B. S., Englehart, M. D., Furst, E. J., Hill, W. H., & Krathwohl, D. R. (1956). *Taxonomy of educational objectives. Handbook 1: Cognitive domain.* New York: Longman.

Bull, J., & Hesketh, I. (in press). Computer-assisted assessment and higher-order skills. *Assessment series: Briefing for learning technologists.* York, UK: Learning and Teaching Support Network Generic Centre.

Bull, J., & McKenna, C. (2003). *Blueprint on CAA.* London: Routledge Falmer.

Cleave-Hogg, D., Morgan, P., & Guest, C. (2000). Evaluation of medical students' performance in anaesthesia using a CAE Med-Link Simulator System. *Proceedings of the Fourth International Computer Assisted Assessment Conference,* Leicestershire, UK. Retrieved September 28, 2004, from *http://www.lboro.ac.uk/service/fli/flicaa/conf2000/pdfs/cleavehogg.pdf*

Cook, J., Hornby, J., & Scott, L. (2001). Assessment driven learning. Retrieved September 28, 2004, from *http://ltsn.mathstore.ac.uk/articles/maths-caa-series/dec2001/*

Elshout-Mohr, M., Oöstdam, P., & Overmaat, M. (2002). Student assessment within the context of constructivist educational settings. *Studies in Educational Evaluation, 28,* 369-390.

Harding, R., & Craven, P. (2001). ICT in assessment: A three legged race. *University of Cambridge Local Examination Syndicate.* Retrieved September 28, 2004, from *http://ital.ucles-red.cam.ac.uk/downloads/ictassessmnt.pdf*

LaPointe, J., & Robert, J. (2000). Using VR for effective training of forestry machine operators. *Education and Information Technologies, 5,* 237-250.

Livingston, K., & Condie, R. (2004). *Evaluation of phase 2 of the scholar programme, University of Strathclyde, Glasgow, UK.* Retrieved September 28, 2004, from *http://www.flatprojects.org.uk/scholarreport.asp*

Mackenzie, D. (1999). Recent developments in the Tripartite Interactive Assessment Delivery System (TRIADS). *Proceedings of the Third International Computer Assisted Assessment Conference,* Leicestershire, UK. Retrieved September 28, 2004, from *http://www.lboro.ac.uk/service/fli/flicaa/conf99/pdf/mckenzie.pdf*

McGuire, G., Youngson, M., Korabinski, A., & McMillan, D. (2002). Partial credit in mathematics exams: A comparison between traditional and CAA. *Proceedings of the Sixth International CAA Conference,* Leicestershire, UK (pp. 223-230).

Nicol, D., & Macfarlane-Dick, D. (2004). *Rethinking formative assessment in HE: A theoretical model and seven principles of good feedback practice.* Retrieved September 28, 2004, from *http://www.ltsn.ac.uk/embedded_obj ect.asp?do cid=21300*

Paterson, J. S. (2002). *The CUE assessment system.* Retrieved September 28, 2004, from *http://ltsn.mathstore.ac.uk/articles/maths-caa-series/apr2002/*

Ramsden, P. (2004). *Fresh questions, free expressions: METRIC's Web-based self-test exercises.* Retrieved September 28, 2004, from *http://ltsn.mathstore.ac.uk/ articles/maths-caa-series/june2004/*

Thomas, R. C., Ashton, H. S., Austin, W. J., Beevers, C. E., Edwards, D., & Milligan, C. D. (2004). Assessing higher-order skills using simulations. *Proceedings of the Eighth International CAA Conference,* Leicestershire, UK (pp. 417-427).

Thomas, R. C., & Milligan, C. D. (2003). Online assessment of practical experiments. *Proceedings of the Seventh International CAA Conference,* Leicestershire, UK (Vol. 20, pp. 421-430).

Thomas, R. C., & Milligan, C. D. (2004). Putting teachers in the loop: Tools for creating and customising simulations. *Journal of Interactive Media in Education, (Designing and Developing for the Disciplines Special Issue),* (15). Retrieved May 16, 2005, from *http://www-jime.open.ac.uk/2004/15*

Section II

Elementary and Secondary Education (K-12)

Chapter IX

Development of a Computerized Adaptive Test for a Large-Scale Testing Program:

A Case Study of the Development of the North Carolina Computerized Adaptive Testing System

Lori McLeod, RTI International, USA

Albert Bethke, RTI International, USA

Cheryl Hill, University of North Carolina at Chapel Hill, USA

Pamela Van Dyk, North Carolina Department of Public Instruction, USA

Kelly Burling, North Carolina Department of Public Instruction, USA

Abstract

In 1997, the Individuals with Disabilities Education Act (IDEA) amendments stated that "children with disabilities must be included in general state-and district-wide assessment programs, with appropriate accommodations, where necessary." Where accommodations alone could not make the testing program accessible, the amendment required that the agencies develop alternative assessments so that every child would be included in the accountability programs. In response to the IDEA Amendments, the

North Carolina Department of Public Instruction (NCDPI) reviewed its testing program and identified areas where additional accommodations were necessary. Based on this review, a research plan was developed for a computerized adaptive testing (CAT) accommodation, where computers and the Internet are used for administration of an adaptive test. This chapter explores several of the issues and lessons learned in the development of a computerized adaptive test in a case study of the design, development, and delivery of such a test in a large-scale testing environment. Findings from the case study have implications for item-pool development, curriculum alignment, and comparability to the paper and pencil tests, scoring and scaling of the computerized adaptive test accommodation, test reliability, validity, programming for the computer-adaptive test, and state and local technology infrastructure. The chapter concludes with lessons learned and future directions.

Background

For a large-scale testing program, computer administration offers several student advantages over paper and pencil administration, as suggested by Wainer (2000):

a. testing can be scheduled so that students have their own block of time for testing rather than large classroom administrations;

b. the environment for the computer exam is more controlled than a large-scale administration;

c. the test can be tailored (or adapted) to each individual student so that more proficient test takers do not waste time on easy items and less proficient students do not become frustrated by having to answer the more difficult items. The adaptive nature of the test eliminates some of the impact of extraneous variables such as boredom and frustration;

d. for the same precision of a conventional test, an adaptive test can administer a reduced number of items;

e. score reports can be generated immediately instead of hours, days, or weeks later.

Although computer-adaptive testing, with its many advantages, allows more students to participate in a large-scale testing program, there are practical issues to consider when implementing a computer-adaptive test in a large-scale assessment environment. Mills and Stocking (1996) identify some of these issues as dealing with test design, programming and testing the adaptive algorithm, establishing comparability, developing and maintaining item pools, and calibrating the test items.

North Carolina Testing Program

The development of all tests in North Carolina is based on principles from the *ABCs of Public Education,* a plan to reorganize public education in North Carolina based on the belief that *all* children can learn. The *ABCs of Public Education* emphasizes that the mission of the public school community is to challenge each child to learn, achieve, and fulfill his or her potential. The State Board of Education initially implemented the *ABCs* accountability program at grades K-8, effective with the 1996–97 school year, and grades 9-12, effective during the 1997-1998 school year, to test students' mastery of basic skills (reading, writing, and mathematics).

Two federal mandates have been the impetus for reviewing existing accommodations in the North Carolina Testing Program. In 1997, the IDEA Amendment initiated the requirement that all disabled children be included in state and district assessment. In addition, the federal No Child Left Behind legislation, signed into law in 2001, sets high academic standards for all students. Key elements of the legislation include closing the achievement gap, having a highly qualified teacher in every classroom, and holding schools accountable for all students' performance at a high level (U.S. Department of Education, n.d.).

Although statewide accountability standards for students have been in existence since 1996, these two key pieces of federal legislation required the Division of Accountability Services to consider how best to serve the needs of all children to ensure their participation in the North Carolina Testing Program. The traditional paper and pencil end-of-grade tests, while offering an adequate opportunity to assess children functioning at their nominal grade level, do not provide opportunities to measure the achievement of those students functioning below their nominal grade level.

Computerized Adaptive Testing in North Carolina

In response to the IDEA Amendments, the North Carolina Department of Public Instruction (NCDPI) reviewed its testing program to identify areas where additional accommodations were necessary. Based on this review, a research plan was developed for a novel testing system that uses computers and the Internet for administration of an adaptive test. In January of 2001, NCDPI, collaborating with the RTI International and the L. L. Thurstone Psychometric Laboratory at the University of North Carolina at Chapel Hill, began the development of the North Carolina Computerized Adaptive Testing System (NCCATS).

The NCCATS would be an accommodation for the North Carolina End-of-Grade tests (NCEOG), which assess students in grades three through eight in mathematics and reading comprehension. The NCEOG tests already had existing accommodations, such as both large print and Braille forms. The addition of an NCCATS accommodation would provide accessibility for exceptional students performing up to two grades below their nominal grade level who also have proficiency with basic computer skills, including familiarity with using a mouse, keyboard, and scroll bars.

The adaptive nature of the NCCATS would allow the test to be more tailored to each individual's proficiency level, increasing the precision of proficiency estimates. Scores derived from the NCCATS were to be on the same scoring scale as the paper and pencil tests, so performance and accountability programs could report and use these scores as they report scores based on other accommodations, such as large print or Braille.

Issues in the Development of a Large-Scale Computer-Adaptive Test

System Design and Operations

The initial hurdle in the research and development of NCCATS was to create an interface that would have high usability for exceptional children and that would also be similar to the paper and pencil tests. During February 2001 preliminary mathematics and reading selection interface designs were developed with various layouts for items and answer choices. A set of released mathematics and reading items was used to prototype the various designs. Initial internal reviews of the mathematics designs showed some to be inadequate for the types of answer choices used on the paper and pencil mathematics tests. For example, answer choices with graphics and a background color were difficult to read. Some of the response button designs were difficult to select because of their shapes. Finally, the use of color in the answer choices was rejected. After the internal reviews, two designs were chosen for further testing.

The interfaces were submitted to usability testing in late February at two schools in a local county. Students participating in the usability study indicated that they were quite comfortable with answering test questions on the computer. When asked to give feedback about the system, all the students indicated that they liked using the computer and would choose it over a paper and pencil method for testing. In general, students found the response choices easy to find on the screen and knew that clicking on the response would select it. The majority of the students used the mouse during the exercise, stating that it was much easier to use than the keyboard. Problems occurred with the server during the usability test, resulting in a slow test delivery and loss of data. As a result of the server issues, a priority was placed on examining server capacity and potential loss of test data in Phase II of the research and development process.

Feasibility of a Large-Scale Online Test

Phase II of NCCATS development, occurring in the spring of 2001, was designated as a feasibility pilot in order to evaluate the overall performance of the testing system, the accessibility and stability of Internet-based delivery, and the number of students who could be tested simultaneously. The pilot included an adaptive test, where the most informative items were selected on an item-by-item basis with final scores reported on the NCEOG scale. Test results from the pilot were not to be included in student permanent records or counted towards the state's accountability requirements.

The first challenge for the pilot occurred on the first day of testing. Students participating in the pilot were selected by their Individualized Education Program (IEP) teams as being students who might ultimately participate in an operational computerized adaptive test. Many of these students were among those performing slightly below their nominal grade level. About 27,000 students, five times more students than originally anticipated, registered to take the pilot administration of NCCATS. The limited server capacity and increased number of students testing simultaneously created problems in test delivery. The server capacity resulted in delays in updating the database to save student responses during testing. In the single-server configuration, the database could not keep up with the demand of more than several dozen simultaneous tests. The loss of test data continued to be a primary concern.

During the testing period, changes were made in the system code and an additional server was added to accommodate additional test loads. By the end of the testing period, these two servers could handle approximately 40 simultaneous tests; however, the servers were still occasionally overwhelmed by the test load. By the end of the testing period, many students had made multiple attempts in order to complete their tests. Just over 12,000 students were able to complete tests in reading, and approximately 11,000 completed tests in mathematics. Technology issues that were external to the organization also proved to be problematic during the pilot. Those problems were characterized by the use of proxy servers, firewalls, configuration problems, and general connectivity issues at the local school level. In many cases, these external technology problems prevented students from accessing the NCCATS test.

In addition to technology issues, teachers in the field were concerned about the quality of the items and the target population for whom the pilot was intended. Feedback from test administrators in the field about the test items indicated that the quality of the items was less than what a child might receive on the paper and pencil tests. Also, observations of actual test administrations revealed that the NCCATS accommodation proved to be too difficult for some of the students registered.

The data collected during the pilot provided the first opportunity to evaluate end-of-grade scores based on NCCATS versus end-of-grade test scores on the paper and pencil tests. The mean scores from the NCCATS population at each grade were much lower than the state mean at the nominal grade level. The NCCATS mean scores, when compared to mean scores of the functioning grade level as assigned by each teacher, were similar to the state mean. These results indicated that a CAT may be more appropriate for students functioning below their nominal grade; however, more research was needed with a stable system to determine precisely for whom the NCCATS would be an appropriate accommodation.

Item-Pool Development, Scale Calibration, and Mode Study

The focus of Phase III, which occurred in spring of 2003, was to determine whether NCCATS scores would be comparable to the paper and pencil end-of-grade tests at each grade and for each subject. If modal differences were discovered, then accounting for the differences would be important. The objectives for Phase III development of the NCCATS were

a.   to conduct a large-scale comparability study in each subject at each grade by analyzing mean scores on the paper and pencil test with mean scores on the NCCATS and

b.   to field test a large number of paper and pencil items in the online format so online item parameters could be obtained.

The large-scale comparability study was designed to evaluate the performance of NCCATS at all grades for both reading and mathematics. Specifically, the investigation focused on the impact of the mode of administration (paper and pencil vs. online) for all grades and subjects in which NCCATS would be utilized as an accommodation. By gathering data at each grade for each subject, grade and subject adjustments could then be made to scores to align them to the paper and pencil test scale prior to reporting. Students were randomly selected from the general population to participate in either an online, linear form of the test or the same form as a paper and pencil test.

Overall, the results indicated that the NCCATS test forms behaved similarly for the gender and ethnicity subgroups. However, results also identified a shift in both reading and math scores between online and paper and pencil formats. This shift indicated that item parameters should be calibrated separately for items administered online instead of using item parameter estimates based on their paper and pencil versions. Based on the item calibrations, score translation tables could then be created so that scores for online NCEOG tests could be directly "linked" and compared to those scores for paper and pencil tests.

To implement the linkage, the NCCATS item pool was finalized. This finalization was accomplished by using an Item Response Theory (IRT) based linkage and student data from the comparability study test forms (NCEOG test forms that were administered both in online and paper and pencil form to random samples of students from across the state and were designed to be equivalent for each grade and school subject). Along with the comparability forms, additional tryout forms comprising operational items were administered online. These forms, along with the comparability forms, constituted the final NCCATS item pool, and the data collected during the comparability study effort were utilized for the final item calibrations (Bethke et al., 2004).

Using linear equating, the average and standard deviation (on the IRT proficiency scale) were computed for the paper and pencil samples for each grade and subject in the comparability study. These became the reference means and standard deviations for scores on the CAT scale, as well as the item parameter estimates for the subsequent item pool (Thissen, Edwards, & Coon, 2004).

In addition to providing information about the impact of mode at the form and item level, data from this phase of development also evaluated performance by gender and ethnicity subgroups. Results indicated that varying the mode of administration does not close the test score gap between gender and ethnicity subgroups. The comparability study also revealed that in many cases, local schools were ill equipped to handle the online testing of a large number of students at one time.

Pilot Testing the Adaptive Algorithm

In Phase IV of the research and development process, occurring in spring of 2004, the primary objectives were to develop a CAT structure that minimized item exposure and met curriculum blueprint or content constraints. In addition, it was to be a pilot of the adaptive format. The adaptive structure developed during Phase II of CAT development provided a relatively accurate method of evaluating a student's proficiency level without requiring a lengthy test; however, the process of developing the initial adaptive structure revealed two primary concerns. First, at each step in adaptation, a highly informative item was chosen regardless of the amount of exposure the item may have received. By design, this type of item selection would overexpose the most informative items and, therefore, create a test security risk. Second, the system did not constrain items to be selected from specific item content areas. The CAT structure was developed to choose a high-quality item as measured by its information at the student's current proficiency estimate. It did not ensure that a student would receive items from all relevant content areas or topics. The desire to restrict item exposure control as well as specify content covered by each item required that the item selection and general structure of the CAT be reevaluated.

Thissen (2003) proposes an alternative to the traditional CAT (where adaptation occurs after each item), which addresses both issues of concern. This method, referred to as the *uniform item exposure multiform structure,* or uMFS, assigns examinees to a routing block of items to begin the test. A preliminary proficiency estimate is computed based on responses to the routing block of items. Those who obtain a low score are then administered an easier block of items at the next stage, whereas those who obtain a high score are administered a more difficult block of items at the next stage. Those who scored in the middle are given a new block of items of similar difficulty. This process repeats for as many stages as defined in the test design. Block size (the number of items that comprise a block) is equivalent within a stage so that each examinee responds to an equal number of items.

Instead of adapting after each item and having a nearly infinite number of potential tests as is done in traditional CAT, a uMFS CAT adapts after a block of items, which reduces the potential test forms to a manageable number. For instance, if each of three stages has three blocks, then 21 forms are possible (when restricting the difficulty of an administered block to be only one level more or less difficult than the previous block administered to that examinee). The ability to examine each of these possible forms allows for content balancing, and the structure allows for test specialist (human) review of all possible test routes for any other constraints desired.

The issue of item exposure control is managed by requiring that as many routing blocks (in the first stage) exist as there are blocks in the subsequent stages and carefully choosing the cut scores for routing to subsequent blocks. Examinees are randomly assigned to these routing blocks. This constraint stipulates that each item is exposed to approximately $1/L$ of the examinees, where L is the number of levels (or blocks) in a stage. This fraction can be maintained by careful selection of cut scores that determine branching to the next block.

Based on simulation results it was determined that a three-level, three-stage uMFS was most appropriate for the NCCATS. This design would ensure adequate measurement precision and test reliability balanced with a smaller item-pool burden. Figure 1 shows a schematic illustration of a three-level, three-stage uMFS design with 12 items within each stage, for a total test length of 36 scored items (Thissen, 2003). The proportions of examinees routed to each block are also shown in Figure 1.

Pilot testing of the adaptive algorithm concluded the research and development of the NCCATS. Overall, the results indicated that the NCCATS algorithm correctly routed

Figure 1. A schematic illustration of a three-level, three-stage uMFS design with 12 items per stage

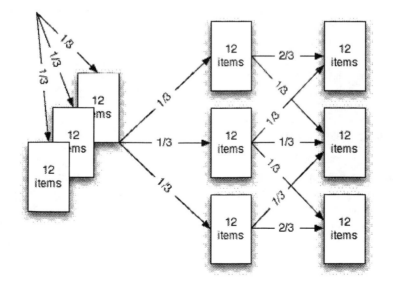

students and assigned scale scores. In addition, the results showed that demographic characteristics and testing environment (as defined by a test administrator survey) had little effect on scale scores. Upon the writing of this case study, NCDPI has made no formal decision regarding the operational use of the NCCATS as an accommodation. However, based on all results to dat it will be imperative that the target population be well-defined and that local testing coordinators be trained so that only those students for which the test is appropriate are tested shoudl NCCATS become operational.

Lesson Learned from the Development of NCCATS

Several lessons can be gleaned from the research and development of the NCCATS that may prove useful to other large-scale testing programs considering the use of a computerized adaptive test as an accommodation. Those lessons concern usability, mode comparability, development of the item pool, use of a developmental scale, test security, state and local technology infrastructure, and gaining buy-in from test consumers.

Lesson One: Usability

There are several concerns regarding the usability of online tests. If the online test is to be used as an accommodation for the paper and pencil test, then the items on both must appear similar. This can be difficult given that online items must also be interactive. Determining an appropriate interface for item delivery is a critical step in the process. Getting both student input in a cognitive lab setting and psychometric input from test development experts will help increase the potential for mode comparability. During the development of the NCCATS, a usability study was conducted at two local schools. Student feedback was extremely useful in determining how the questions and response choices should be formatted. Psychometric staff members had final approval of the interface based on their determination that the interface would not impact the construct being measured.

Lesson Two: Comparability

If a CAT is to be used as an accommodation to a paper and pencil test, then content and mode comparability must be addressed. Students taking the computer-adaptive version of the test must be administered a CAT with content that is parallel to the paper and pencil version. Parallel content can be ensured by building the CAT test with the same content specifications as the paper and pencil test. An item-by-item adaptive test structure will require significantly more programming to accomplish this task. The

NCCATS team addressed the issue by using the uMFS structure consisting of blocks or groups of items that had the same percentage of items in each strand as the paper and pencil tests. After the test specifications were laid out, psychometric consultants were able to run simulations to determine appropriate levels of difficulty for each block. The ultimate goal was that a student could receive a test with parallel content and an eventual scale score could be placed on the existing developmental scale.

In addition to content comparability, it is important that the mode of administration not interfere with a student's score. In the early stages of NCCATS, when modal differences were determined, the decision was made to extend the research and development phase so that a large-scale comparability study in each grade and subject could be conducted. The large-scale comparability study made it possible to link the NCCATS test scores to the existing scale.

Lesson Three: Development of the Item Pool

An adequate item pool is critical to the development of a computer-adaptive test. Computer-adaptive tests require a broad range of difficulty within the item pool to build a test that minimizes floor and ceiling effects, which is one of the primary advantages of the adaptive structure. In addition, when used as an accommodation, the computer-adaptive test content specifications must match the paper and pencil content specifications. Because multiple pathways exist in any given CAT administration, items matching both content and precision requirements will quickly become overexposed. This increases the need for a large pool of items that have parameters derived from an online field-test administration.

Lesson Four: Test Security

Although policies and procedures have long been in place to minimize security issues for the paper and pencil tests in North Carolina, no such policies exist to cover testing in an online environment. The test security issues are in many cases similar (e.g., securing test items and forms); however, the mode of administration introduces new issues. For example, NCCATS is administered through the Internet. Items are delivered to the student, the student answers the items, and then the items are returned to the server. Cookies are used on the local desktop computer so that a student's test can be recovered if testing is interrupted. This temporary storing of information on a local desktop was a source of concern for the test developers and was addressed in NCCATS by requiring a login user name and password. These names and passwords were provided only to test administrators who were responsible for logging on to and out of the test. In addition, specific instructions and training were provided to the test administrator on how to clear the computer's cache and cookies.

Lesson Five: State and Local Infrastructure

Equity dictates that if one school has access to an accommodation, then all schools must have access to the same accommodation. In the early phases of NCCATS, problems occurred with state level technology infrastructure. These problems prompted a review of the technology architecture and some eventual changes to it. After state level problems were addressed, it became clear that local technology problems would also need to be resolved. When technology problems occurred at the local level, it was difficult to ascertain the cause of the problem. In most cases, the test administrator was not the technology support person at the school and could not accurately articulate the technology problems. NCDPI staff addressed the problem in a number of ways. Initially, data from the third phase of implementation were analyzed. Based on the results of this analysis, NCCATS technology staff were able to further identify specific minimum technology requirements that would be necessary for a school to participate in NCCATS. Technology plans from schools experiencing problems during the previous development phases were reviewed to identify the cause of the problem. Local schools were strongly encouraged to utilize the practice activity available on an NCCATS Web site and to report any problems that occurred during the practice activity. Finally, two additional persons were hired to staff a helpdesk, resulting in a two-tiered helpdesk system. The first tier was immediate assistance for typical technology problems. When the first tier support could not address the issue, the calls were routed to second-tier support staff, who could then work with the local technology support staff to resolve the issues.

Local and state technology problems, should they occur during test administration, will result in invalid test scores. In addition, students cannot be expected to remain seated for an extended period of time while staff members work to resolve technology problems. When possible, steps should be taken to minimize technology problems prior to test administration, and policies should be drafted to address how problems occurring during a test administration will be handled.

Lesson Six: Buy-In from Test Consumers

Without consumer buy-in, a large-scale administration of a computer-adaptive test will only be nominally successful. When changes to a large-scale test format are made, the field (teachers, principals, test administrators) needs to be prepared in advance. They need to know when the test will be administered, what it will look like, and what guidelines they should use in determining for whom the accommodation is most appropriate. They need time and other resources to be properly trained in the administration of the test. In short, communication is a key component in the successful implementation of a computer-adaptive test.

Future Directions

Research and development activities for the NCCATS have resulted in a computer-adaptive test that is comparable to the paper and pencil test and yields a test score that is linked to North Carolina's developmental scale. As with most research activities, the development of NCCATS raises other questions related to federal requirements for state testing programs, curriculum and subsequent item-pool development, and validation of the developmental scale. Are computer-adaptive tests compatible with federal requirements? No Child Left Behind legislation requires that students be tested on grade-level material if they are to be considered proficient against grade-level standards. This presents a problem when grade level item pools do not maintain a sufficient number of items at all levels of difficulty. This question raises yet another question. Can grade-level curriculum or content standards be designed to accommodate a computer-adaptive test? In developing content standards and a resulting item pool, consideration should be given to developing a core bank of items that can be mapped to different grade-level content standards. These items can then be field-tested at multiple grade levels so that item parameters can be grade-level item parameters. The items can then be used to build CAT tests that have flexibility around grade levels but still test only grade-level content. This process requires prior planning and buy-in from policymakers who are responsible for codifying curriculum standards. Finally, will a developmental scale that has been developed largely on test data collected from a general population of students hold for a special population of students? Programs have to assess whether special student populations fit the assumptions of the developmental scale and consider what it means to translate item parameter estimates from more than one grade level. How much error does this introduce? If one were to calibrate items based only on the special student population, even with the ability to use only students functioning one or two grade levels below, the parameter estimates are not likely to match the paper and pencil parameters. This is significant, but what it means for the utility of the NCCATS is unclear. Additional research must be conducted to validate the use of the developmental scale for all populations of students.

Conclusion

NCCATS began as a concept four years before the research and development process concluded. The first phase was an opportunity to design a user-friendly prototype. The second phase was necessary to determine the feasibility, from both a test and a technology perspective, of implementing a large-scale computer-adaptive test. From the feasibility study emerged the question of how comparable the online and the paper-and-pencil tests were. The third phase focused on establishing comparability and gaining online item parameters from paper and pencil items. The final phase of research and development provided an opportunity to test the adaptive structure designed to accomplish the task of meeting content guidelines. Many questions still need to be researched. Considering the duration of the research and development process and the lessons learned from the research activities, perhaps the most important conclusion to be derived from the development of NCCATS is that the development of a computerized adaptive test for use in a large-scale testing program requires technological expertise, test development expertise, testing policy expertise, and, above all, patience.

References

Bethke, A., Hill, C., McLeod, L., VanDyk, P., Zhao, L., Zhou, X., & Thissen, D. (2004). *North Carolina Computerized Adaptive Testing System: 2003 Comparability Study Results*. On file at NCDPI.

Mills, C., & Stocking, M. (1996). Practical issues in large-scale computerized adaptive testing. *Applied Measurement in Education, 9*(4), 287-304.

Thissen, D. (2003). *Construction of the North Carolina Computerized Adaptive Tests (NCCATS) uniform multiform structure.* Unpublished manuscript, University of North Carolina at Chapel Hill.

Thissen, D., Edwards, M., & Coon, C. (2003). *Adaptive simulations of the uniform multiform structure (uMFS).* Unpublished manuscript, University of North Carolina at Chapel Hill.

U. S. Department of Education. (n.d.). *No child left behind.* Retrieved June 7, 2004, from *http://www.ed.gov/nclb*

Wainer, H. (2000). Introduction and history. In H. Wainer (Ed.), *Computer adaptive testing: A primer* (pp. 1-19). Hillsdale, NJ: Lawrence Erlbaum.

Chapter X

Introducing a Computer-Adaptive Testing System to a Small School District

Timothy Pelton, University of Victoria, Canada

Leslee Francis Pelton, University of Victoria, Canada

Abstract

A computer-adaptive test (CAT) is a relatively new type of technology in which a computer program "intelligently" selects and presents questions to examinees according to an evolving estimate of achievement and a prescribed test plan. A well written CAT can be expected to efficiently produce student achievement estimates that are more accurate and more meaningful than a typical teacher-generated paper and pencil (P&P) test with a similar number of questions. Although this method of testing sounds good in theory, many schools and districts are waiting for positive examples of practical applications and observable benefits before adopting a CAT. This chapter begins by describing the essential elements of meaningful measurement in education and the features of a typical CAT. Next, we describe the Measures of Academic Progress (MAP) system of the Northwest Evaluation Association (NWEA; 2004) and observations made during the introduction of this system into a small semirural school district. Finally, as independent observers, we provide a set of recommendations to help guide other districts as they consider the potentials of implementing a CAT system to guide instruction within their schools.

Background

A Need for Meaningful Measurement

Underlying the implementation of a CAT is the assumption that there is a meaningful interval scale of development and growth upon which the curricular strands or constructs identified in the test specifications can be mapped.

To support meaningful measurement, construct-linked items must fit within a stable hierarchy of difficulty, such that if a person were to be presented with the entire set of items for a particular construct starting from least difficult and progressing to most difficult, the resulting response vector would consist of a sequence of almost entirely correct responses followed by a sequence of almost entirely incorrect responses (i.e., approximating a Guttman response vector; Guttman, 1944). The expectation of an approximate hierarchy of item difficulties is not a great barrier—master teachers implicitly use this type of internal hierarchy as they adjust their diagnostic questioning to more accurately understand the achievement level and needs of individual students—but the requirement is important and needs to be attended to when examining a test item bank. Without this hierarchy of construct-linked items, a valid adaptive test is not possible.

Given a well refined hierarchical set of construct-linked items and a substantial set of responses from members within the target audience, it is possible to obtain a meaningful measurement scale by analysis using item response theory (IRT) or the Rasch measurement model (Lord, 1980; Pelton, 2003; Rasch, 1993; Wright, 1991). Difficulties inevitably arise when an attempt is made to build a unitary assessment device for an entire curriculum that in reality is a very complex collection or network of constructs. Here, pragmatism and optimism tend to lead test developers to implicitly assert that each of the curricular strands approximates a well defined construct and that these constructs load primarily onto a common scale in such a way as to maintain a meaningful hierarchy of difficulty both within the constructs and between them.

The limitations of a finite calibrating data set and the pragmatic binding together of a complex domain of constructs onto a single achievement scale mean that the assumptions of the measurement model being used (i.e., Rasch or IRT) are being broken, and therefore the underlying domain scale should really be described only as quasi-interval. Although this type of measurement scale is not perfect—indeed, the error levels are likely to be understated (Pelton, 2003; Pelton & Bunderson, 2003; Pelton & Francis-Pelton, 2004)—it can be argued that the units have a relatively stable meaning and, as such, allow for more appropriate mathematical and statistical analysis than traditional test score values.

What is a CAT?

CAT software typically uses an evolving estimate of achievement level (starting from a random guess or based upon a teacher-generated estimate) to locate items in an item bank that are likely to be effective in testing the student's knowledge and skills (i.e., at or near the student's achievement level). The student response (correct or incorrect) is then incorporated into the information used to generate the next achievement estimate. This iterative process typically continues until the error estimate associated with the current achievement estimate diminishes to an acceptable level (i.e., increasing the reliability of the test until it reaches an acceptable level), or until the test specification requirements have been met.

The test specifications are used in CAT systems to support validity by ensuring that a sufficient number of questions are asked for each of the specified constructs (curricular strands) in the domain and that the test includes sufficient coverage of the cognitive skill levels. With some test specifications, longer CATs may also be able to generate valid estimates of achievement for each individual construct in the domain (albeit with larger error estimates), thereby improving the potential utility of the test results.

An adaptive test and its associated item bank have several natural advantages over a traditional test:

1. Items presented to the student are almost ideal with respect to the student's achievement level; the resulting adaptive test can either be equal in length to a traditional test and much more reliable, or much shorter and equally reliable.

2. The individualized nature of adaptive testing increases test security because all students are given an almost unique exam (e.g., 50 items selected from an item bank of 2,000 items), reducing the potential for copying.

3. Item banks support the efficient management of items with respect to renewal, general exposure level, and the tracking of prior item presentations to individuals.

4. Testing flexibility is also enhanced with a large item bank because a CAT provides support for make up, early, challenge, and practice exams.

Greater efficiency occurs because P&P tests typically present a broad range of questions (very easy to very difficult) in order to encompass all achievement levels within the target range of the test, while adaptive tests present questions selected to be near the achievement level of each student being tested. With CATs, students are not compelled to waste time responding to very easy questions (where construct-irrelevant errors associated with transcription, interpretation, attention, etc., are the largest sources of error) or very hard questions (where guessing, item interactions, cheating, etc., might be the largest sources of error). In addition, the effective target range of a CAT can be much broader (i.e., covering a multiyear span of development). Teachers and administrators can compare student achievement estimates in a mathematically valid way to items in the item bank, past performance (i.e., gain), other students (for grouping), norms, and so forth. Wainer (1990) more completely describes these and other advantages associated with a CAT over a P&P test.

CAT, a New Experience for Students

The idea of completing a test on a computer and receiving almost immediate feedback appears to be encouraging or motivating to most students, but some differences in the CAT process may be troublesome and frustrating.

The computer-based nature of the test may be unhelpful to students who have only had minimal prior exposure to computers and must learn to deal with this mode shift. During a CAT administration, the items are presented on the computer screen one at a time and the student answers each item by selecting one of the options provided by using the keyboard or the mouse. However, the use of computers to present items allows for a richer item format and presentation through the inclusion of multimedia components for stems or response options.

Because most of the questions presented in a CAT are selected to be near their achievement level, students will typically correctly answer about 50% of the questions presented. This experience may be unfamiliar to weak students and potentially unpleasant for strong students. Although the effect on the students' scores should be low overall, additional efforts should be made to explain the testing process to those students who might be distressed by this paradigm shift.

Perhaps the most dramatic difference that a student will observe when taking a CAT is that the subsequent review or revision of past questions and answers is not permitted. Although this change in testing approach may result in slightly lower achievement estimates for testwise students, it may also result in slightly higher achievement estimates for students who traditionally struggle with bubble sheets or are distracted by multiple questions on a page (e.g., students with visual or figure-ground disabilities; Bley & Thornton, 2001).

CAT, a New Experience for Educators

The multiple choice question (MCQ) format is commonly used in a CAT because it is very easy to mark. Although both intuition and research suggests that teacher-generated MCQs and other selected response types of questions tend to be fact-based and do not attend well to higher-order thinking skills (e.g., Fleming & Chambers, 1983), this tendency is not a natural deficiency of the question type, but rather an issue of time, effort, knowledge, and skill on the part of the item writers (Worthen, White, Fan, & Sudweeks, 1999). Skilled item writers can create, pilot, and validate selected response items that assess higher-level cognitive skills (i.e., application, analysis, synthesis, and evaluation) if given sufficient time and opportunity to do so.

When proctoring an exam, the teachers and administrators have an opportunity to vet and flag inappropriate or erroneous items as well as comment on the usability of the software interface and features (both testing and administrative). By sending this feedback to the developers, educators can support the continual improvement of the quality of item pools and the efficacy and efficiency of the CAT process. In addition, some CAT producers often have mechanisms to support the construction of jurisdiction-specific CATs by allowing for the creation of test specifications and item banks that are more closely aligned with the local curriculum.

With a meaningful measurement scale being a foundational component of a CAT system, every scale value is linked to a collection of construct-linked items (and ideally a theory of development). Interpretation grids can help teachers to interpret student results (scale estimates) by supplying meaningful examples of items that are likely to be too easy, just right, or too hard for a student at any given scale position. This information may then be used to support low-stakes decision making at the macro level for the individual student (e.g., assign groupings, plan follow-up diagnostic interviews, and present lessons). If the results are aggregated across students (e.g., a classroom), then teachers may use these aggregated results to guide lesson and unit planning and professional development. An important caveat, however, is that educators need to understand that achievement estimates are always accompanied by error estimates, and these error estimates should be accounted for in any evaluation or reporting process—a measurement without error is not a measurement.

CAT systems can support improvements in educational processes if the educators using the results are able to interpret the results easily and adjust their approach in a timely manner to meet the specific needs of individual children. Still, CATs do not represent a perfect form of assessment. Although a 50 item CAT may be much more valid (i.e., has better coverage of construct-related conceptual and procedural knowledge) and reliable (i.e., has a lower error estimate for most students) than a typical 50 item test constructed by a teacher, it is still a relatively crude snapshot estimate of achievement with respect to the curriculum (written, taught, learned, or desired) and is subject to many unknown and uncontrollable factors. Because of these uncertainties, using a CAT achievement estimate (or any other type of assessment result) as a single source for high-stakes decisions is not advisable.

The NWEA MAP System

NWEA

The NWEA is a well established (1977) nonprofit organization that has created a comprehensive set of computer-adaptive assessment instruments called the Measures of Academic Progress (MAP). The MAP system currently covers the curricular areas of mathematics, reading, language usage, and science (Northwest Evaluation Association, 2004).

The NWEA's stated mandate is to support student learning by providing educational growth measures and professional support. All users of the NWEA MAP system are invited to become active partners with the organization (they have 1,200 such partners). Although they are currently focused within the U.S. educational market (claiming 42 states; 1,500 districts; and 3.2 million students), they are working with schools and jurisdictions in Canada as well (2004).

Curricular Links

As the foundation for the MAP system, the NWEA has developed a comprehensive model of the curricular domains being tested. Each curricular domain is subdivided into goal areas (constructs or curricular strands) that support more meaningful interpretations of test results.

Item Banks

Starting with a large existing item bank of approximately 15,000 items and employing subject-matter experts, the NWEA has been able to identify useful collections of items that (a) are consistent with goals and theoretical underpinnings of each of the MAP areas, (b) have performed well in other assessment contexts, and (c) have historical response data that are relatively consistent with the measurement scales and the Rasch measurement model, which were used to calibrate the items. Using this process, substantial item banks (1,500-2,000 items) were developed for each of the curricular areas in the MAP system.

NWEA MAP CATs

For each of the curricular areas in the MAP system, the tests come in three lengths- a locator, a survey (short adaptive 20 questions), and a goals survey (long adaptive 40- 52 questions). Although many adaptive tests present a variable number of items depending on the error estimate, the underlying content requirements for the MAP tests result in a fixed number of items in each test. The time required for any individual student to complete any CAT still remains highly variable (e.g., 30-90 minutes for the goals survey test).

Scale score estimates are reported in Rasch Units (RITs) and can be effectively interpreted by educators with a *reference* chart supplied by NWEA for each of the curricular areas. To support more detailed analysis, the goals survey MAP test provides both an overall scale estimate and less precise scale range estimates for each of the goal areas (constructs) within each of the domains.

In addition to the RIT scale reference charts, a second resource—the Learning Continuum (Northwest Evaluation Association, 2004)—is available to guide the instructional planning process. This guide consists of sets of appropriate curricular goals that are within reach of persons achieving any given subscale score range. By considering these suggested goals in concert with their local curricula, teachers are supported in their development of appropriately targeted and differentiated instructional programs.

The MAP domain scales are designed to produce values that are typically between 160 and 260 RITs (note that these values are distinct from, and cannot be easily confused with, either percentages or number correct). The continuous, extended nature of these scales (from grades 2 through 10) allows for a meaningful comparison of scores over time.

A School District Adopts a CAT

Context

This case study focuses on a pilot implementation of the NWEA's MAP system within a small (fewer than 5,000 students) semirural school district. This pilot was designed to help the district assess the potentials and limitations of a comprehensive CAT program with respect to supporting their instructional mandate. We were invited observers of this pilot process and had the opportunity to observe the testing process in the district, review the NWEA MAP documentation, and discuss the process and outcomes with district administrators and NWEA personnel.

The district administrators are progressive in their outlook with respect to using a comprehensive and objective assessment system to support the improvement of the quality of education in their schools. It appears that they are committed to the ideal that this assessment resource should be used primarily to support student learning by providing timely information to teachers in the classroom and school administrators. They also appear to be aware that any heavy-handed use of these assessment results for school accountability or teacher evaluation would be unhelpful.

The schools involved are "self-selected" in that the staff and the administration at each school had to agree to participate in the process before they were considered for inclusion. Other considerations that affected inclusion were funding limitations, hardware availability, technical capability, and association with other participating schools (i.e., Was an elementary school a feeder school for a participating high school?).

Goals

The overarching goal of this pilot process was to assess the potential suitability of the NWEA MAP system software for supporting instruction in the district. More specifically, the following goals/needs have been explicitly articulated or implied:

- Provide timely, detailed estimates of student achievement on meaningful scales to allow for effective communication of individual and aggregate student abilities to students, parents, teachers, and administrators. The results should be available within days of testing in contrast to the several weeks or months typical with other external estimates of achievement.

- Support grouping of students according to achievement level (homogeneous or heterogeneous) to maximize the efficiency of various learning activities.

- Provide a mechanism whereby student progress can be tracked over time (i.e., within and across grades) by using a system with scale values that span all grade levels.

- Support program analysis, teacher-directed professional development, and research on the efficacy of new pedagogical interventions.

- Review and revise items in each of the existing MAP item banks to remove references that may be affected by local cultural differences (e.g., unfamiliar terms), curricular differences (e.g., order of instruction and content covered), and defects in the item stems or response options (e.g., missing elements from graphics, symbols that are difficult to read, and questions that may not have correct answers).

- Review and adjust the MAP reference charts score translation charts to reflect changes in the item bank in order to maximize the potential for meaningful interpretation of students' scale scores in the local context.

Equipment Required

The NWEA MAP CAT software is compatible with most current Mac OS systems and Windows OS machines. Some upgrades were required in elementary schools to provide in-school secure server space for the testing system database, as the local Internet service was incapable of supporting timely testing. The data management and report generation processes requires a Windows based CPU, while the generated PDF reports may be viewed on any computer capable of accessing the Internet and having a current version of Adobe Acrobat. Administrators and teachers involved in the management and proctoring of the test were able to set up the equipment and manage the assessment process with relatively few technical issues.

Planning and Preparation

The district assessed all students in grades two through nine (grade 10 students were dropped from the pilot process because of conflicts with other external testing requirements) with domain tests for math, reading, and language usage. This testing required three to four hours of computer lab time to assess each class across all three MAP CATs.

To minimize the disruption of computer lab time for other courses in the second and third rounds of testing, the schedule was laid out in advance of the school term so that teachers could plan around testing. Completing all the tests in a short period of time (one to two weeks) resulted in some degree of test fatigue and yielded some negative effects in teacher attitude and student response to the test. The administrators are now considering offering only one domain test at a time over a short period (e.g., one week) and then having a two or three week break before the next testing period to allow for a rest and for computer classes to have sufficient access to the labs so they can accomplish their curricular objectives. The district is assessing the students in both the fall and the spring, which is well within NWEA's recommended limit of four assessments per year.

Administrators upload the database of students, teachers, classes, and schools within the district to the NWEA central database before each testing session begins. This information is used in both the proctoring and reporting process (maintaining the integrity of the testing system and the information generated). Although administrators are able to make small adjustments to the database during a testing session (e.g., add new students), some found this process cumbersome.

The Testing Process

When a test is administered, the *proctor* (a teacher or administrator trained in proctoring the NWEA MAP) must access the server containing the software and select the NWEA testing software. Then, to run the NWEA MAP system, the proctor must enter an ID and password. After the testing software is loaded, the proctor selects the student (from the student database) and the test to be presented. At this point the computer is ready for the student to begin the test.

The first round of testing (in May-June 2003) was used to identify equipment and labs that needed to be upgraded, confirm that the results were in line with teacher evaluations of student understanding (i.e., to validate), and identify items that needed to be corrected or adjusted to align with the local curriculum. Ongoing testing (September 2003 and May 2004) has continued with this process of refinement and validation.

The students' motivation to participate in CAT-based assessment appears to be fairly high, although there was some novelty effect. The majority of students observed were attending well to the questions presented to them and working diligently to answer them to the best of their abilities. However, test fatigue and time frustrations did have a negative effect on the enthusiasm and attitudes of some teachers and students with respect to the CAT.

Major sources of student motivation associated with a CAT appear to include (a) the potential for immediate feedback, (b) the self-paced nature of the test, which allows students to spend as much time as they need to complete any item, and (c) the appropriately challenging nature of the questions (not too simple, not too frustrating). However, each of these sources of motivation also proved to be a challenge in some way: (a) The on screen display of results was not appreciated by some students who were concerned about privacy; (b) some students would spend an inordinate amount of time seeking a solution for a question; and (c) the challenging nature of the exam was uncomfortable for some students accustomed to answering most questions correctly.

Analysis and Reporting

The results presented by the MAP system on the screen immediately after completion of a CAT include an overall score (without error estimates) and a score range (± 1 SE) for each of the goal subscales.

At the end of each testing day an administrator uploads student response data to NWEA for analysis, and the class reports are available to the teacher within 24 hours. Summary reports for the district are available at the end of the testing window.

The MAP postprocessing system flags a *test event* (student response set) as invalid (or anomalous) when it is out of range, the time taken was too short, or the error associated with the response pattern was unusual (i.e., substantially different from a Guttman pattern). The results from all invalidated tests are retained in the record and are reported to the teacher and school but are not used in the calculation of overall statistics (classroom, school, district, regional, or national) or any refinement of the related item bank (Northwest Evaluation Association, 2004). Administrators observed that about half of the students with interrupted (paused) tests were flagged as invalid. This seems to be a pragmatic compromise-no student information is lost to the school, but any potentially questionable data is not used to refine the item banks or to bias the overall results.

Interpreting and Using the Results

Because this is only the end of the first full year of testing, most teachers are still evaluating the validity of the MAP system. As of May 2004, only a few LA teachers were using the results to directly guide instruction. The administrators felt that it will likely take five to seven years before the NWEA MAP results are fully integrated into teachers' programs and supporting instructional practice.

Effective interpretation of the results of a MAP test requires some inservice training. In order to effectively interpret MAP system scores, teachers and administrators need to acquire and refine (a) an understanding of the relationship between the scale values and the MAP reference charts, (b) an understanding of the hierarchical nature of NWEA's MAP scales and the Learning Continuum, (c) an awareness of the nature of error distributions, (d) an awareness of the underlying theory of measurement that allows the results from this system to be properly compared and aggregated and that provides for meaningful estimates of growth within and across grades, and e) confidence in the validity of the scale estimates. The latter point appears to be the first hurdle for the teachers. They are just now able to examine correlations between MAP scale estimates, grades, and other external assessments. As validity evidence builds (e.g., correlational) and as results are further refined through reduction of inconsistencies (through retesting or score invalidation), teacher confidence in this assessment instrument should rise. As teacher confidence builds, it is likely that the testing process will be more rigorously followed and the quality of the achievement estimates will further improve.

The typical range of scale values associated with each grade is fairly narrow. The greatest fall/spring gains on continuum scale scores appear in the earliest grades (e.g., math grade 2: 15 RITs; grade 5: 8.8 RITs; and grade 9: 5.8 RITs). This means that the potential for observing individual growth through the error noise associated with the standard error estimate (typically 3.0-3.2 RITs) is much greater in the earlier grades. Confidence intervals (CI) for student achievement estimates often range beyond a single grade level, and individual goal or strand estimate CIs can span two or more grade levels. Class results typically show wide (multigrade), approximately normal distributions of student achievement in each of the subject areas.

Responding to MAP Test Results

The NWEA MAP appears to provide a manageable and effective assessment strategy that has the potential to support appropriate and helpful classroom grouping and selection of appropriate tasks or challenges. This use of assessment is consistent with good teaching practice and the trend toward differentiated instruction (e.g., Tomlinson, 1999). It is anticipated that specific, individualized instructional benefits will be more achievable in the elementary grades (e.g., two to five) because the errors associated with student achievement estimates are much smaller in relation to the typical growth interval for students at these grade levels.

Because the standard error estimates are fairly large relative to the growth intervals expected in the higher grades, it is not uncommon for some individuals in each class to appear to have zero or negative movement in relation to previous MAP scale estimates (during the last testing process, some students appeared to drop by as much as 15-20 RITs) . Here, a solid understanding of the nature of the instrument, the measurement error, and the potential factors that may impact the estimation process is important. When the student has obviously underperformed (i.e., when suffering from illness or apathy or when results are highly inconsistent with other assessments, etc.), a retest is possible and may be recommended. In addition, whenever such an anomaly is observed, a review of other evidence of progress (i.e., portfolio and other assessments) should also be used in the evaluation.

The testing also identified some students who were exceptionally advanced (even when error was considered). With this information teachers and administrators are able to adjust programming or provide enrichment opportunities for students who otherwise may have "flown under the radar."

Aggregate estimates of class achievement are more reliable than individual student estimates (i.e., smaller error estimates relative to grade-level intervals on the scale). Class-level charts of student achievement can be generated by the system that show the distribution of student achievement levels within each goal area. Although only a few teachers are currently using this information to make macrolevel classroom-planning decisions, improve instructional targeting, or manage grouping, these results are becoming part of the context in which the teachers are operating and are again contributing to the pool of validity evidence.

The periodic nature of this testing program and the continuous scale underlying each curricular area allow for the effective collection of a series of observations of student achievement and growth. This information may be helpful to teachers and schools in two major ways: (a) identifying effective strategies and programs that should be shared with other teachers and (b) identifying programs in need of revision or additional support.

Administrators interviewed at the end of the third testing cycle were positively disposed toward the system. The issues mentioned seemed to focus mostly on logistics of accomplishing the testing process and training teachers to interpret and make use of the results in their classrooms. Perhaps the greatest endorsement of CATs in general, and the NWEA MAP system in specific, is the district administrator's expressed intention to continue with, and expand, the process.

Recommendations

A long term commitment is required to allow for a CAT to become an integral part of the educational process. The administrators in this district have suggested that they expect the process to take five to seven more years. The majority of teachers will need to see several cycles of student results that are consistent with traditional mark estimates of student achievement (and their own intuitive estimates) in order to be confident in the validity of the instrument. After the system results are locally validated, several more years will be required for the results to be fully utilized in supporting instruction. It is expected that the time required for this validation and acceptance process will compress as evidence of the system's utility is introduced into the public domain (i.e., through journals, books, etc.).

Comprehensive in-service training should be available to support all teachers who are interested in applying MAP scale scores to assist in planning their classroom activities. Specifically, teachers need to understand the nature of the measures generated, the uncertainty implied by the errors, the pragmatic interpretation of measurement scale scores, and the use of supplementary information (e.g., the Learning Continuum and interpretation charts) to guide unit and lesson planning. Although including all students in the assessment process is ideal, the pushback (i.e., nonparticipation and apathy) by some less enthusiastic teachers and students suggests that a phased voluntary adoption may be helpful.

It is recommended that the application of the results should be left to the teachers' discretion rather than by administrative decree. As evidence is shared on successful (and unsuccessful) applications and interventions, the potential utility of the system will be illuminated, and teachers will gradually adopt those techniques that are most fruitful.

The need for public accountability appears to be in conflict with the need to maintain the integrity of the measurement system in order to maximize its utility with respect to helping students learn more efficiently. The use of average gain in MAP scale scores to evaluate teacher or school effectiveness would likely invalidate assessment by subverting the cooperative process and destroying the potential utility of the instruments with respect to supporting instruction. Protocols for the use of data collected by this system should be developed to manage the dissemination of the data to support appropriate uses and maintain validity. Perhaps a balance between the needs of the students and the needs of the public might be found by allowing a delayed (e.g., one year) release of district-level growth results concurrently with school and district growth plans. Administrators in the district have repeatedly committed to the ideal of using this assessment solely for the benefit of instruction.

The NWEA MAP system is intended to be an external benchmark that describes the pattern of growth through the curricular content independent of the local curriculum. The advantages associated with having a standard set of goals and items calibrated to common scales include (a) consistent and meaningful results across time and geography, (b) economies of scale for developing and maintaining software and test items, and (c) potential to support research efforts across jurisdictions. However, the validity of an assessment instrument for use in classrooms is also dependent upon its alignment with the local curriculum and the teachers' awareness of any discrepancies. As topics are presented in different orders to differing grade levels or not presented at all, the students' scores can be affected. The district is taking advantage of the available opportunities to refine the NWEA item banks and test specifications so that they are more closely aligned with the local curricula, and it is anticipated that any new initiatives to further enhance the validity of the test will be embraced.

Conclusion

It seems that the introduction of the NWEA MAP system within this district is well underway, and the system appears to have the potential to evolve and improve over time. The school district has also done well in its first year of implementing the system and is anticipating that meaningful educational benefits will be realized over time, with the CAT system becoming an integral component of their instructional process.

References

Bley, N. S., & Thornton, C. A. (2001). *Teaching mathematics to students with learning disabilities.* Austin, TX: Pro-ed.

Fleming, M., & Chambers, B. (1983). Teacher-made tests: Windows on the classroom. In W. E. Hathaway (Ed.), *Testing in the schools: New directions for testing and measurement* (pp. 29-38). San Francisco: Jossey-Bass.

Guttman, L. (1944). A basis for scaling qualitative data. *American Sociological Review, 9,* 139–150.

Lord, F. M. (1980). *Applications of item response theory to practical testing problems.* Hillsdale, NJ: Lawrence Erlbaum Associates.

Northwest Evaluation Association. (2004). Assessments should make a difference. Retrieved August 4, 2004, from *http://www.nwea.org*

Pelton, T. (2003, April). *What are the effects of allowing crossing item characteristic curves into our measurement model?* Paper presented at the meeting of the American Educational Research Association, Chicago, IL.

Pelton, T., & Francis-Pelton, L. (2004, April). *Exploring the Rasch model's potentials and limitations by rediscovering length?* Paper presented at the meeting of the American Educational Research Association, San Diego, CA.

Pelton, T. W., & Bunderson, C. V. (2003). The recovery of the density scale using a stochastic quasi-realization of additive conjoint measurement. *Journal of Applied Measurement, 4*(3), 269-281.

Rasch, G. (1993). *Probabilistic models for some intelligence and attainment tests.* Chicago: MESA Press.

Tomlinson, C. A. (1999). *The differentiated classroom: Responding to the needs of all learners.* Alexandria, VA: Association for Supervision and Curriculum and Development.

Wainer, H. (1990). Introduction and history. In H. Wainer (Ed.), *Computerized adaptive testing: A primer.* Hillsdale, NJ: Lawrence Erlbaum Associates.

Worthen, B. R., White, K. R., Fan, X., & Sudweeks, R. R. (1999). *Measurement and assessment in schools.* New York: Longman.

Wright, B. (1991). Rasch vs. Birnbaum. *Rasch Measurement Transactions, 5*(4), 178-179.

Chapter XI

A Computer-Adaptive Mathematics Test Accommodates Third Grade Students with Special Needs in the Pacific Northwest

Luke Duesbery, University of Oregon, USA

Leanne R. Ketterlin-Geller, University of Oregon, USA

Jan D. McCoy, Learning Point Associates, USA

Gerald Tindal, University of Oregon, USA

Abstract

Assessment of student ability is often clouded by the interaction between content knowledge and prerequisite access skills. These ancillary skills can influence the students' level of engagement with the test material by limiting their ability to access the test information or respond to the questions. In the case of mathematics, for example, reading and writing are viewed as access skills in that a student is required to be proficient in these skills in order to succeed on the multiple choice mathematics items (Helwig, Rozek-Tedesco, Tindal, Heath, & Almond, 1999). Students with deficiencies in these access skills are unable to demonstrate their knowledge and skills in the construct under investigation by the test (Elliott, Kratochwill, & McKevitt, 2001). To compensate for these access barriers, test accommodations are provided that change the manner in which the test items are delivered, the setting in which the test is taken, the timing of the test, and/or the administration procedures employed during testing. In a traditional paper and pencil test, these changes to the test are only possible by retrofitting existing materials. In an online computerized testing platform, however, accommodations can be embedded within the design and delivery of the items, thereby creating a seamless testing environment that integrates the necessary support structures to provide all students with an equal opportunity to succeed. The purpose of this chapter is to highlight the process we used to create an accommodated mathematics test for third grade students in an online environment.

Introduction

Online assessments incorporate design features of static computer-based tests with the dynamic delivery mechanism of the Internet. Computer-based tests allow for the integration of sound measurement principles with burgeoning technologies to address such issues as accommodating students with disabilities and English language learners, while the Internet provides a network for efficient delivery and scoring as well as secure storage of student performance data. Together, these components make a powerful system for meeting the needs of schools, districts, and states.

Although an online assessment has the potential to be a powerful complement to existing assessment systems, this testing platform can be difficult to navigate. In 2001 the American Psychological Association (APA) formed the Task Force on Psychological Testing on the Internet (Naglieri, Drasgow, Schmidt, Handler, Prifitera, Margolis, et al., 2004), in which a diverse array of field scholars was assembled to address those testing issues exclusive to online assessment. The report from this task force highlights some of the issues central to the design, development, and delivery of online tests. In this chapter, we integrate the task force's recommendations with a practical application of an online test to provide an example of how to use these technologies to create dynamic, efficient, and technically adequate online assessments.

The Context for Our Online-Accommodated Mathematics Test

Under recent federal legislation, annual testing of all students is required in grades three through eight in the areas of reading and mathematics (U.S. Department of Education, n.d.). Among other requirements, state assessments must meaningfully include students with disabilities in general education assessments. In order to support the needs of all students, appropriate accommodations must be provided. In mathematics, accommodations are often needed to support deficiencies in reading skills such as comprehension and decoding fluency. As these skills may influence access to information or expression of knowledge and ability, support mechanisms are required to mediate these extraneous sources of non-construct-related difficulty. Such accommodations include verbatim audio presentation of information (read-aloud accommodations) and reduction of the complexity of the vocabulary demand (simplified language accommodations).

Researchers in mathematics achievement have found that a read-aloud accommodation may remove the barriers caused by low reading skills and, therefore, may provide students with the opportunity to perform closer to their ability level (Fuchs, Fuchs, Eaton, Hamlett, & Karns, 2000; Helwig et al., 1999; Helwig, Rozek-Tedesco, & Tindal, 2002; Johnson, 2000; Tindal, Heath, Hollenbeck, Almond, & Harniss, 1998). To further validate these findings, Tindal et al. (1998) compared results from a standard and accommodated test administered to low-performing general education students and students receiving special education services. Although the read-aloud accommodation benefited the special education population, no benefit was observed in the general education population. Effect sizes were not reported in the research, but when comparing the accommodated special education group to the lowest performing accommodated general education group, significant differences were still evident ($p <$ 0.001). Therefore, this accommodation appears to remove construct-irrelevant limitations caused by a disability, enabling students to more accurately demonstrate their mathematical knowledge and skills.

Similarly, simplified language accommodations reduce the language demands of word-based mathematics problems. Linguistic simplification decreases the complexity of the language and non-mathematics related vocabulary in the item without changing the content or difficulty of the item (Kiplinger, Haug, & Abedi, 2000). This accommodation reduces the level of English language proficiency needed to interpret the problem (Stansfield, 2002) by reducing the number of words, removing multi-syllabic words, and omitting conditional statements (Tindal, Anderson, Helwig, Miller, & Glasgow, 2000). Therefore, simplified mathematics word-based problems may permit students with limited decoding skills to accurately demonstrate their knowledge and skills.

In keeping with this research, we designed a third grade mathematics test to support students with limited access skills by providing reading-based accommodations. Reading deficiencies were identified through a series of preliminary reading tests. Based on performance on the reading tests, students were accommodated on the mathematics test with either having the text read aloud, having the text presented in simplified language, or both. Additional supports were built, such as 18 point font and clear graphics for ease in viewing, full screen images to eliminate the need for scrolling, and multiple choice question formatting to avoid the interference of writing skills. To reduce the length of time in each testing session, we created a computer-adapted mathematics test. Therefore, we created an online test that included a series of basic reading tests and a computer-adapted mathematics test in order to provide a testing environment that supported the needs of the larger student population. What follows is a description of how we created and integrated these components into a seamless online delivery system.

Instrument Design

Issues in design primarily center on psychometric concerns. Meaningful measurement dictates the evaluation of evidence for both reliability and validity. The facets of psychometric integrity in traditional assessment are well documented in academic literature, but interpretation of them in terms of online assessment is warranted. Along with the evaluation of traditional sources of data for establishing reliability and validity of any assessment, an online assessment should provide dependable and consistent results each time the test is administered, ensured by (a) consistent administration and (b) appropriate design specifications that encourage consistent delivery. Although the basic premises of reliability and validity remain the same, when we speak of online assessment, a new array of variables must be considered.

Consistent Administration

Consistent administration refers to the property of the assessment that causes it to be the same across administrations, regardless of who participates, which computer hardware is used, or the time of day. The Standards for Educational and Psychological Testing call for "comparable measurement for everyone, and unfair advantage to no one" (American Psychological Association, American Educational Research Association, & National Council on Measurement in Education, 1999, p. 61). Early in the era of computer-based testing, Green (1990) referred to these elements of consistency as system issues. They include elements such as platform, screen size and resolution, image color depth and file size, and screen layout, and should be considered to maximize the likelihood that consistent administration takes place. These issues are particularly important in an online testing environment, where hardware and software may vary across administration sites.

Platform must be the first decision because it will likely direct many subsequent development and delivery decisions. Next, optimal screen size and resolution should be considered during this phase of development. Guidelines must be set for minimum requirements to avoid differences in test administration. For example, if screen size and resolution vary, students in one location may see the items on a single screen, whereas students in another location may need to scroll to see the items. These subtle differences may impact student performance and, therefore, jeopardize the validity and reliability of the measure.

Image color depth and file size must be addressed due to the interdependence between these features and delivery speed. The more color information in the images, the larger the file sizes and the slower the delivery. Put simply, delivering more information over a fixed bandwidth takes more time than delivering less information and threatens the consistency of delivery.

Lastly, in the design stages of the assessment it is important to establish whether single or multiple items will appear on each screen. Although delivering several questions on a single screen may be appropriate for some computer-based tests such as survey instruments, an advantage to computer-based technology is the ability to deliver a single item per screen. Students may benefit from this format because they may be less distracted by upcoming items, thereby providing accurate information about their abilities. Additionally, this flexible format allows for delivery of individually tailored assessments such as accommodations and audio support for directions. These design issues must be discussed and guidelines established prior to development and delivery of any online assessment.

In the context of our online-accommodated mathematics test, we administered the test to over 250 third grade students in computer labs across public elementary schools in one state in the Pacific Northwest. In order to maintain consistent administration across different platforms found at these sites, we designed our test to run under both Windows and Macintosh operating systems. Additionally, we designed our system to mirror the screen size and resolution requirements imposed by the state's online assessment system, a fixed screen size of 800 x 600 pixels displaying 24 bit color images. In our situation, items were delivered as a set of images, thereby bringing issues of color depth and image file size to the forefront. Because of concerns about the speed of item delivery, we used Macromedia Fireworks, a bitmap graphics editing software, to compress each image and optimize file size. Finally, to accomplish our goals of creating an individually tailored assessment that incorporated accommodations, we elected to present one item per screen. In this way, each item could be delivered with a customized accommodation, whether it be read-aloud or simplified text. Although not specifically tested in this case, these items could have also been presented in increased font size, if necessary, for those with vision impairments. Carefully considering all these design issues prior to development helped us create an online test that could be consistently administered across sites.

Design Specifications for Consistent Delivery

Three distinct strategies can be employed to inform layout decisions: community-based review panels, prior practices, and current research. Thompson, Thurlow, and Moore (2002) suggest that one method for creating an appropriate computer testing interface is to incorporate members of the educational community throughout the test development process. Community review panels can be structured to gather input from software designers, test developers, and test administrators, as well as test takers, to provide a well balanced perspective of design issues. Software designers can collaborate with assessment experts to review the purpose of the test and devise technological solutions for maintaining these goals while providing accessibility and flexibility. Next, the test developers should consider creating a flexible design that still maintains the integrity of the construct being tested. Flexible designs will allow the widest range of options to support the variety of student needs. The appropriateness of the response format of the instrument should be evaluated in light of the construct being measured. For example, a multiple choice test may be appropriate for measuring subject matter knowledge but may be inappropriate for measuring performance-based skills.

Additional sources of information that can guide layout decisions come from (a) leaders in the field of online assessment such as Educational Testing Services (ETS), (b) building on existing state-of-the-art assessments, and (c) investigating the work of prominent people in graphical design to focus design issues on proven best practices. Edward Tufte (1990), for example, provides valuable insights into the interplay between making our assessment appealing in appearance while simultaneously making it practical in performance.

For the online-accommodated mathematics test, we incorporated aspects from these approaches to inform our layout design. To determine how members of the educational community would respond to our test, we gathered input from teachers, administrators, parents, and students. To determine how teachers and administrators would respond to the assessment, we conducted a guided interview with 10 participants. We solicited information about the appropriateness of the item format, layout design, and test content. Additionally, we conducted focus groups with parents and students from our target populations. We displayed the test to these participants and asked for specific feedback. Responses related to such features as the size of the "next" button, color indicators when a response has been selected, and font style. Comments from both the interviews and focus groups were used to align the design of the test with the needs of the test users and takers.

Next, we researched practices used by ETS and the Center for Applied Special Technology (CAST) to determine how to effectively design assessments to support the needs of a diverse student population. Additionally, research on universal design was integrated into the test layout. We designed the test to include audio recordings of all directions as well as written text to provide redundancy of material and to support students with low reading skills. All information that was read aloud to the student was formatted with an icon that resembled a speaker to the left of the text. The student could access the audio recordings by clicking on the speaker icon. There was no limit to the number of times a student could listen to the information.

For consistency with the state assessment format and to reduce the complexity of the test (Bennett, 2002; Burk, 1998), items were written in a multiple choice format. Problems were formatted with the question on the left of the screen and the answer choices listed vertically on the right (see Figure 1). Answers could be selected with the computer mouse or keys on the keyboard, thereby allowing students with a range of motor skills and physical abilities to access the material. An answer choice was selected when the student tabbed to or clicked anywhere within the box containing the answer. After an answer was selected, the box containing the answer changed color to indicate that a choice had been made. The students were allowed to change their answer choices at any time prior to submitting their responses. Responses were recorded when the student progressed to the next screen. These features help to ensure that all students are able to interact easily with the test format and that the design facilitates equal access to the test.

Figure 1. Interface design for the online-accommodated mathematics test

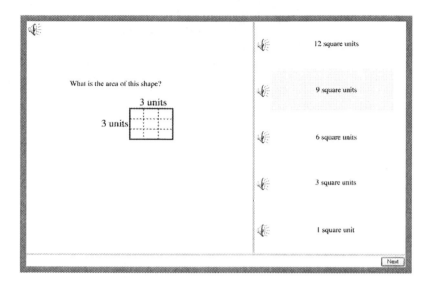

Instrument Development

As with a traditional paper and pencil test, creating an online assessment requires two distinct development phases: (a) item development and (b) structural development. First, items must be developed that are representative of the constructs being assessed and known to reliably measure those constructs. To assess efficiently, items should be at the appropriate difficulty level for the test takers. Second, the structure of the computer-based assessment must be developed. Software must be chosen, algorithms written, graphics created, and data collected and analyzed. These two distinct phases can be seen as mutually exclusive yet equally important.

Item Development

Item development, whether for computer-based or paper and pencil tests, must be considered in the context of the construct under investigation and the intended use of the observed results. Evidence for construct, content, and criterion validity must be gathered to ensure that the items are meaningful and lead to trustworthy data. Item bias should also be examined to determine whether the items function differently for different populations. Additionally, reliability data should be evaluated to make sure that the items are consistent across time, settings, and raters (American Psychological Association et al., 1999).

Our online-accommodated mathematics test included a series of basic reading tests as well as a computer-adapted mathematics test. To develop the items for all these tests, we followed a series of steps. First, we determined the purpose of the assessment and brainstormed possible formats for measuring the intended construct. After we decided on the type of assessment tool we were going to use, we formatted a preliminary paper and pencil-based test, created a key, and wrote the test administration instructions and student directions. Next, we asked three third grade teachers and three content experts to review the tests to make sure the items were appropriate in their content, format, and language and to make sure that they aligned with the standards and accurately represented the construct. After revising the items based on this input, we pilot-tested all the items. The results were analyzed by using Item Response Theory (IRT) to determine the difficulty and discrimination parameters. Differential Item Functioning (DIF) analysis was also possible with IRT modeling and provided information about item bias.

For the mathematics test, we decided to create a computer-adapted test (CAT). A CAT uses student responses to select subsequent problems, closely matching the test taker's ability level and thereby increasing the precision and efficiency of the test and reducing measurement errors (Rudner, 1998). These variations from the standard paper and pencil format increase the accessibility of the information and allow greater flexibility for the learner (Dolan, 2000).

At the heart of the CAT lies the logic of IRT, a method by which student responses are used to calculate a latent ability in the construct. That calculated latent trait could be used in turn to target and deliver items more appropriate to a student's ability level. When developing a test to determine entry-level computer programmer's skill, Zicker, Overton, Taylor, and Harms (1999) isolated three advantages of IRT in online assessment. First, IRT allows for increased security, because it is unlikely that any two test takers will face the same set of items. Second, IRT reduces testing time by delivering fewer items than a traditional test, which is better targeted to the test taker's ability. Third, IRT is able to distinguish item difficulty levels with more precision, allowing for the delivery of targeted items strategically drawn from the item bank.

Structural Development

Apart from the item development, a mechanism by which the items will be delivered must also be created. Myriad approaches exist for the structural development of online assessments. At one end of the spectrum, the easiest and most expensive route would be to contract the work out to assessment and software developers. A more cost-effective approach, however, is to develop assessments purely in-house. At the beginning of the development process, it is critical to assess the strengths of those involved and determine where external support will be needed. For example, an organization may be fully capable of designing the test specifications but may need to contract external technical expertise to program the software engine that drives the assessment.

For the online-accommodated mathematics test, we had access to a wide array of resources; therefore, we developed the test in-house. Staff included a videographer with editing experience, a computer programmer to code the software, a methodologist to write

Copyright © 2006, Idea Group Inc. Copying or distributing in print or electronic forms without written permission of Idea Group Inc. is prohibited.

the computer algorithms for the CAT, and a software designer to create the graphical interface, in addition to the management staff needed to organize and implement the project.

Graphics

The magnitude of developing even a small online assessment necessitates a high degree of automation in the development of item graphics. For delivery over the Internet, it is desirable for each item to have separate image files for the stem and all possible responses. This alleviated the concern that plain text might be re-sized on different computer platforms. By using fixed-size images we could assure consistency across administrations. In our case, the image development program Adobe Photoshop was the primary graphics tool to craft and design the item images. In addition, we used Macromedia Fireworks to fine tune the images and slice the items into separate image files. Photoshop enabled a high degree of automation in the re-sizing and recoloring of images when necessary. Fireworks allowed us to specify final dimensions of the individual image files and automatically name them sequentially. This enabled us to create more than 10,000 images and automatically generate file names according to a consistent naming convention. During the process, item image sets were tracked and stored in a database.

Tool Choice

Several tools are needed to efficiently develop an online assessment, such as Web development software to make test pages, a simple to use scripting language to manage variables, and a secure database to store data.

Web development tools allow a variety of multimedia, such as images, text, and sound, to be delivered at the same time in accordance with the design specifications. We chose Macromedia Dreamweaver, given its simple click-and-drag interface and widespread use. The decision to adopt this tool also meant that we could easily move between online and local administration and multiple platforms if necessary. It is noteworthy to mention that requiring the latest browser version is advisable. Later versions of browsers seem less prone to crashing when encountering more complex scripts. In the end, the Web browser through which the assessment was delivered was set to run in kiosk mode, thereby preventing students from accessing any distracting menus and navigation buttons.

By using hypertext preprocessor (PHP) as our scripting language to manage variables, we were better able to employ an uncomplicated data retrieval and manipulation mechanism. As test takers selected answers to questions, responses were moved over the Internet into a table in a MySQL (My Structured Query Language) database on our server. This move was important, because it removed any possibility of data entry error. It also meant that the table could be quickly accessed to make IRT calibrations and deliver the next targeted item without delay. MySQL is an open source relational database, freely available for download on the Web. Having a relational database was necessary in our case, because we needed to estimate the IRT ability parameters for test takers after each response in order for the CAT to function. Within the database, Bayesian iterative calculations were made based on item response patterns, and values were passed back to the assessment engine to deliver the next appropriate item. Using PHP embedded in HTML to pass variables to a MySQL database on a Linux server was the most economical choice in our situation.

As information was passed from server to client and back again, it was critical that we embed features to ensure secure transmission of data. As the stakes of the assessment increase, so should the attention paid to security issues (Naglieri et al., 2004). To account for security, students entered the testing session through a secure login system. After information was entered, a secure socket layer (SSL) at the server was established with little difficulty, enhancing the protection of data. In order to take advantage of this more secure connection, a modern Web browser was used that could handle encrypted data and thereby ensure data security.

In summary, item development and structural development issues must be considered when creating an online assessment. In order to get valuable information, items must be created that accurately and appropriately measure the intended construct. Additional structural considerations, such as the graphics development and Web tools, must also be addressed. In our example, we were able to develop a complex online-accommodated math test by using commonly available software and local personnel.

Planning for Online Delivery

In an ideal setting, we could deliver assessments seamlessly, without delay or pause. Unfortunately, this may not be a reality. Although many Internet users are moving to high-speed broadband connections, some continue to use dial-up connections. Additionally, public school districts are often constrained by sharing a single connection among many schools' sites. Furthermore, even those with broadband connections, such as cable or DSL, may not have sufficient bandwidth to deliver an assessment without noticeable delay. Delays and other technological limitations of delivering tests over the Internet influence the standardization of administration, which is critical for consistency of results. In the delivery process, then, it is important that only essential data be sent to a test taker's computer. During the design and development stages, this constraint means minimizing the use of graphics, optimizing image file size, and limiting image resolution and color depth. To further overcome bandwidth constraints, issues of software choice and the establishment of minimum test-bed requirements should be addressed.

The choice of development software can make a difference in file sizes and thereby impact the bandwidth constraint. Some software does a better job of compressing and delivering graphics over the Internet than others. Specifically, Macromedia Director or Flash may be more suited than HTML at developing intensive multimedia deliveries.

In the context of our online-accommodated mathematics test, we were delivering our test to students within one state. As such, we were able to use the minimum test-bed specifications set by the State Department of Education for use on their computer-based assessment system. By limiting access of our assessment to these testing sites, we ensured the hardware capabilities of the test site met a pre-specified set of requirements, thereby alleviating design pressure. We also took 20 laptops to test sites that did not meet the requirements and delivered the test over a wireless network. With this, we circumvented both hardware and bandwidth constraints when we ran the assessment over a local area network.

Limitations of Online Assessments

Issues of differential access to computers serve as limiting features for all forms of computer-based tests. Exposure to technology can vary across individuals based on incomparable resources at home and school. Prohibitive costs of computer hardware and software influence the quantity and quality of resources available. As a result, families and schools with limited financial resources or priorities that redirect funds from technology may be disadvantaged when computers are used for assessments. This concept of a digital divide is ever present. Additionally, personal attributes, such as a short attention span or underdeveloped fine motor skills, may negatively interact with technology and, therefore, must be considered in the development (Naglieri et al., 2004). These and other issues associated with computer-based assessment must be taken into account in the design, delivery, and development of online assessments to ensure equal access by all users.

Costs can also be a constraint in the use of online assessments. Computer-delivered tests, whether CBT or CAT, can be difficult to develop; add to that the intent to distribute the administration via a Web browser, and difficulties multiply. The question to answer, then, is whether the constraints and their concomitant challenges present barriers limiting the usefulness of online assessment delivery. In other words, do the benefits outweigh the costs?

Conclusion

Where paper and pencil tests were governed by the Committee on Psychological Tests and Assessment (CPTA) and the Standards for Educational and Psychological Measurement (American Psychological Association et al., 1999), the Task Force on Psychological Testing on the Internet has developed a document addressing those issues specific to online assessment (Naglieri et al., 2004). We attempted to apply these principles in a practical setting in the design, development, and delivery of our online-accommodated mathematics test.

We feel that our effort represents a small success and that the creation of the delivery engine used here will have a beneficial impact on similar future efforts. As mentioned earlier, our fundamental goal was to assess student achievement in mathematics at the third grade level. This goal was achieved (Ketterlin-Geller, 2003). Beyond merely assessing student mathematics achievement, however, was the goal of offering appropriate accommodations to those students needing support in accessing the mathematics assessment. This measurement of student access skills and delivery of appropriate accommodations required a computer to make it as expeditious as possible and to function without the intervention of teaching staff. Both of these goals could have been achieved by using stand alone workstations rather than delivery over the Internet. But without the use of an online assessment, it would not have been possible to collect information on student performance for rapid analysis, nor to broadly deliver the questions across multiple classrooms and schools simultaneously. These two functions require a model of the sort described in this chapter and provide more than adequate justification for the development of an online delivery system. Now that the model is in place and functional, the steps necessary for development of additional, similar tests revert largely to those necessary for more traditional testing. Replication has already begun and is proving successful.

References

American Psychological Association, American Educational Research Association, & National Council on Measurement in Education. (1999). *Standards for educational and psychological testing.* Washington, DC: Author.

Bennett, R. E. (2002). Inexorable and inevitable: The continuing story of technology and assessment. *Journal of Technology, Learning, and Assessment, 1*(1), 3-22. Retrieved May 20, 2003, from *http://www.bc.edu/research/intasc/jtla.html*

Burk, M. (1998). *Computerized test accommodations: A new approach for inclusion and success for students with disabilities.* Washington, DC: A. U. Software.

Dolan, B. (2000). Universal design for learning. *Journal of Special Education Technology, 15*(4), 47-51.

Elliott, S. N., Kratochwill, T. R., & McKevitt, B. C. (2001). Experimental analysis of the effects of testing accommodations on the scores of students with and without disabilities. *Journal of School Psychology, 39*(1), 3-24.

Fuchs, L. S., Fuchs, D., Eaton, S. B., Hamlett, C. L., & Karns, K. M. (2000). Supplementing teacher judgment of mathematics test accommodations with objective data sources. *School Psychology Review, 29*(1), 65-85.

Green, B. F. (1990). System design and operation. In H. Wainer, N. Dorans, R. Flaughter, B. Green, R. Mislevy, L. Steinberg, et al. (Eds.), *Computerized adaptive testing: A primer* (pp. 23-36). Hillsdale, NJ: Lawrence Erlbaum Associates.

Helwig, R., Rozek-Tedesco, M. A., & Tindal, G. (2002). An oral versus a standard administration of a large-scale mathematics test. *Journal of Special Education, 36*(1), 39-47.

Helwig, R., Rozek-Tedesco, M. A., Tindal, G., Heath, B., & Almond, P. J. (1999). Reading as an access to mathematics problem solving on multiple choice tests for sixth grade students. *Journal of Educational Research, 93*(2), 113-125.

Johnson, E. S. (2000). The effects of accommodations on performance assessments. *Remedial and Special Education, 21*(5), 261-267.

Ketterlin-Geller, L. R. (2003). *Establishing a validity argument for universally designed assessments.* Unpublished doctoral dissertation, University of Oregon, Eugene.

Kiplinger, V. L., Haug, C. A., & Abedi, J. (2000, April). Measuring math—not reading—on a math assessment: A language accommodations study of English language learners and other special populations. Paper presented at the *Annual Meetings of the American Educational Research Association*, New Orleans, LA. (ERIC Document Reproduction Service No. ED441813.)

Naglieri, J., Drasgow, F., Schmidt, M., Handler, L., Prifitera, A., Margolis, A., et al. (2004). Psychological testing on the Internet: New problems, old issues. *American Psychologist, 59*, 150–162.

Rudner, L. (1998). *An online tutorial for computer adaptive testing.* Retrieved May 25, 2003, from *http://edres.org/scripts/cat/catdemo.htm*

Stansfield, C. W. (2002). Linguistic simplification: A promising test accommodation for LEP students? *Practical Assessment, Research & Evaluation, 8*(7), 1-5. Retrieved April 30, 2003, from *http://ericae.net/pare/getvn.asp?v=8&n=7*

Tindal, G., Anderson, L., Helwig, R., Miller, S., & Glasgow, A. (2000). *Accommodating students with learning disabilities on math tests using language simplification.* Eugene: University of Oregon, College of Education, RCTP.

Tindal, G., Heath, B., Hollenbeck, K., Almond, P., & Harniss, M. (1998). Accommodating students with disabilities on large scale tests: An empirical study of student response and test administration demands. *Exceptional Children, 64*(4), 439-450.

Tufte, E. (1990). *Envisioning information.* Cheshire, CT: Graphics Press.

U.S. Department of Education. (n.d.). *The no child left behind act of 2001 executive summary.* Retrieved July 1, 2002, from *http://www.ed.gov/nclb/overview/intro/execsumm.html*

Zicker, M., Overton, R., Taylor, L., & Harms, H. (1999). The development of a computerized selection system for computer programmers in a financial services company. In F. Drasgow & J. B. Olson-Buchanan (Eds.), *Innovations in computerized assessment* (pp. 7-34). Mahwah, NJ: Lawrence Erlbaum Associates.

Chapter XII

Designing an Online Formative Assessment that Helps Prepare Students and Teachers for a Summative Assessment:

A Case Study—A Two-Year Pilot Project Pairing an Online Classroom Assessment with a Statewide High- Stakes Test

Stephanie JL Gertz, Riverside Publishing, USA

Sally Askman, Bill & Melinda Gates Foundation, USA

Abstract

Across the nation, even prior to the passage of the No Child Left Behind Act in 2001, many states had instituted statewide assessment programs. In response to these initiatives, school systems were interested in how to better prepare their students and teachers for the statewide assessment. The Bill and Melinda Gates Foundation, founded in January 2000, was, and is, committed to exploring the ways in which the improved technology in the 21ˢᵗ century can be utilized to improve educational processes and programs. Based in Seattle, the foundation was interested in working closely within its home state.   So the Washington State Education Department, the Office of the Superintendent of Public Instruction (OSPI), and the foundation worked together on funding and managing an online formative assessment system. From 2000 to 2002, a classroom online assessment system was piloted in several districts in the state of Washington. The goals were threefold:

1. *To determine the effectiveness of classroom online assessment*
2. *To give teachers a tool to help them assess student competency during the course of the year toward meeting or exceeding state-required standards*
3. *To increase teacher knowledge of the state standards*

Background

In 1997, the state of Washington introduced its new standards-based statewide assessment program, the Washington Assessment of Student Learning (WASL). The state assessment program initially assessed reading, writing, and mathematics in Grades 4, 7, and 10. Although the high stakes accountability era ushered in by No Child Left Behind was still to come, a high stakes aura was already attached to the state tests. The Grade 10 tests were eventually going to be required for graduation. The score releases each fall for all grades were big media events, and the teachers and students were feeling the pressure. In 2000, a parent of a fourth grade student said, " . . . despite our efforts to convince her this isn't a life or death thing, she's starting to get worried about passing the official test" (Hunt, 2000).

At the 2000 Annual Office of Superintendent of Public Instruction Conference, WASL was one of the main topics. "People [teachers and administrators] are afraid that they won't know enough to help their kids or that someone will take their job away," said State Schools Superintendent Terry Bergeson. "They hear all this stuff about accountability and that someone will come if their kids don't have high enough scores next year and fire them" (Harris, 2000).

Although no one was being fired over the test results, it was true that those teachers might not receive the test results from the WASL in time to help their students. Paper and pencil tests, the predominant assessment method throughout the state and the nation, did not provide quick turnaround time and feedback. It seemed that something else was needed to help prepare students and teachers and to reduce the anxiety that was only growing (Bennett, 2001).

The corporate sector had been turning to technology to process information more efficiently for years, and there was a growing realization that technology could also be applied in the classroom to help teachers process information about their students more effectively (Palaich, Good, Stout, & Vickery, 2000). Specifically, online assessment models offer a number of advantages over paper and pencil classroom testing, including the following:

- **Faster score report turnaround:** For multiple choice questions, true/false, or other dichotomous questions that can be scored by a machine, the results can be reported immediately. For tests requiring hand scoring, the reports are generated as soon as the manual scores are input.

- **Student familiarity:** More and more students are using computers as a part of their everyday lives, so taking a test online is becoming a more familiar experience, and less anxiety producing, than taking a paper and pencil test.

- **Integration of curriculum and assessment:** The results generated from an online assessment can be easily tied to state standards and curriculum, allowing teachers to modify their instruction in response to student scores (Thomas, 2003).

In addition, previous research has shown evidence that students' ability to achieve higher proficiency on the state's academic standards is directly related to teachers' ability to accurately diagnose their students' strengths and weaknesses and therefore teachers' ability to accurately target instruction and remediation (Frederiksen & White, 1997; Stiggins, 1997). Therefore, a diagnostic assessment prior to WASL that helped teachers pinpoint students' strengths and weaknesses could prove to be effective in raising student proficiency levels.

Into this environment the OSPI, in cooperation with the Bill and Melinda Gates Foundation, released a request for information (RFI) for formative assessments to help the students prepare for the tests-the online assessment was to "provide teachers with a diagnostic and assessment tool they can use to make adjustments in instructional strategies to align more closely with EALRs [Essential Academic Learning Requirements], benchmarks, and frameworks" (State of Washington Office of Public Instruction & the Bill and Melinda Gates Foundation, 2000). These tests were to be standards-based tests that would be delivered via the Web. The full program would entail tests in reading, writing, and mathematics three times a year in Grades 3, 5, 6, 8, and 9, and two times a year in Grades 4 and 7. These online assessments were supposed to help the teachers diagnose and identify weaknesses and, hopefully, allow them a chance to address these weaknesses before the students took the WASL.

Additionally, it was hoped that the program would provide professional development to the teachers. The pilot program was designed to give maximal input from the teachers throughout the development process so that they could gain greater insight into the test development process and learn more about WASL. Moreover, the open-ended items were scored by the classroom teachers by using the same scoring rubrics as were used on the WASL, thereby providing the teachers with a greater understanding of what was required on the state test. These tests would thus help prepare both students and teachers for the high stakes state test. A number of districts throughout the state of Washington had previously been selected as *Gates grantee* districts, which were districts selected to receive grants to improve teaching and learning in Washington State schools. These districts would be the ones invited to participate.

Design of the Tool

According to the original request from OSPI and the Gates Foundation, the program requirements (State of Washington Office of Public Instruction & the Bill and Melinda Gates Foundation, 2000) were:

a.   Web-based tests that provide for online testing, assessment, and reporting

b.   Subject-based tests for math, reading, and writing, initially for Grades 3, 6, and 9

c.   Preferably grade level (pretest, midterm, and posttest)

d.   Preferred format is a combination of multiple choice, short, and long answers

e.   Web-based reporting capabilities for parents, staff, and students as appropriate

f.   Teacher/administrative training component

The final product consisted of a series of mini-WASL tests (not actual subsets of WASL tests, but tests built using WASL-like items) across Grades 3 through 9. Each test was approximately 25-50% of the length of the WASL so that the online assessment could be taken within one class period. At each grade a series of tests in the three subject areas was developed. The administration schedule is detailed in Table 1.

The reading and mathematics tests for all grades had a range of 14 to 17 total items, with two to three short answer items per test; the rest were multiple choice. The writing test consisted of one writing prompt at each grade. The teacher manually scored all open-ended items, including the writing test.

After inputting the scores for the constructed response items, 13 different score reports were available to the teacher.

Table 1. Subject area administration of the online assessment

	Fall 2000	Winter 2001	Spring 2001	Fall 2001	Winter 2002	Spring 2002*
Reading	Grades 3, 6, 9	Grades 3, 6, 9	Grades 3, 6, 9	Grades 3-9	Grades 3-9	Grades 3, 5, 6, 8, 9
Writing	Grades 3, 6, 9	Grades 3, 6, 9	Grades 3, 6, 9	Grades 3-9	Grades 3-9	Grades 3, 5, 6, 8, 9
Mathematics	Grades 3, 6, 9	Grades 3, 6, 9	Grades 3, 6, 9	Grades 3-9	Grades 3-9	Grades 3, 5, 6, 8, 9

These reports (Assess2Learn Administrator Reference Guide 4.8.0, 2003) were:

- **Class List Report:** This report lists the number of questions each student got correct out of the total number of questions on the test. It also lists the overall score (percent) for the test.

- **Class Roster Report by Test:** This report lists the name, login ID, and password for each student in a class by test.

- **History Report by Student:** This report lists each instance of every test taken by that student, including the date and test score for each test. Gain or loss percentages are shown between the first test instance and consecutive test instances. The grade percentage hyperlink displays the Skill Proficiency Report (SPR) for that test, which shows the score for each strand, standard, and benchmark tested.

- **Item Analysis Report:** This report lists questions along with their corresponding objectives and gives an account of the number of students who answered incorrectly, correctly, or not at all.

- **Paper Test Information Log:** This report allows the printing of student ID information for bubble sheet tests.

- **Playback Report:** This report shows the teacher exactly what the student sees upon completing a test. It looks just like the student's results page.

- **Proctor Information Log:** This report lists the proctor ID(s) and password(s) for tests set for the proctor login(s).

- **Skill Gap Analysis:** This report provides information on a student's proficiency levels based on specific objectives.

- **Skill Proficiency Report by Class:** This report includes the same information as the *Skill Proficiency Report by Student* and includes the combined scores showing a class average for each category and section.

- **Skill Proficiency Report by Student:** This report provides detailed information on individual student performance for each strand tested, section averages for each standard and benchmark, averages for each strand, and an average for the test as a whole. Correlations to state standards of learning are listed within each section to show skill proficiency as it relates to state expectations. This report is used to determine a student's strengths and weaknesses.

- **Teacher Information Log for School:** This report lists the name, login ID, and password for each teacher and administrator.

- **Test History by Class:** This report provides the overall test score for each student in the class. If the student has taken the test more than once, the report will display the maximum score, the minimum score, and the average on that test assignment. It lists all students in the class for that particular test assignment.

- **User Roster Report:** This report is an administrator-level report that provides a list of administrator, teacher, and/or student IDs and passwords. You can select which IDs you want to include in the report (administrator, teacher, and/or student).

Table 2. Demographics of users in Washington schools (Brown, 2003)

	# of Gates grantee schools using or piloting Assess2Learn by June 2003	# of students in Gates grantee schools using Assess2Learn by June 2003	Total # of Assess2Learn test instances in Gates grantee schools by June 2003
March	153	12,351	30,189
April	164	13,109	31,519
May	169	14,146	35,236
June	172	14,978	38,998

At the administrator level, typically district office personnel, the results for the districts were available in "drill-down" reports so that the administrator could see the results for the district and could then drill down all the way to the individual student results.

The numbers of students, tests taken, and schools using the program gradually increased over the course of the year (see Table 2), so that by June 2003, when the system was fully operational, 172 schools were using the online formative assessment.

Methodology

At each step of the development of the online assessment, every attempt was made to replicate the process used in creating the WASL. Using the state standards, the EALRs, the same development team that worked on the item development for the WASL developed the initial pool of items for the online assessment. After the initial pool of items was developed, the teachers involved in the pilot served as the content review committee. Their directions were to review the items for

* Alignment to the EALRs
* Content accuracy
* Grade appropriateness

The training they received was based on the training given to the content review committee members for the WASL. The content committees approved all items used in the online assessment. Regular meetings and training sessions were scheduled throughout the pilot program.

Grades 3, 6, and 9 Trainings

In October 2000, teachers from Gates grantee districts were nominated by the district to participate. Later that month, these teachers met with the test publisher, OSPI, and Gates personnel to review the item pool. The publisher made revisions as necessary and entered the items into the online system. In November, the same teachers were invited to the foundation offices to review the items to see how they would appear online. After this meeting the tests were finalized on the system. At the end of November, teachers came back to the foundation for training in scoring the open-ended items and for training on the technology. The scoring training used was a modified version of the same training used for the scorers for the WASL. The teachers started to pilot the system in December. There was a feedback videoconference in mid-December. In February there was an additional item review session for the winter and spring test forms, and in March there was a final scoring training session and additional technology training for the teachers who were implementing the program. Based on the feedback from the November online item review, it was deemed unnecessary to have the online item review meeting. By spring 2001, the teachers were ready to implement the full series of tests (all three forms) for Grades 3, 6, and 9.

Grades 4, 5, 7, and 8 Trainings

A similar pattern was followed for the teachers in Grades 4, 5, 7, and 8. Teachers were nominated in January 2001. The first item review session was held at the end of May. The hand scoring and technology training was delayed until the beginning of the next school year so it would be fresh in the teachers' minds when they were ready to first use the tool in fall 2001. Therefore, the scoring and technology training was held in September 2001. The second item review meeting was held in November, and the second training on hand scoring and the technology was conducted in December. By mid-month, all tests were loaded into the system, ready for use in Grades 3 through 9.

Conclusion

The high level of teacher involvement in the development of the project was very successful.

> *Teachers were enthusiastic about the training they received in preparation for administering the online assessments. Being able to participate in the development of test items, including how to score various types of questions, was invaluable. It helped them understand assessment in a larger context and gave greater meaning to the WASL. In addition, teachers believed their participation in the online training would be valuable in providing similar training to their building colleagues in those cases where the program was to be expanded. Teachers need not be technology experts to use the system, they said, and could be brought on board with relative ease.* (Brown, 2002)

Teachers were also very excited about the opportunity to receive scoring feedback so quickly. Because the teachers had to enter the constructed response scores, the turnaround time was not immediate, as it would have been with an all multiple choice test, but the teachers did not have to wait weeks for results, as they did for the state test.

Information gathered from the assessments was used to identify learning strengths and weaknesses and allowed teachers to modify and adjust instruction to meet specific individual and classroom needs. In addition, immediate feedback proved helpful in the analysis of errors and academic goal-setting. (Brown, 2002, p. iv)

In addition, the score reports had high approval. "Both the format and content of the reports were useful to teachers, parents, and students. Particularly informative were those that allowed analysis of errors and those that helped teachers identify deficiencies around specific EALRs" (Brown, 2002, p. 14).

But the hand-scoring activity generated more negative responses. Although scoring the tests taught the WASL rubric to the teachers, it was quite time consuming, and the teachers did not believe that keyboarding their written responses showed students' writing at its best. Because the WASL itself is not given online, it was not seen as helpful practice.

We do not believe the writing portion of the test is practical for third graders. Their keyboarding skills are not yet at a level that allows them to quickly type or easily edit their stories. Writing and editing a story on the computer is an entirely different process than the one students experience taking the WASL.

I had the most problems trying to get in and score the open-ended items. The time factor to score was too high . . . even though it is good for students to experience the need to write out their answers, I think that this may not be the format to do it in. Eliminating the open-ended questions might make the test quicker for the students to take and easier for the teachers to manage.

Writing is easier to do with pencil and paper. I like the prompts and use them for the kids, but I have them do it with paper and pencil. I am concerned about the amount of time that it will take to administer this assessment three times during the year. As a writing teacher (primarily), I found last year that the online assessment didn't give me any additional feedback on a student's writing skills and progress than what I was already receiving by assessing their in-classroom work. Since the writing assessment is just that, writing, it doesn't enhance my knowledge of student performance any more than a nonelectronic assessment, but takes up a significant amount of time that could be spent on instruction and coaching . . . if the purpose of this assessment is formative and is intended to inform classroom instruction, then I am not sure it is the most efficient means to do so. (Brown, 2002, p. 17)

There were also problems in getting the technology component to work properly. One teacher reported, "… we tried a few things and never got it to work. Maybe it runs now, but I haven't been back and I'm not planning on going back right now (Brown, 2003, p. 24).

> *[School] personnel cooperated with Assess2Learn; however, operational issues emerged throughout the year, and the June progress report stated that teachers were "discouraged by the difficulties." While teachers viewed the assessment as a potentially useful tool, the judgment was that "there is still more frustration than usefulness being experienced."* (Brown, 2003)

In addition to learning how to use the specific assessments, several felt the training had improved their understanding of the WASL and the way it is scored. Because of this training they felt better equipped to prepare their students for the WASL experience, whether or not they continued using the online assessments. One teacher reflected that the training was "incredible. I have a much better idea of how to prepare kids for the WASL. . . . It is good to involve them in the grading process" (Brown, 2002, p. 18).

Recommendations

The two most significant complaints were with the writing portion and the technology difficulties.

Because WASL writing is not administered online, it may not be helpful to have a formative assessment given online in this area. Until or unless the state assessment is online, it is recommended that the teachers be provided with prompts and rubrics so that they can administer formative writing assessments offline in the classroom.

The technology issues were exacerbated by the lack of participation by the technology personnel at each school site. Our original plan was to work directly with the classroom teachers. On one hand, this plan was an excellent idea. The state testing program was definitely a "top-down" situation, and it was hypothesized that working directly with the teachers, involving them each step of the way, would be an excellent tactic to get their buy-in and support. In many ways this approach was successful. Many of the teachers who had been involved felt positively about the project. However, the information technology personnel from each school should have been included from the beginning. There were issues related to each school's hardware/software configuration and firewall. Had technology staff been involved from the outset, the configuration issues could have been addressed ahead of time, rather than reactively when the teachers were trying to administer the test.

Evaluating the program by looking at its original goals, it was a qualified success because it:

1. Determined the effectiveness of classroom online assessment
2. Gave teachers a tool to help them assess student competency during the course of the year towards meeting or exceeding state-required standards
3. Increased teacher knowledge of the state standards

Initial technology barriers slowed the adoption of the online assessment. However, in the short time that has passed since the pilot project, teacher familiarity and comfort level with technology has dramatically increased (Murray, 2004). If technology problems were addressed proactively, then participation likely would have been much higher. Even with a glitch free testing and delivery system, the biggest challenge facing teachers today is knowing how to analyze the real-time data presented through online assessments and take action to intervene or supplement a child's or classroom's instructional plan.

The teachers who did participate, however, felt better able to prepare their students for WASL. And the teachers did report a greater familiarity with WASL (Brown, 2002, 2003).

> *In the same way that the Internet is already helping to revolutionize commerce, education, and even social interaction, this technological advance will help revolutionize the business and substance of large scale assessment. . . . However, as the history of innovation suggests, this reinvention won't come immediately, without significant investment, or without setback. With few exceptions, we are not yet ready for large scale assessment via the Internet (at least in our schools). However, as suggested above, this story is not so much about today. It really is about tomorrow.* (Bennett, 2001, p. 16)

It seems clear that online assessment has a role to play in formative assessments in the classroom. But in order for a program to be successful, the support at the school level, from teachers and technology staff, must be in place.

References

Assess2Learn Administrator Reference Guide 4.8.0. (2003). Itasca, IL: Riverside.

Bennett, R. E. (2001). How the Internet will help large-scale assessment reinvent itself [Electronic version]. *Education Policy Analysis Archives, 9*(5), 1-29.

Brown, C. J. (2002). Online classroom assessment project evaluation report #1. Paper prepared for the *Bill and Melinda Gates Foundation*, Seattle, WA.

Brown, C. J. (2003). Assess2Learn: An online classroom assessment project evaluation report #2. Paper prepared for the *Bill and Melinda Gates Foundation*, Seattle, WA.

Frederiksen, J. R., & White, B. J. (1997, April). Reflective assessment of students' research within an inquiry-based middle school science curriculum. Paper presented at the meeting of the *American Educational Research Association*, Chicago, IL.

Harris, W. (2000, January 19). Teachers focus on new graduation rule. *The Spokesman-Review, 101.* Article 0001190005. Retrieved June 29, 2004, from *www.spokesmanreview.com*

Hunt, J. (2000, April 12). Anxiety about test boosts sales of WASL workbook. *Seattle Post-Intelligencer, 137.* Article 04122000. Retrieved June 29, 2004, from *seattlepi.nwsource.com*

Murray, C. (2004, June 24). Teachers: Limited time, access cut school tech use. *eSchool News.*

Palaich, R. M., Good, D. G., Stout, C., & Vickery, E. (2000). *Smart desktops for teachers.* Denver, CO: Education Commission of the States.

State of Washington Office of Public Instruction & the Bill and Melinda Gates Foundation. (2000). *Request for Information No. DE-21.* Olympia, WA: Author.

Stiggins, R. (1997). *Student-centered classroom assessment* (2nd ed.). Upper Saddle River, NJ: Merrill.

Thomas, W. R. (2003). *Status of online testing in SREB states.* Atlanta, GA: Southern Regional Education Board.

Chapter XIII

Online Assessment in the K-12 Classroom:
A Formative Assessment Model for Improving Student Performance on Standardized Tests

Jacqueline B. Shrago, ThinkLink Learning, USA

Michael K. Smith, ThinkLink Learning, USA

Abstract

ThinkLink Learning has developed an online formative assessment model that helps teachers and students prepare throughout the year for end-of-year state and national summative assessments. Four aspects of the ThinkLink system are discussed in this chapter: (a) how online formative assessment can help improve student learning on standards tested at a state or national level, (b) the advantages and disadvantages of using online assessment, (c) three case studies that demonstrate the predictive validity of this system and its use in improving student learning, and (d) future trends in the use of online assessment and directions in measuring student learning on standardized tests. In general, ThinkLink Learning has pioneered online solutions to large-scale assessment problems.

Introduction

One of the problems that face the teacher in the K-12 classroom is the disjuncture between classroom instruction and assessment during the regular school year and the standardized state or national assessments that are often given near the end of a school year. These end-of-year mandated tests, often called *summative assessments,* measure a student's progress toward state or national standards. Summative assessments have been used for many high-stakes purposes: for student promotion to the next grade, as a graduation requirement, as a measure of teacher effectiveness, and as a measure of school or district progress toward state or national goals.

Given the importance attached to these summative assessments, numerous problems exist with integrating the standards measured on these tests and the goals of classroom instruction. For instance, the objectives on these standardized tests are sometimes not sufficiently aligned with curriculum standards, and practice materials for these tests are inadequate or unavailable. Furthermore, teachers and students are almost never provided with the questions from these standardized assessments, making review of specific weaknesses almost impossible (see Bracey, 2002; Kohn, 2000; Popham, 1999; Sacks, 1999). Thus, a classroom teacher is faced with the dilemma of how to prepare students for standardized tests that are often used for accountability, with no practical way of measuring throughout the year a student's progress toward the objectives tested on these exams.

Preparation for classroom assessments is not so problematic. Teachers can more easily ensure that tests cover material that is taught. Teachers can even use assessments as a teaching tool. These formative assessments can improve student learning on a variety of topics. Procedures of formative assessment make it easier to align instructional objectives directly with assessment. Formative assessments can be effectively integrated into classroom learning when the following characteristics are met: test objectives are clearly identified for teachers and students, a mechanism of assessment or self-assessment exists within the classroom environment, and data from these assessments can be directly connected to subsequent assessments. Formative assessments can be used continuously within the classroom setting to provide feedback to both students and teachers on progress toward identifiable goals. The question then becomes the following: How can formative assessments be used to improve student performance on summative assessments?

ThinkLink Learning has developed an online formative assessment model that helps teachers and students prepare throughout the year for end-of-year state and national summative assessments. This assessment model has been in practice since 2001 in these states: Tennessee, Kentucky, Alabama, Mississippi, West Virginia, and New Mexico. During the school year 2003-2004, over 200,000 students used the ThinkLink system. Thus, ThinkLink Learning has pioneered online solutions to large-scale assessment problems (Tindal & Haladyna, 2002). Four aspects of the ThinkLink system are discussed in this chapter: (a) how online formative assessment can help improve student learning on standards tested at a state or national level, (b) the advantages and disadvantages of using online assessment, (c) three case studies that demonstrate the predictive validity of this system and its use in improving student learning, and (d) future trends in the use of online assessment and directions in measuring student learning on standardized tests. We first review the research evidence for formative assessment, and then we address these four aspects of the ThinkLink model.

The Value of Formative Assessment

The use of tests to improve student learning and evaluate instruction has a long history. Even the computer presentation of test items has coexisted with the use of computers in the classroom. The fact that a test or assessment can be directly used as a vehicle for improving student learning has a shorter research past. Foos and Fisher (1988) showed that students who completed an initial test after studying a unit on American Civil War history did better on the final test than students who did not complete the initial test. Fuchs and Fuchs (1986) showed that systematic formative evaluation improved the achievements of special education students.

More recently, Black, Harrison, Lee, Marshall, and Wiliam (2003), in reviewing the research evidence for formative assessment, suggested that significant learning gains might be achieved by using this method. These authors defined formative assessment as follows:

> *An assessment activity can help learning if it provides information to be used as feedback by teachers, and by their students in assessing themselves and each other, to modify the teaching and learning activities in which they are engaged. Such assessment becomes formative assessment when the evidence is used to adapt the teaching work to meet learning needs.* (p. 2)

For formative assessment to work effectively, teachers and students must understand its value and accept its use in the classroom. Two actions must be clearly defined:

> *The first is the perception by the learner of a gap between a desired goal and his or her present state (of knowledge and/or understanding and/or skill). The second is the action taken by the learner to close that gap to attain the desired goal.* (Black et al., 2003, p. 14)

The recognition of the learning gap and the actions taken to close this gap define the concept of feedback, the key components of which are as follows (Sadler, 1989): (a) data on the actual level of some measurable attribute, (b) data on the desirable level of that attribute, (c) a mechanism for comparing the two levels and assessing the gap between them, and (d) a mechanism by which the information can be used to alter the gap.

Much of this work thus far has been strictly focused on formative assessment used in the classroom to improve student learning on instructional objectives. In fact, the use of formative assessment has not been seen as useful or appropriate for improving student performance on summative assessments, such as standardized multiple choice tests. Sadler (1989) suggested that his theory of formative assessment has less relevance for outcomes in which student responses are judged as correct or incorrect. Black et al. (2003) feel that their techniques are less concerned with assessments that hold schools accountable. Thus, the use of formative assessment, especially in an online environment, has yet to be demonstrated as effective in improving student learning on summative assessments.

How Online Formative Assessment Improves Performance on Summative Assessments

For formative assessment to work, data on student achievement must be continuously available, easy to understand, and capable of being integrated into instructional practices. The ThinkLink model, called the Predictive Assessment Series (PAS), develops high quality simulations of summative assessments that can then be easily used for classroom formative assessments. More specifically, ThinkLink has developed a series of equivalent assessments designed to measure the knowledge and skills tested by nationally normed tests in many states, including Terra Nova and Stanford-10, and state-developed criterion-referenced assessments, such as Kentucky's Core Content Test and Tennessee's Criterion Referenced Test. These assessments have reliabilities and content validities equivalent to those associated with standardized summative assessments.

Consider the Terra Nova as an example of a nationally normed assessment used by many states as part of their school accountability programs. This test provides domain scores in reading, language arts, and mathematics, as well as other subject scores. The domain of mathematics also provides scores and mastery levels for eight objectives across Grades 2 through 8: number and number relations; computation and numerical estimation; operation concepts; measurement; geometry and spatial sense; data analysis, statistics, and probability; patterns, functions, and algebra; and problem solving and reasoning. Students are often expected to display mastery of each objective. When the Terra Nova is used as a summative measure, students are usually tested near the end of a grade level, and feedback about performance is not provided until after a student has already completed that grade. Thus, this test's ability to be used for formative assessment is nonexistent. Feedback on performance during the school year is also dramatically limited. Teachers are seldom provided sufficient practice materials, and objectives are not clearly defined. Thus, teachers do not know if a student is nearing the mastery level. This difficulty raises an obvious question: How is a teacher to improve a student's performance on the objective "Geometry and Spatial Sense" without a mechanism for measuring a student's progress on this objective and a specific way for data on student achievement to be used for formative assessment?

The ThinkLink model has tried to remedy some of these problems by developing a system based on formative assessment principles that provides measures of student progress in the midst of instruction. Assessments are provided via the Internet and are automatically scored. Thus, teachers are able to adjust instruction based upon measurable data rather than intuition. Three assessments enable teachers to provide feedback to students at regular intervals. The characteristics of these feedback points are as follows.

Feedback Point 1: Beginning of School Year (Fall)

The first assessment measures how well students have retained knowledge completed at the end of the previous grade. For example, a beginning fourth grade student is measured on end-of-year third grade knowledge. Using this data, teachers can determine how much of the previous grade level's skills have been retained by current students and where to start instruction.

Feedback Point 2: Middle of School Year (Winter)

The second assessment is typically administered at midyear (usually December). This assessment provides an accurate measurement of how well students have mastered grade-level objectives at this point in the curriculum. Using this data, teachers can implement strategies to bolster skills that have not yet been mastered. The data help teachers focus on the need to reinforce skills taught at an earlier point in the year.

Feedback Point 3: Prior to Standardized Test Dates (Spring)

The third assessment is administered approximately six weeks before the official state mandated test. This assessment provides an accurate measurement of how well students have mastered objectives that will be tested in an individual state's testing program. Furthermore, this assessment allows teachers time to improve student skills, particularly in partial mastery areas. With focused review and reteaching, this time represents an opportunity for improvement.

Teachers revise instruction after each of these feedback points, using the data to guide their selection of lessons, units, and teaching approaches. Unlike standardized assessments, ThinkLink is able to release all its test items after each administration. Thus, with a predictive measure and a full view of the items and the individual performance results on each item, ThinkLink has overcome the inability to use standardized assessments for instruction due to security issues. This item detail also identifies more specifically the subskills that are not being mastered and the difficulty level. With this information, an online tool that displays relevant test objectives and the associated subskills becomes a "just in time" resource for teachers. The efficiency of such a display offers a more complete grasp of the objective that is being tested and highlights subskills for revised instruction. Thus, ThinkLink has overcome another problem, allowing more effective use of teachers' time with information immediately accessible.

Students, in addition, can be assigned formative assessment items so they have the opportunity to learn the skill and try again. They can receive a "hint" or mini-lesson in the midst of assessment. Furthermore, ThinkLink has developed procedures to supply the feedback that Sadler (1989) found so crucial to a formative assessment system: Data are provided on how close a student is to mastery, information is detailed on how to reach mastery, the ThinkLink assessments provide a mechanism for comparing actual student performance with the desired level, and formative assessment procedures are supplied to help teachers and students close the gap between the actual and desired levels of performance.

Advantages and Disadvantages of Using Online Assessment

By developing data that can be directly incorporated into teaching and learning plans of classes and individual students, ThinkLink has increased the usefulness of testing from a high-stakes measure that demands high security to one that focuses on instructional support. This change reduces the concern for security and permits schools to use assessments effectively to promote classroom learning.

Online assessments can draw on the strengths of current computer technologies to deliver items that use color, graphics, and testing aids, such as calculators or large print, to facilitate testing. The availability of data on student achievement, however, is the greatest advantage to online assessment. This access to data can facilitate formative assessment in numerous ways:

- immediate feedback to students
- immediate data for teachers to use to revise instruction
- data available for parent conferences during the school year
- data available for individual education plans that focus on academic achievement and not exclusively behavior
- shared data, by teacher teams in middle school, allows integration of curriculum and a focus on student achievement
- data available for teachers to group students in various ways, depending on the skill
- assessment data that can be immediately made available when new students enter at times other than the beginning of the school year

- progress points that can be identified for individual students who follow something other than a regular school calendar, such as those in juvenile justice centers, those who are homebound, schools with year-round calendars, and special tutoring or other intervention programs

- students who are absent can be tested easily upon return without delaying the processing of all other students

- staggered assessment times so that online testing does not require everyone in the school to take the test at the same time

An online formative assessment system has some obvious disadvantages. It has technical limitations. For instance, schools must have either a physical or wireless lab of computers so that students in a class can take tests simultaneously, they must organize a testing schedule so that the labs can be available to reach all students, and they must have Internet access equivalent to half to a full T-1 to support testing. This system has technical design limitations as well. For instance, because bandwidth availability is always an issue, presentation of items must be small and modest to preclude students' having to wait for items. Furthermore, graphics can be used but must be simple enough to be displayed on a wide range of computers purchased over many years. Finally, a recognition that the network or the Internet may go down at any moment necessitates adjustments to make it easy to complete testing for any student.

Of more concern, however, is the issue of professional development. For any assessment system to work, teachers must be involved in its implementation and trained on how to use the data and reports provided. The ThinkLink model has facilitated professional development by making the measurement of student achievement and the reports easy to understand. However, these features are still not enough; adequate professional development is needed before any assessment system can significantly improve student performance.

ThinkLink routinely offers professional development workshops that encourage a more complete understanding of standardized testing results. Using the ThinkLink tool and actual student results encourages a collegial dialogue. This dialogue helps teachers focus on data and identify strategies that refocus instruction and improve student performance.

ThinkLink's tool also has become a part of the activities of other organizations. As part of a professional development program, the Appalachia Eisenhower Regional Consortium for Mathematics and Science Education at the Appalachian Educational Laboratory (AEL) provided the ThinkLink tool to several school sites during the 2003-2004 school year and continued to do so in 2004-2005. Four of the current six sites have received training and support from AEL to assist them in enhancing their data-driven decision-making capabilities, using the ThinkLink tool. Each of these four sites is using the data in grade-level cross-curricular teams. AEL's overall approach to professional development has been to facilitate a plan for sustained professional development training and technical assistance to meet each school's specific situation. AEL's work in these schools is designed to build collaborative communities with professional dialogue around student outcomes while encouraging teacher sharing and reflection in reviewing their instructional practices.

Predictive Validity and Improvement of Student Learning: Three Case Studies from K-12

For an online formative assessment system to work, it must be capable of predicting performance on summative measures and improving student performance on these same assessments. The predictive validity of a measurement system demonstrates that these formative assessments of student achievement are actually comparable to levels of student achievement on the summative standardized measures. Improvement of student performance is one of the main goals of this system; it must also be demonstrated that the use of this online system improves scores to a significant degree. The use of this system to help with summative measures assumes that the knowledge and skills measured by standardized tests are important reflections of student learning. The criticism that standardized tests do not adequately measure the most important aspects of student learning are addressed later in this chapter. Three case studies are presented: one that addresses the predictive validity of this system and two that outline its use in improving student learning.

Case Study 1: Predicting Student Proficiency for No Child Left Behind

The No Child Left Behind (NCLB) federal education act requires schools to demonstrate that all students are meeting rigorously defined proficiency levels in math, reading, and language arts in order to receive federal funding. NCLB mandated that schools meet these proficiency benchmarks in nine subgroups, including five race and ethnic groups, students with disabilities, students with limited English proficiency, and economically disadvantaged students. Furthermore, schools must show yearly progress toward the meeting of proficiency levels by all students. Many states are using nationally normed assessments or state-developed criterion-referenced tests to measure student progress in math, reading, and language arts. As such, NCLB has sparked an increased emphasis on summative measures.

If a school demonstrates student proficiency in all nine subgroups, the school passes the federal requirements for that year. If all schools in a school system pass, then the system as a whole passes. If any subgroup fails or any school fails, then the school or system as a whole does not meet the yearly federal requirements.

Is the ThinkLink online formative assessment system valid for predicting performance on these NCLB requirements? For the 2002-2003 academic year, 223 elementary schools in Tennessee and Kentucky used the PAS system. Scores on these assessments from Grade 3 were used to predict fulfillment of NCLB requirements for elementary schools. A discriminant analysis was conducted trying to use the PAS measures of math, reading, and language arts to classify schools and systems as to whether or not they were meeting federal requirements. The results of this analysis indicated that the PAS system correctly classified 80% of schools and 88% of systems (chi-square values were significant at the 0.01 level in both analyses). In other words, ThinkLink's online formative assessment system can predict proficiency levels on summative measures used to satisfy NCLB requirements. This information, provided during the school year, can help schools avoid NCLB sanctions.

Case Study 2: Improving Student Performance on Tennessee's Comprehensive Assessment Program

In an effort to demonstrate improvement across a much broader use of ThinkLink's tool, schools in Tennessee, representing 35,300 students across Grades 3 through 8, were examined for the 2001-2002 school year. To evaluate wide-scale effectiveness, test scores from the Tennessee Comprehensive Assessment Program (TCAP) were collected for each school grade level for the 2000-2001 and 2001-2002 school years. Median national percentiles in reading, language, and mathematics for each school were converted to Normal Curve Equivalent (NCE) scores. A gain score was calculated for each school. An NCE gain of 1.5 points or more is considered significant. This gain represents a minimum improvement of at least three national percentile points over the previous year.

The percent of schools with significant gains in reading, language, or mathematics was tabulated for Grades 3 through 5 combined and for Grades 6 through 8 combined. Furthermore, gains were tabulated for four categories of schools with varying percentages of free or reduced lunch students: (a) schools with fewer than 50% free or reduced lunch students, (b) schools with 50 to 59%, (c) schools with 60 to 74%, and (d) schools with 75% or more free or reduced lunch students.

Figure 1 presents the results for Grades 3 through 5. 58% of these schools made significant gains in reading, language, or mathematics. Demonstrating gains in high-poverty schools is often more difficult; however, the ThinkLink system showed especially large gains, with 66% of *high-poverty schools* (comprising 75% or more free or reduced lunch students) making significant gains. Figure 2 presents the results for Grades 6 through 8. Over 40% of these schools made significant gains in reading, language, or mathematics, while the high-poverty schools posted the most impressive results in language (59%), mathematics (46%), and, to some extent, reading (29%), with an overall 42% making significant gains.

The ThinkLink PAS system helped over 64% of the high-poverty schools improve, while 61% of schools overall improved. These gains suggest the usefulness of this type of online assessment in schools that typically have the most difficulty improving student learning and standardized test scores.

Figure 1. Percent of ThinkLink schools in Grades 3, 4, and 5 with significant gains on the Terra Nova

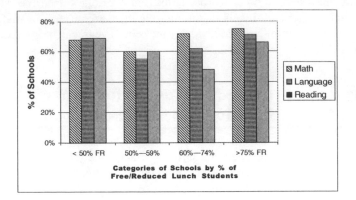

Figure 2. Percent of ThinkLink schools in Grades 6, 7, and 8 with significant gains on the Terra Nova

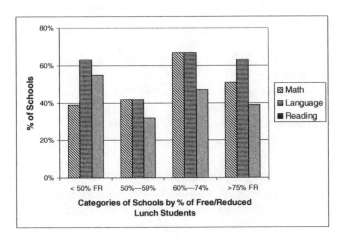

Case Study 3: Alabama Priority Schools and Kentucky Example

Examining the impact on schools where the most progress is needed further supports the experience of improved performance. The state of Alabama uses an accountability system to measure school performance. Part of this system is an index of student learning in math, reading, and language arts using the Stanford-10 assessment series. Schools are classified into three levels: clear, watch, and priority. Priority-level schools must improve performance to avoid state-mandated sanctions.

During the 2003-2004 academic year, several priority schools in Alabama used the PAS system. Improvement in student performance was measured by comparing student scores on the winter and spring administrations. Scores were grouped by grade level within a school. For example, all students in third grade were averaged. Figure 3 presents the percent of grades that demonstrated various levels of NCE gains.

Gains of one NCE or more can help schools improve their status on the state account-ability system. In addition, a positive outcome in one year reinforces that these lowest performing schools can begin to meet NCLB requirements and encourages teachers and school administrators not to give up but rather to try harder the following year.

Figure 4 presents similar information for a priority Kentucky school. It also presents gain information in a format useful to teachers. Gain of 100% shows one full year's gain, and more than 100% shows teachers that students are actually overcoming deficiencies in specific learning objectives. In particular, when teachers start to change their instruction and can see these kinds of gain differences from one feedback to the next, they are strongly encouraged to use the data to make more modifications.

There are many other examples of the impact on schools when they have access to this kind of ThinkLink information. In one school, teachers focused with considerable effort on improving math skills. The ThinkLink tool produced gains of 15 NCEs, equivalent to making two years' progress in six months. As a result, the school was removed from the list of schools scheduled for sanctions.

Future Trends

Given the increased importance of summative measures to satisfy federal requirements, many states have begun implementing online practice assessment systems. Elaborate

Figure 3. Percent of grades achieving various levels of NCE gains by academic subject

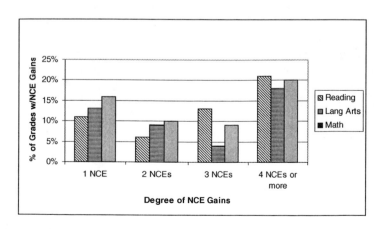

Figure 4. Objectives with more than 1 year's gain by grade level

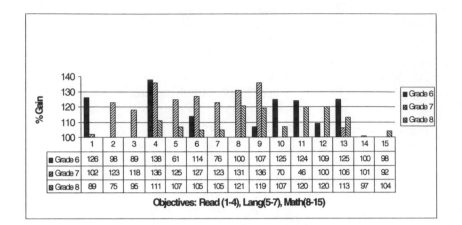

Objectives: Read (1-4), Lang(5-7), Math(8-15)	1	2	3	4	5	6	7	8	9	10	11	12	13	14	15
Grade 6	126	98	89	138	61	114	76	100	107	125	124	109	125	100	98
Grade 7	102	123	118	136	125	127	123	131	136	70	46	100	106	101	92
Grade 8	89	75	95	111	107	105	105	121	119	107	120	120	113	97	104

efforts are underway in such states as Texas, California, Florida, and Georgia. These practice systems supposedly will provide a wide variety of practice items linked to the standards on a state's summative assessment measures. Mechanisms for incorporating these new practice systems are a response to educator concern about high-stakes testing, but they are not generally linked to a research-based approach. In fact, procedures for linking these practice items and tests into a formative assessment system are often not developed. Furthermore, the effectiveness of these practice systems has yet to be demonstrated. The ThinkLink model is one of the first online assessment systems that has demonstrated its effectiveness in improving student performance on summative measures.

The arguments in this chapter have assumed that summative assessments are important measures of student learning. There are obviously many proponents who claim otherwise. Some authors note the discrepancy between these measures and curriculum objectives; thus, placing importance on assessments that do not measure what is taught in the classroom can prove counterproductive to student learning. Other authors argue that an increased emphasis on standardized tests detracts from a teacher's time to teach a wider variety of topics in the classroom; thus, the limits on a standardized test translate into limits on student learning (Jones, Jones, & Hargrove, 2003). Finally, various authors claim that current standardized tests do not measure complex thinking; because of this inadequacy, assessment systems should be redesigned to measure these more important aspects of student learning (Lane, 2004; Pellegrino, Chudowsky, & Glaser, 2001).

The current ThinkLink model is limited to providing formative assessments of skills measured via multiple choice items. The use of constructed-response items in an online environment still faces many obstacles. Assessments that go beyond constructed response, such as more open-ended performance measures, have yet to be adequately developed and tested in an online environment. Thus, the ThinkLink formative assessment system faces no philosophical problem with providing measures of student achievement that go beyond multiple choice items. If these types of items become more prevalent on summative measures, then it is incumbent to change the ThinkLink model to address these more cognitively rich assessments. Until that time, however, the use of multiple choice items in summative assessments must be addressed, and any formative assessment system cannot ignore the fact that student achievement is being measured in this way.

Conclusion

ThinkLink has developed an online formative assessment model that helps students prepare for standardized summative assessments. These online assessments are given at various times during the school year and provide feedback on student performance on objectives measured by standardized tests. This chapter has described how this system is implemented and used by teachers in the classroom. Furthermore, evidence has been presented that describes the validity of this assessment system and how it has helped to significantly improve student achievement.

References

Black, P., Harrison, C., Lee, C., Marshall, B., & Wiliam, D. (2003). *Assessment for learning: Putting it into practice.* Maidenhead, UK: Open University Press.

Bracey, G. W. (2002). *On the death of childhood and the destruction of public schools.* Portsmouth, NH: Heinemann.

Foos, P. W., & Fisher, R. P. (1988). Using tests as learning opportunities. *Journal of Educational Psychology, 80*(2), 179-183.

Fuchs, L., & Fuchs, D. (1986). Effects of systematic formative evaluation: A meta-analysis. *Exceptional Children, 53*(3), 199-208.

Jones, M. G., Jones, B. D., & Hargrove, T. Y. (2003). *The unintended consequences of high-stakes testing.* Oxford, UK: Rowman & Littlefield.

Kohn, A. (2000). *The case against standardized testing.* Portsmouth, NH: Heinemann.

Lane, S. (2004). Validity of high-stakes assessment: Are students engaged in complex thinking? Paper presented at the meeting of the *National Council on Measurement in Education*, San Diego, CA.

Pellegrino, J. W., Chudowsky, N., & Glaser, R. (Eds.). (2001). *Knowing what students know: The science and design of educational assessment.* Washington, DC: National Academy Press.

Popham, W. J. (1999). *The truth about testing.* Alexandria, VA: ASCD.

Sacks, P. (1999). *Standardized minds.* Cambridge, MA: Perseus.

Sadler, D. R. (1989). Formative assessment and the design of instructional systems. *Instructional Science, 18,* 119-144.

Tindal, G., & Haladyna, T. M. (Eds.). (2002). *Large-scale assessment programs for all students: Validity, technical adequacy, and implementation.* Mahwah, NJ: Lawrence Erlbaum.

Section III

Corporate and Government Training

Chapter XIV

Online Assessment Distribution Models for Testing Programs:
Lessons Learned from Operational Experience

Anthony R. Zara, Pearson VUE, USA

Abstract

This chapter discusses three distribution models for online assessments and their characteristics. Since 1999, Pearson VUE has been assisting clients in achieving their goals of providing globally distributed computerized assessments for high-stakes certification and licensure purposes. We have identified three major distribution models for the delivery of online assessments: (a) controlled, (b) global, and (c) ubiquitous. Each of these models is appropriate for some types of online assessments but not others. The characteristics of each model interact with the features of the online assessment program in important ways to either advance or impede the goals of the assessment. Operational program experience shows that these strengths and weaknesses must be analyzed and considered with the assessment goals as part of a good decision-making process.

Introduction

Since 1999, Pearson VUE has been assisting clients in achieving their goals of providing globally distributed computerized assessments for certification and licensure purposes. One thing we have learned is that the grand promise of online assessment can only become reality as the test owner, test developer, and test-delivery organization work through the difficult planning and execution steps of operating on the test owners' ideas. This chapter describes a framework for contemplating the delivery of online assessments and describes some of the lessons learned by high-stakes testing organizations as they brought their assessments from paper and pencil testing to online assessment.

Background

Computers and measurement have been intertwined since the mid-1970s. Early research into concepts related to computerized testing were funded by the U.S. military, which recognized that the power of computing could potentially enhance the conduct of mental measurement activities (e.g., see Weiss, 1978, 1980). The research program of online assessment continued as the science and technology progressed and, in fact, has stretched into the present with growing theoretical and operational knowledge being developed (as evidenced by this volume).

The actual business of computer-based testing (CBT) evolved circa 1978 through a collaboration of the National Association of Security Dealers (NASD) and the Control Data Corporation. Control Data was hired to develop a computer-based testing system for the NASD regulatory examination program. Control Data was a logical partner choice based on its seminal development (with the University of Illinois) of the PLATO™ computer-assisted instructional system. The NASD remained the sole sponsor (test owner) of an operational CBT program until around 1989, when Novell began its testing program for its Certified Network Engineer classification. The Novell program was the pioneer for the information technology industry, which then saw explosive certification program growth during the 1990s as most of the brand name companies developed certification programs with parallel goals (e.g., Microsoft, HP, Cisco, Sun, and Oracle).

Many U.S. regulatory examination programs also began the process of migrating existing paper and pencil examinations to CBT during the early-to mid-1990s. The first two national licensure programs (after the NASD) to move to CBT examination delivery were the American Society of Clinical Pathologists Board of Registry (ASCP:BOR), which launched its CBT transition in 1992, and the National Council of State Boards of Nursing (NCSBN), which transitioned its NCLEX national nurse licensure program to a computerized adaptive testing (CAT) model in 1994. (For a description of the foundational research leading to online assessment for these programs, see Bergstrom, 1992; Lunz & Bergstrom, 1991; Zara, 1994, 1996).

Each of these early CBT programs was faced with important decisions about the appropriate distribution model for implementation of online assessment. Key issues that they considered included distribution reach, testing system security, standardization, and psychometric characteristics.

Over time, professionals in the industry have learned that there are several ways to conceptualize the issues around distributing online assessments. I would like to share with you the lessons we at Pearson VUE have learned in helping our clients to make good decisions. We have identified three major distribution models for delivery of online assessments: (a) controlled, (b) global, and (c) ubiquitous. Each of these distribution models is appropriate for some types of online assessments but not others. The characteristics of each model interact with the features of the online assessment program in important ways that can either advance or impede the goals of the assessment. In this chapter, I discuss each model and its strengths and weaknesses in the context of current ongoing operational CBT programs.

CBT Distribution Models

In today's market, each of the CBT distribution models has several commercial providers. Pearson VUE entered the CBT delivery business in 1999 as a response to a broad lack of competition in the CBT test-delivery market. Before Pearson VUE, the CBT industry was dominated by a single test-delivery provider, and test owners were requesting a more competitive landscape. The company's executive leadership responded to this challenge; the executive team and lead technologists had prior industry experience through their previous work at Control Data Corporation and Drake Training and Technologies, where they developed the first two commercial computer-based testing systems. Through Pearson VUE's entry into the CBT delivery business, it built a third generation testing system to address both the competition needs of the industry and the increasing requirements of test owners for customized and configurable CBT systems. Through our work with many test owners, we have developed commercial distribution channels for each of the online assessment distribution models described in this section. I describe our experience with current clients using each of the distribution channel models.

Controlled Distribution

This model is characterized as providing the most consistent, controlled assessment experience for the examinee and the most limited distribution for the test owner. We define the model as computer-based assessment in a single purpose testing center, with the testing center fully under the control of a test-delivery agent (e.g., as in company owned and operated testing centers). Important features of this model include having the exact same hardware and software at every test center and at every workstation; an identical look and feel of the test centers, including design and ergonomic features; separate testing carrels for examinees; a separate locked file server room; an identical staffing and training model for all test center staff; a dedicated nonpublic Virtual Private Network for data transfer with headquarters; a digital video and audio recording of every test session; layered biometrics including the digital photograph, digital fingerprint, and digital signature of all examinees; and computerized admissions procedures tools customizable by the test owner. This model provides the highest degree of standardization possible for online assessments.

The security and consistent control requirements of our professional licensure test owner clients caused us to develop this distribution channel (named Pearson Professional Centers; PPCs). A new test center technology feature that we implemented, based on our clients' needs to have specialized admissions procedures, was an application, *Admissions Manager™*, which provides the capability to display customized admission steps configurable by the client at the administrator's check-in station. Obviously, different clients would have different rules or procedures regarding examinee identification requirements, admissions documents, and so forth. *Admissions Manager™* displays the unique admissions requirements for each examinee at the time of examinee admission at the check-in station, freeing the test administrator to attend to each candidate according to the test owner's policies without relying on the administrator's memory or causing him or her to check a large procedures manual for each examinee admission. This new technology leads to a large increase in service to examinees and in test center staff compliance with test owners' unique rules.

A number of online assessment owners have chosen the Controlled Distribution model as providing the appropriate level of standardization and control for the assessment and candidate experience. These owners have chosen this model to meet their specific needs in online assessment. Assessments that have high-stakes decisions and consequences and little to no need for global distribution are appropriate candidates for using this distribution model. In this context, *high-stakes* refers to assessments that have important or life-changing consequences based on the inferences made from the assessment's results (e.g., the right to practice a profession granted by a regulatory authority, admissions decisions, mental health diagnoses, or employment decisions). The NCSBN was the first agency to require this level of control within its online assessment distribution channel for NCLEX. The NCLEX program is delivered within the U.S. only, so requirements for global distribution were not factors of its decision-making process. For the NCSBN, the key decision parameters were the need to securely protect the intellectual property of the NCLEX, the need for layered biometric identification processes at the test centers, the need for consistency of examinee assessment experiences, and the need for the capability to deliver high-technology examinations (e.g., computerized adaptive testing, media-rich items, etc.).

Other appropriate online assessment applications for this distribution model include programs in which high-stakes inferences are made based on the assessment outcomes, programs with high complexity computer-based assessments, assessments with valuable intellectual property, assessments in which definite candidate identification is important, assessments that place a high value on preventing cheating, assessments that do not require global distribution, and assessment programs that require that their "face" to the examinees provide the highest quality experience and best customer service. This last example relates to the quality of the examinee experience in the context of online assessment delivery being an outsourced service provided by a contractual partner and the degree to which the test owner desires control over that examinee experience.

In practice, this last point is extremely important for test owners; the very nature of online assessments generally leads to an arm's length relationship between the test owner organization and its primary clients, the examinees. In most online assessment situations, the assessment owner's staff has no direct contact with its examinees. During the assessment process, the assessment delivery agency becomes a de facto surrogate for the test owner and provides the only real human contact with examinees on a personal level. This Controlled Distribution model provides the shortest distance between test owner and examinee (e.g., test owner> test delivery agency's test centers >examinee) and therefore the most consistent messaging.

Global Distribution

This model provides a generally standardized assessment experience for the examinee along with the broadest distribution of the assessment for the test owner. The model provides computer-based assessment in a proctored test center environment. In the current CBT delivery market, it has been actualized as a third party distribution channel. That is, the assessment delivery agency does not "own" the test centers but rather has contractual relationships with test centers that provide the actual test delivery to examinees. These test centers may be located in college computer labs, computer-based training facilities, private businesses, and so forth. Important features of this model include computer workstations for examinees, an available test administrator or proctor, a testing room, a technology to accomplish data transfer with headquarters, and an examinee identification check for admissions.

Given the wide range of computer labs available globally, there is an obvious limit to the level of standardization possible in this model. Test center features that are not currently standardized and cannot be include file server configuration; computer workstations, monitors, examinee work space, and other ergonomic features; staffing models; and technology for data transfer with headquarters. As with any relationship based on contract terms, it is also more difficult for the test delivery agency to compel specific behavior from its contractual partners (the test centers) regarding attending to the test owners' specific requirements. Thus, test owners have an increased relationship distance between themselves and their examinees (e.g., test owner>test delivery agency>test center>examinee) compared to the Controlled Distribution model in the previous section, leading to a less consistent assessment experience across examinees (including messaging, customer service ethic, and compliance with the test owner processes).

A number of online assessment programs have selected Global Distribution as their model of choice, based on their online assessment needs and goals. This model of global distribution was the original CBT delivery model for the information technology certification assessment market. The concept sprang from a "test-where-you-train" approach. Certification candidates would take training at authorized education centers and, upon completion of the program, be eligible for the posteducation certification assessment, which would be delivered at the same premises. This model provides the opportunity for a high capture rate of trainees into certification testing. Novell, Microsoft, Cisco, and many other information technology organizations all believe that this model provides an appropriate balance of security and far reaching global distribution for their programs. As these organizations have evaluated the goals of their certifications and the inferences made based on the certification examinations, they have decided that in weighing the equation of maximum consistency, standardization, and control versus global reach and examinee convenience, global reach is currently more important.

Over the past year or so, many information technology certification programs have begun to discuss the question of test center security and control within the model of global distribution. These organizations have seen the demand for their certifications grow exponentially and the network of people trying to subvert the system increase at similar rates. The market has banded together to form the Information Technology Certification Security Council to begin to address the issues of examinee cheating, fraud, and intellectual property protection (Foster, 2003). To respond to this new market concern, more sophisticated technologies around data analysis and test experience forensics are being developed. For example, Pearson VUE has begun analyzing the test purchasing patterns of credit card accounts to try and determine whether groups of examination registrations are legitimate or a product of an item harvesting group. Patterns of item response data can also possibly be analyzed to uncover examinee wrongdoing. We also routinely check the passing rates for examinations by test center. As these concerns mature for test owners using the Global Distribution model, the issues of standardized conditions, security, and increased control may increase in importance.

Ubiquitous Distribution

This model is characterized as providing a likely nonstandard assessment experience for the examinee and universal distribution for the test owner. For the purposes of this discussion, we define this model as computer-based assessment distributed over the Internet. This model is not test-center based; it provides online assessments that are available anywhere the Internet is accessible. There has been much market and test-owner interest in this distribution model since the Internet achieved broad coverage and popular usage. Important features of this model include browser-based assessment delivery, the widest possible spread of distribution, no standardization of computers or monitors, variance in Internet connectivity, variance in Internet performance, no assurance of examinee identification, very little to no intellectual property protection for the assessment, no control over examinee behavior, and assessments limited to standard psychometric models (e.g., no adaptive testing).

Compared to the previous two distribution models, the Ubiquitous Distribution model has very few characteristics that lend themselves to high-stakes assessments. For example, using a browser as the testing engine doesn't allow for much of the normal testing system functionality present in the center-based distribution models. For assessments with high importance, it is good practice for the testing system to be able to gracefully shut down (due to technical problems) and just as gracefully recover the examinee's work; system recovery processes are very limited or absent with most browser-based testing systems. Also, the degree of standardization and control is not sufficient for assessments with important consequences. The compelling distribution advantage of not requiring a test center for the assessment causes the condition that examinee control is nonexistent for identification purposes, behavior monitoring purposes, and intellectual property control purposes.

Even with the model's negative characteristics, some types of online assessments may be appropriately distributed by using this model, based on their goals, including assessments that have no-or low-stakes inferences as an outcome. Other examples include assessments in which examinees have no incentive to misbehave. Good examples include practice testing exercises and diagnostic assessments. It is also important for test owners to contemplate the lack of intellectual property control when making decisions about implementing this distribution model: Anyone with a browser can have unfettered access to the assessment content. Obviously, there are ways to attempt to limit access through a password or other types of authentication models, but no technology is available to ensure that the person on the other end of the keyboard is the actual person who has been awarded access. There is also no way to know exactly how the person behind the keyboard is behaving when he or she has access to the assessment content.

Future Trends

Each of the Controlled, Global, and Ubiquitous Distribution models will likely progress in quality as test professionals learn more about delivering online assessments. The power of the computer for assessment allows for very interesting and "blue sky" assessment procedures to be contemplated. However, many of the interesting theoretical and "bleeding edge" benefits of online assessment cannot be obtained after the requirements and constraints of actual assessment distribution channels are incorporated into the design of assessment models. This reality reflects neither a weakness in the distribution models nor the theoretical models but rather a lack of operational understanding by assessment designers. Currently, a bit of a gap exists between the research and theories forwarded by assessment thought leaders and their knowledge of operational online assessment realities. One of the important lessons learned as the field of online assessment matures is that as test owners become more sophisticated in their knowledge of the advantages and disadvantages of each specific assessment distribution model, their choices of distribution modality will necessarily become more informed. Their choices will become less based on the specific technology involved and/or hypothetical benefits and more on preserving and enhancing the validity of the inferences made from the assessments. The level and likelihood of the specific threats to validity vary based on the specific distribution model implemented (e.g., level of standardized conditions and level of control of examinee behavior).

The trend of increasing test owner concerns about item and test security and examinee wrongdoing will continue. Growing numbers of assessments are being developed and delivered for a reason-that is, the inferences made on the basis of assessment performance have increasingly important consequences. Many life decisions are based on the outcomes of assessments in general and, more specifically, on these online assessments. As such, the value of the assessments and the need for confidence in their results are also increasing, leading to the requirement for more security surrounding the entire online assessment process. This trend seems to be in conceptual opposition to the also growing trend towards active consideration of the Ubiquitous Distribution model as appropriate for online assessments. A rational analysis would suggest that the death knell for test center-based assessment is a bit premature (and I would suggest not forthcoming).

Complementing the increasing need for secured online assessments is the growing emphasis on using sophisticated data mining analyses techniques for understanding the data transactions in an online testing system. For security purposes, there is a need to use pretest registration data, data gathered during the testing session, and postassessment data. One example of an appropriate data mining includes checking the registration records across examinees for troublesome patterns (e.g., multiple registrations for the same credit card and many score reports going to the same address). A wealth of data is generated during the test session that is also appropriate for security analysis, including (depending on the distribution model chosen) analysis of the gathered biometrics, real time analysis of the digital video and audio recording, analysis of item latencies for suspicious patterns, and so forth. Postassessment, security-appropriate analyses could include investigating item response patterns and analyzing pass/fail patterns, item performance shifts, delivery times, and so forth.

With respect to the online assessments themselves, it is apparent that there will be a large increase in the types of items that are delivered online. From a behavior stimulus perspective, more rich-media items will be developed and delivered. It is not far-fetched to imagine streaming video and audio items, adding to the construct measurement for many different assessment areas. Conversely, on the response side of the equation, utilization of different response types will undoubtedly increase. The appeal of performance-type items is compelling. Drag and drop, short answer, long answer, fill in the blank, multiple response, point and click, and so forth are all response modalities that have been investigated and are becoming more commonplace in operational online assessments.

Conclusion

There is a large societal/environmental trend towards more assessment in people's lives as they progress throughout their lifespan (e.g., school assessments, placement assessments, admissions assessments, employment assessments, licensure and certification assessments, and continued competence assessments). Much of this testing may be accomplished through online assessment. However, effective use of online assessments cannot be realized without implementing the appropriate distribution models to meet the assessments' goals.

Many decisions need to be made when deciding how to best use online assessments and distribute them into the market. Test owners, test developers, and test-delivery agencies must work together to develop optimal distribution of assessment content, taking into account the purposes of the assessments, their form, their value, and the intended examinee population.

Experience to date has taught us that not all of the three distribution models (controlled, global, and ubiquitous) are appropriate for all online assessments. Each has specific strengths and weaknesses that interact with assessments in important ways; these strengths and weaknesses must be analyzed as part of a good decision-making process. Appropriate assessment distribution decisions must flow from adherence to good testing practice and an understanding of fundamental psychometric concepts (e.g., standardized testing needs standardized conditions). The strengths and weaknesses outlined in this chapter can help professionals make appropriate assessment distribution decisions.

References

Bergstrom, B. A. (1992, April). The ability to measure the equivalence of computer-adaptive and paper and pencil tests: A research synthesis. Paper presented at the meeting of the *American Educational Research Association*, San Francisco, CA.

Foster, D. (2003, January). Test piracy: The darker side of certification. *Certification Magazine*. Retrieved from *http://www.certmag.com/articles/templates/cmag_feature.asp?articleid=2&zoneid=1*

Lunz, M. E., & Bergstrom, B. A. (1991). Comparability of decisions for computer adaptive and written examinations. *Journal of Allied Health, 20*(1), 15-22.

Weiss, D. J. (Ed.). (1978). *Proceedings of the 1977 Computerized Adaptive Testing Conference*. Minneapolis: University of Minnesota, Department of Psychology, Psychometric Methods Program.

Weiss, D. J. (Ed.). (1980). *Proceedings of the 1979 Item Response Theory and Computerized Adaptive Testing Conference*. Minneapolis: University of Minnesota, Department of Psychology, Psychometric Methods Program.

Zara, A. R. (1994, April). An overview of the NCLEX/CAT beta test. Paper presented at the annual meeting of the *American Educational Research Association*, New Orleans, LA.

Zara, A. R. (1996). Overview of a successful conversion. In E. L. Mancall, P. G. Bashook, & J. L. Dockery (Eds.), *Computer-based examinations for board certification* (pp. 79-90). Evanston, IL: American Board of Medical Specialties.

Chapter XV

From Paper and Pencil to Computerized: A Dental Board's Perspective

G. Eric Jenson, Thomson Prometric, USA

Abstract

Computerized testing offers many advantages over paper and pencil exams. Advantages can include increased security, greater availability of the exam, rapid scoring, and reduced administrative costs. Possible disadvantages can include the need for computer hardware and software, computer glitches, and computer anxiety. This chapter discusses the advantages and disadvantages of computerized testing followed by a description of the experience of a state-based dental board as they transitioned from a paper and pencil exam to a computerized exam.

Introduction

In a relatively short time, computers have gone from huge behemoths accessible only to obscure scientists to small machines in homes throughout the world. Many household tasks previously done manually are now being completed by computers. As access to computers has increased, software applications have multiplied. The testing world has also experienced major changes driven by the prevalence of computers in society. Because of the benefits offered by computers, many exams are being converted from their original paper and pencil format to a computerized format or being developed and delivered completely via the computer. Prior to converting a paper and pencil-based program into a computer-based program, test sponsors should consider the advantages and disadvantages. If the decision to computerize the exam is made, the transition from old to new delivery modes should be planned carefully. This chapter seeks to briefly review historical advantages and disadvantages of computer-based testing, discuss current advantages, and then offer a case study.

Early studies of computerized testing mention as potential drawbacks the lack of available computer hardware and frequent hardware and software glitches. In their article titled "Testing by Computer: Findings in Six Years of Use, 1982-1988," Bugbee and Bernt (1990) state that "computer equipment and performance is perhaps the greatest potential problem in this type of testing" ("Negative features" section, ¶5). Although access to computers and hardware and software glitches are still problematic, computers are now common fixtures in school labs, businesses, and homes. Early DOS-based programs have been replaced with programs developed on more stable operating systems, reducing the software challenges faced earlier.

In addition to the physical problems, much early research was done comparing candidate scores from exams delivered via paper and pencil and computerized versions. Results from these studies were mixed; several studies found no difference in exam modes, while others found relatively large differences (Bugbee, 1996). A likely addition to early findings of differences between modes was the concept of computer anxiety. As computers have been assimilated and normalized in our environment, the concept of computer anxiety has become less worrisome. As stated by Bugbee (1996), "It is not unreasonable to expect that although test anxiety will never disappear, computer test anxiety could become extinct in the near future with increased computer knowledge and comfort" ("Discussion" section, ¶6). In addition to being challenged by computer anxiety, test-takers may perform differently due to the limitations of the mode of presentation. For example, lengthy passages may require a page break in a paper and pencil exam but employ a scroll bar when computerized. Both of these artifacts may affect item performance (Pommerich & Burden, 2000). Clearly, when considering conversion from paper and pencil to computerized examinations, administrators must consider the level of comfort with computers and appropriateness of the items to computerized environments. As computers have become more accepted and common in our environments, many of these concerns have diminished. For the older generation, reading long passages requiring the use of a scroll bar may still be uncomfortable, but for the younger generation, such a reading environment may be more common than turning pages.

One finding that has remained constant through the research is the preference that candidates have for computerized exams (Glasnapp, Poggio, Yang, & Poggio, 2004). Even candidates taking early forms of computerized tests reported a preference for the computerized versions due to their rapid scoring and flexible scheduling (Bugbee & Bernt, 1990). Currently, computerized testing offers many advantages over paper and pencil delivery. A brief listing and explanation of some of these advantages includes the following.

Security

When exams are delivered electronically, printed copies of the exam are not available for theft. Electronic delivery alleviates the security problems of sending large numbers of printed copies of the test to remote test sites. Computerized exams can be manipulated to present random item ordering, multiple forms, or adaptive testing, all of which make cheating more difficult.

Authentic Testing Experience

Many computerized testing systems support a variety of item types, including simulations. Depending on the content covered by the exam, innovative item types may more closely align with the actual skills being tested.

Greater Availability of the Exam

Paper and pencil exams require printing and often shipping of test materials. Because of these administrative burdens, it can be difficult and costly to provide frequent testing opportunities for the candidates. Computerized exams do not require printing, and they can potentially be sent to worldwide testing locations with the click of a mouse.

Scoring

Candidates name the ability to receive instant or rapid scoring as a major advantage of computerized testing. In addition to the mental stress that occurs while waiting for scores, for many people, the wait for final score decisions delays job promotions, employment, and graduation. Slow scoring response can also make educational remediation less effective. Schools using paper and pencil exams frequently administer exams in the fall but do not provide the results to teachers until spring. This delay effectively lessens the amount of time teachers have to provide intervention in needed content areas (Woodfield & Lewis, 2003).

Additional Data Can Be Collected

Computerized exams allow additional data to be collected that is not possible with paper and pencil exams. A common example of such data is time data. Time data can be used to customize the exam to allow candidates only the amount of time needed to complete the exam or to check for aberrant time response patterns that could indicate cheating.

Although it possesses many advantages over paper and pencil administration, computerized testing presents several drawbacks. These drawbacks can include the need to install and maintain standardized computer hardware and software across administration sites and over time, the need for additional training for proctors, limited seating, differences in item and form functioning across the two modes of delivery, computer glitches, and cost.

Case Study:
The Conversion Experience of a
State Dental Board Exam

Background of the Testing Company
Used for the Conversion

Operating a network of over 3,000 testing centers in 134 countries, Thomson Prometric is a company familiar with the advantages and challenges of computerized testing. Tests are published via secure networks to testing centers. At the testing center, multiple tests are hosted simultaneously by the local server and delivered to individual testing stations in monitored carrels. The test center is supervised by trained and certified proctors. In addition to its testing centers, Thomson Prometric also delivers exams via the Internet. This delivery solution is combined with data management and psychometric services to allow clients a full range of testing options. As an electronic test delivery vendor, Thomson Prometric has helped many test sponsors through the conversion from paper and pencil to computerized testing. Although each of these programs is unique in its experience, the following case study is typical of what clients undergo as they make this transition.

Past History of the Dental Board

The state dental board used for this case study has a long and storied history in licensing dentists, hygienists, and dental assistants. In 1889 the state passed a law requiring county judges to be responsible for testing new dentists. This law required the judges to appoint a team of three dentists to interview the prospective dentists and then consult with the judge to decide who would be licensed as a dentist in the county. In 1905 the state opened two dental schools and created a dental board to oversee the licensure process. The dental schools were given the responsibility to test candidates to determine which candidates would be credentialed to practice. In 1950 the program was expanded to license dental hygienists, and in 1989 licenses were granted for dental assistants.

Current testing volumes range from about 900 candidates a year for the dentist exam to 2,500 a year for the dental assistant exam. The testing program has a wide and varied population to which exams are delivered. This population ranges from dental school graduates possessing multiple years of post-bachelors' education to dental assistants just graduating from high school.

Paper and Pencil Program

Prior to the test's computerization, the state board exams were delivered in a paper and pencil format. The method used to administer the three exams was customized to the needs of the testing populations. Test delivery and proctoring for the dental assistant exam was the responsibility of dentists trying to get licensure for their assistants. After a candidate signed up to take the exam, a packet was sent out to the dentist employer. This packet contained study materials, the test, a Scantron, and a document to be signed by the dentist verifying that the dental assistant did not cheat while taking the exam. The dentist was given 6 months to return the packet to the dental board. This format produced a number of problems; most obvious was the conflict of interest for the dentist. The employer-employee relationship between the dentist proctor and the candidate would have heightened the temptation to allow cheating and/or to provide an advantageous testing environment. In addition, the administrative costs for the program were burdensome, requiring printing and tracking of test forms and so forth.

The dentist and the hygienist exams were both administered on-site at schools and association conferences. Depending on the needs of the graduating classes, each of these exams was delivered 12 to 15 times a year. Often one proctor was charged with supervising a roomful of 200 candidates. Registration was generally handled on a first-come, first-serve basis at the testing event. Due to the limited size of the rooms, particularly at the dental schools, candidates often had to be turned away.

After the delivery of the exams, the dental board would scan the answer sheets, create score reports, and mail certificates to those passing the exam. The goal was to get the results back to the candidates within two days of the examination. Many hours were required to print photocopies of the exams, travel to and proctor the exams, scan the results, score candidates, and send out certificates.

During the spring of 2001 the program was jolted by a security breach. During a testing session, the proctor ran out of copies of the exam. Not having a backup or assistant, the proctor relied on the integrity of the candidates and left the room to obtain more copies. During the proctor's absence, multiple candidates left the room with copies of the exam and several candidates verbally shared answers back and forth. The resulting outcry provided the impetus for computerized testing.

The Transition to Computerized Testing

Following the security breach in 2001, the dental board began searching for ways to provide better security for their high-stakes exams. By the fall they had completed their internal assessment of computerized testing and voted to move the exams to this format. Accordingly, the dental board contracted with Thomson Prometric to transition three exams to computer-based testing (CBT) and to create two new CBT exams. Two of the exams that were transitioned to CBT were also reviewed to verify the testing objectives and item performance and to create multiple equated forms of the exams. The new CBT exams rolled out in 2002.

Prior to the CBT rollout, the dental board conducted a large-scale educational and public relations campaign to notify the candidates of the change in delivery modes. Due to the diverse population of candidates, the dental board had to employ many methods to reach the candidates. These methods included posting the information on the board's Web site, informing associations and groups of the change and requesting that they communicate the message to their members, putting the message on the voicemail system, and passing the message through contacts at various schools.

The Benefits of CBT for One State Dental Board

With the rollout of the new computerized exams in 2002, the dental board entered the computerized testing world. The transition to computerized testing was a major change for both the sponsoring agency and the testing candidates. The new testing format has created many positive changes within the dental board's testing program as well as introduced some challenges for both the board and its candidates. The board reports that the benefits are as follows:

- **Improved exam security:** Security concerns have been reduced by delivery of the exams through the Prometric secure network of testing sites. Each of these sites has trained proctors, video surveillance, and a secure data system. In addition, each exam has multiple forms, and items are delivered in random order. By delivering the exams via the computer, there are no hard copies of the exam that can be removed from the testing centers.

- **Reduced administrative burden:** The huge administrative burden of copying, delivering, and scoring exams has been simplified through computerized delivery and scoring at the testing centers. Candidates are now issued pass or fail decisions immediately following the exam instead of being required to wait 2 days. Previously, multiple persons were needed to handle scheduling and proctoring of exams. Scheduling is now handled via the Internet, and dental board personnel are freed from their duties of traveling the state as proctors. The test is now available in more locations and is available for the candidates to take at their scheduling convenience.

- **Data collection and storing:** Additional data from the candidates are now collected and tracked, which allows the dental board to better understand their population of test candidates. Further data from each testing session are easily stored and reaccessed if needed. Previously, only final scores were recorded and accessible.

Future Changes

During the next year, the dental board plans to add new item types made possible by the computerized environment. These types will require candidates to demonstrate skills that are more in-line with actual dental tasks.

Challenges Experienced by the State Dental Board

The conversion to CBT has required the state dental board to grapple with the following new challenges:

- **Selling the idea to the candidates:** Initial and continuing enthusiasm for the conversion has been tempered slightly by candidates accustomed to the test coming to them. Taking the test at school at the end of the educational program became tradition. The transition to requiring students to be responsible for traveling to the test centers has been a subject of complaint among many students.

- **Getting candidates to take responsibility for registration:** Prior to CBT, candidates would register for the exams on a first-come, first-served basis the day of the exam. Students accustomed to this process have complained about the need to register in advance on the Internet. In addition, students accustomed to taking the exams on the last day of class have procrastinated taking the exam until the deadline for the exam. The testing seats the day of the deadline have been limited due to the number of students vying for those seats. The paradigm shift of advanced registration and multiple testing days will be difficult for students accustomed to different processes but will likely be less of a problem with future graduating classes.

- **Lack of a personalized face to the testing program:** While the exam was delivered via paper and pencil, the dental board had the opportunity to meet and interact with the students as they registered and took the exam. This allowed students to sense the humanness of the people administering the testing program. With the change to computerized testing, the human touch is gone. The dental board reports feeling more detached and less current with the needs and desires of the testing population.

- **Discomfort with computers:** The dental board has reported that some candidates have reported being uncomfortable with the use of computers. This appears to be more prevalent among those for whom English is a second language. This anecdotal observation is potentially quite significant for diverse testing populations; in the move from paper and pencil to CBT, we may not be able to assume that computer familiarity is distributed evenly among subpopulations.

- **Complaints about the payment options:** Many candidates have expressed concerns with the payment process. Prior to the conversion, candidates paid the fees the day of the testing. Payment options were limited to checks and cash. Internet registration now requires payment via a credit card. Many of the dental assistants are very recent high-school graduates and do not have credit cards. The dental board reports that many of the candidates struggle to understand why they cannot pay for the exams at the testing center with cash or check.

Conclusion

Based on the experiences of this dental board and experiences of other test sponsors, before converting from paper and pencil exams to computerized exams, a testing sponsor should carefully weigh the advantages and disadvantages of computerized testing. Careful thought should be given to the effect the transition would have on the budget, candidates, and goals of the testing program. Programs deciding to convert to computerized testing should plan ample time and set a schedule for the transition. The conversion should be carefully communicated to the candidates and other key stakeholders. The message should be delivered frequently via multiple outlets and should be clear and simple. Where possible, explaining the steps that will occur and even providing examples of items in computerized formats is helpful.

Exams converting from a paper and pencil legacy should carefully consider the validity of comparisons between item and form functioning. Programs planning to make such comparisons or offer both modes of delivery for the same exam should collect data and analyze item and form functioning. Finally, all exams, both paper and pencil and computerized, should review item performance regularly to ensure that items are performing in the intended manner and are not subject to method-of-delivery artifacts.

References

Bugbee, A. C. (1996). The equivalence of paper and pencil and computer-based testing. *Journal of Research on Computing in Education, 28*(3), 282-290.

Bugbee, A. C., & Bernt, F. M. (1990). Testing by computer: Findings in six years of use, 1982–1988. *Journal of Research on Computing in Education, 23*(1), 87-101.

Glasnapp, J. P., Poggio, J., Yang, X., & Poggio, A. (2004, April). Student attitudes and perceptions regarding computerized testing as a method for formal assessment. Paper presented at the annual meeting of the *National Council on Measurement in Education*, San Diego, CA.

Pommerich, M., & Burden, T. (2000, April). From simulation to application: Examinees react to computerized testing. Paper presented at the annual meeting of the *National Council on Measurement in Education*, New Orleans, LA.

Woodfield, K., & Lewis, K. (2003). Getting on board with online testing. *T.H.E Journal, 30*(6), 32-37.

Chapter XVI

Assessment Elements in Web-Based Training

Kimberly Payne, Imedia.it, USA

Abstract

Web-based training is a field that advances rapidly. Rapid advancement leads to the development of industry standards and best practices. This case study will review some of those practices related to assessment design and evaluation and how each was applied to a U.S. Army Web-based training product. These best practices include adaptive learning, immediate and meaningful feedback, and assessment security. In addition, the problems that the army faced and the solutions that the development company designed will also be discussed. Towards the end of the case study, the results of the validation will be examined. The case study concludes with a look at future trends that may become best practices.

Introduction

As technology rapidly advances, so does the training medium. In the early days of computer-based training, distance learning merely consisted of simple text on a Web page. The content was generally followed by some type of knowledge-level assessment. This assessment consisted of multiple choice, true/false, and/or matching questions. Computer-based training and the assessment methods have advanced with the addition of audio, video, and other media forms. Now training can be scenario-based and offer learners multiple ways to experience the courseware. Scenario-based training can be considered a simulation. A *simulation* places the student in a real-world situation that poses problems to the student that he or she must solve. As such, assessments can measure the performance of the learner without being limited to traditional knowledge-level questions. The objective of this case study is to discuss some of the ways in which Imedia.it incorporated certain elements into the 97B10 project for the U.S. Army. This chapter includes a literature review, background project information, problems encountered, implemented solutions, validation results, and future trends.

Literature Review

This section of the case study is intended to define the terms and provide background information about several of the educational theories and models that Imedia.it incorporates into its Web-based training (WBT) products. At the end of this section, I provide a brief overview of the training that I discuss at length.

Adaptive Learning

Training "is intended to build on individual knowledge, skills, and attitudes to meet present or future work requirements" (Rothwell & Sredl, 2000, p. 48). In most training facilities and classrooms, one would likely find everyone being taught exactly the same way. Teachers predominately teach to the average, middle-of-the-road learners. However, learners differ in many ways. "Whether it is in appearance, learning style, multiple intelligence, prior experience, personal preference, or social/emotional development, students differ" (Gregory & Kuzmich, 2004, p. 2). So if educators know this information, why do they continue to teach in this way? Some may wonder what other options are available. One possible option is adaptive learning. Adaptive learning addresses the differences of each learner. Adaptive learning, as applied to the training referred to in this case study, starts with a preassessment of the learner and resultant placement in a skill-level group. Everyone has his or her own strong and weak areas of ability. "Students need to be placed in groups that maximize their instructional time based on their performance levels" (Gregory & Chapman, 2002, p. 70). These different skill-level groups address the same content, but at different learning levels. This differentiation allows for "modification in content, process, and product based on the needs of the student" (Auld et al., 2000, p. 3).

Feedback

Proponents of constructivism, Stolovitch and Keeps state, "Knowledge cannot simply be imprinted onto an individual's mind; rather each individual constructs meaning in interaction with the specific environment" (1999, p. 886). It is believed that the student will construct knowledge based on his or her experience (Smith & Ragan,

1999). One method used in constructivism is termed *coaching*. Coaching depends on the "types of students and their needs" (Gregory & Kuzmich, 2004, p. 18) and is achieved by adding feedback to the course. Appropriate feedback "helps students maintain a sense of control, reduces uncertainty, and encourages a higher level of thinking" (Gregory & Kuzmich, 2004, p. 17). As such, useful feedback must be descriptive so as to offer the learner detailed, constructive information. Feedback is meant to "support learners at points where their own aptitudes or attitudes might infringe on learning" (Smith & Ragan, 1999, p. 25). It is the "process of providing just-in-time, just-enough assistance" to the learner (Dabbagh, 2003, p. 39). Feedback is especially important when "supporting novice learners by limiting the complexities of the learning context" (Dabbagh, 2003, p. 39). Feedback that is "planned and tuned to specific student behaviors and needs is effective" (Gregory & Kuzmich, 2004, p. 20). Feedback should be given to a learner throughout the course and at the end of the training to recap the performance and review the learner's progress.

Assessment Security

Assessment security is not a new concept; however, it has gained new attention as more people begin utilizing online assessment. The issues are broad and include measures to prevent hacking (such as implementing firewalls) and verifying learner identity. For the purpose of this case study, assessment security will refer to keeping the test content from being compromised in WBT. I will examine the way in which Imedia.it has been able to implement a program that makes it difficult for learners to compromise the integrity of the performance assessment.

Project Background

In November 2001, the U.S. Army Distance Learning Center tasked Imedia.it with creating a WBT product that would be used to train a 97B10 Counterintelligence Army Reserve or National Guard soldier on interviewing procedures and techniques. A 97B10 conducts police-like investigations and works on cases involving espionage and other threatening activities. The interview training, which is part of a 500-hour course, is conducted in the final phase of the course after classroom prerequisite training has been completed.

The Web-based product is similar in many ways to the classroom training. Before the learner starts conducting interviews, he or she is required to have prerequisite knowledge of the procedures, interviewing techniques, and the governing regulations. This information is given in the face-to-face classes. Both courses use the same scenarios. The traditional setting uses the same eight scenarios as the WBT but also has several more from which the instructors can choose. The learner is required to execute the correct procedure before and after the interview.

Each scenario has three interviews-walk-in, source, and subject-that must be sequentially completed and passed. The first interview conducted by the learner is the walk-

Figure 1. 97B10 question interface

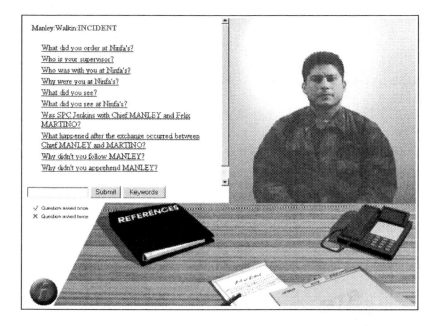

in. The *walk-in* is someone who alerts the learner about the probable incident or violation. The second interview is a source. For the WBT, there is just one source. However, a real case could have many sources. *Sources* are various individuals who verify and validate the information that the walk-in provided. The last interview that the learner conducts is the *subject*-the person who has allegedly committed the violation. In both the WBT and face-to-face interviews, the scenarios are randomized so the learner does not know which case he or she will receive.

Displayed in Figure 1 is an array of questions available for the student to choose. These questions are responded to in the form of video clips. For purposes of scoring the performance, the questions that the student can ask the interviewee are grouped in three categories: critical, good, or irrelevant. The first type of question is *critical*. Critical questions are phrased correctly and are specific. If the learner asks a critical question, he or she is given all available information that answers that question and scores the maximum number of points. The second category is a *good* question. A good question is usually correctly worded but might be missing some specific information. If the learner asks a good question, he or she is given some information and scores the minimum number of points. A learner would have to ask several good question to receive all the information that was given in a critical question. The third type is an *irrelevant* questions. An irrelevant question yields no information of value, and the student receives a negative score. The irrelevant question type has several subcategories. A question may not have relevance, may not be specific enough, or should be avoided. Questions that should be avoided are ones that are generally protected by law. For example, the learner should not ask about religious or political beliefs. During the interview, the learner has to ask as many critical and good questions as possible in order to obtain the facts of the case. The final product was delivered to the army in August 2003.

Problems and Solutions

In this section, I discuss the problems that the project team faced and the solutions they incorporated into the training.

Problem: Lack of Instructors

Historically, this training was done face-to-face. The learners had to successfully complete all classes, conduct three live interviews, and write reports based on information obtained during each interview in order to finish their military occupational specialty (MOS) training. The live interviews required one instructor for every two learners. In a class of 20 students, you would need 10 instructors. With increased overseas missions, instructors cannot always be found, resulting in class cancellations and a growing backlog of students awaiting training.

Solution: Web-Based Training

With increasing instructor shortages, the army sought help in delivering this course. In this case study validation, one instructor sat in a computer lab with 10 to 15 learners and monitored their progress. Instead of needing 10 instructors, the course required only 1 or 2. If this course is taken online from a remote location, more students can be reached per instructor. By incorporating e-learning, the instructor requirements were reduced to a manageable number, which enabled the army to conduct more classes and relieve the backlog.

Problem: Diverse Learners

When joining the active army, many learners come straight from high schools and colleges. These learners have little or no military knowledge. The army then trains them in their occupational specialty. The students taking the 97B10 WBT are reclassification soldiers. As *reclassification soldiers,* the students have previously been in the army and have had other job specialties before joining the Army Reserve force. Some soldiers come from the intelligence MOS, some from combat positions, and others from communications, engineering, and medical jobs. Each field has special rules, regulations, and vocabulary. The amount of prior knowledge the 97B10 students have depends on the field they are coming from.

Figure 2. Adaptive learning for 97B10

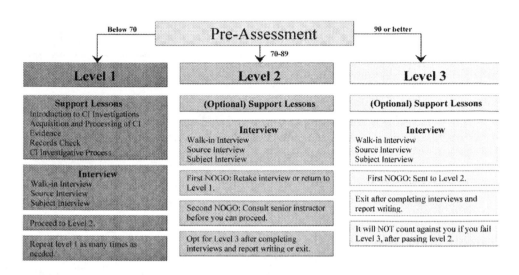

Solution: Adaptive Learning

In order to assess each student's capability and ensure that all students finish the training at a competent level, adaptive learning was incorporated into the WBT. Figure 2 shows the different levels and paths a learner could take to complete the training.

The preassessment in this adaptive learning model is equal in difficulty to the final assessment that the learner has to take in order to pass and receive credit for the course. All learners must take the preassessment. If the learner does not pass the preassessment (with a score below 70), then he or she is placed in a Level 1 (practice) path. Each learner can execute Level 1 training as many times as needed without being penalized. For every mistake the learner makes, he or she receives feedback and remedial training. The learner must progress to a Level 2 scenario and successfully complete it in order to pass the training.

If the learner does pass the preassessment but does not score exceptionally high (with a score between 70 and 89), then the learner is placed in a Level 2 (competency) path. The competency path is more difficult than the practice path. The learner is offered feedback, but only after making several mistakes. After the learner successfully passes the walk-in, source, and subject interviews at this level, he or she is finished with the training program. The learner then has the option of attempting the Level 3 scenario.

If the learner does exceptionally well on the preassessment (with a score of 90 or better), then the learner is placed in the Level 3 (advanced) path. This level is the most difficult. The learner receives no feedback. If the learner is unable to successfully complete this path, it does not count against him or her. The learner has already demonstrated the mastery of the content in the preassessment or in a Level 2 scenario and has successfully passed the training course.

Sample Learners

To show how adaptive learning benefits all learners, Figure 3 shows a sample of the students from the validation study.

Because Mike has been in the army only a short time and his previous MOS is food service operations, he will not be familiar with the specifics of the human intelligence field. Mike had a fairly difficult time with the preassessment and began his training on Level 1. This is a good level for him because he can practice interviewing techniques as many times as necessary in order to construct knowledge. When he can pass a Level 1 scenario, he will move on to a Level 2 scenario. By practicing on Level 1, he is not frustrated by the difficulty of the course.

Chris has more education than Mike and has spent twice the time in service. Although her prior MOS is not in human intelligence, she still has a slight advantage over Mike. Chris took the preassessment and performed at a competent level. She started her training on Level 2. By doing the preassessment, she has already started assimilating knowledge of how the interview process should be approached. Level 2 is a great place for her to start because it is still challenging but not exceedingly difficult.

James has been in the army longer than Chris or Mike. In addition, he has a law degree, and his prior MOS as an infantry soldier provided some training in processing prisoners of war. These three elements combined give James a greater advantage over his colleagues. James took the preassessment and passed it very easily. His score was almost high enough to place him in the Level 3 training. He will begin his training at Level 2 and move on to Level 3. Level 3 looks similar to Level 2; however, it delves into denial and deception. Not only does James have to know what questions to ask and when to ask them, but he also has to know when the person might be withholding information. Then James must figure out how to make the interviewee divulge information about informants and contacts.

Adaptive learning is a viable learning methodology for many reasons. Courses that implement adaptive learning help easily frustrated learners work at their own pace

Figure 3. Cross-section of learners

Name	Mike	Chris	James
Education	High-School Diploma	Bachelor's Degree in Education	Juris Doctor Degree
Military Occupational Specialty	92G–Food Service Operations	31U–Signal Support System Specialist	11B–Infantryman
Time in Service (Years)	3	6	14

until they feel comfortable with the content. Learners who have not mastered the content are allowed more time to gain experience in the practice mode, increasing their confidence level. Learners who have mastered the content have the opportunity to show their skills and advance to learning that is more challenging and beneficial to them. This method increases time efficiency by allowing students to work on their skill level and not waste time with content that may be too easy or too difficult.

Problem: Consistent and Immediate Feedback

Consistency of feedback can be an issue. In the live interview portion of the face-to-face classes, the instructors are the responsible parties for role-playing the scenario and taking notes about the learner's performance. However, because instructors are human, they can make mistakes, and there is no simple way to accurately evaluate every aspect of a learner's performance. A student's learning experience and/or evaluation can be dramatically impacted by which instructor a student is assigned to work with. Instructors have different experiences and styles of teaching. What one instructor may pick up on, another may miss. Learners are at a disadvantage when feedback is inconsistent.

In a classroom setting, an instructor is present and can give feedback instantly and in numerous ways to all students. Online courses do not have an instructor to monitor every interaction that the student executes. Learners taking online courses rarely, if ever, see an instructor, yet they too need detailed, immediate feedback about their performance, just as if they were sitting in a classroom.

Solution: Database Tracking and Feedback

In the WBT, learners receive consistent, immediate feedback because their performance is tracked in the database. The database can record which scenarios the learner has completed, how he or she scored on each interview, and every question that the learner asks. For example, Chris clicks on the question "What color is your car?" She receives feedback to avoid that question because it has no relevance to the case. If James clicks on the same question as Chris, he will get the exact same response that Chris did. Would that always happen in a classroom setting? The answer is *no*. Not all instructors would provide feedback on that question, and some instructors might not think that anything is wrong with the question asked. Maybe the learner has a larger problem that needs more attention. This is where inconsistencies come into play. Learners are at a disadvantage when feedback is not consistent. In this project, immediate feedback occurs as the learner is taking the training and is delivered by an animated avatar. For learners on Level 1, feedback is given for every mistake that they make. In Level 2, the learner is given feedback after several mistakes. The Level 3 learner does not receive any feedback until the after action review (AAR). Utilizing detailed tracking of a learner's performance is a major advantage of online assessment and greatly reduces inconsistencies in learner feedback.

Figure 4. Sample AAR from the 97B10 WBT

Questions:		AAR:
INCIDENT:		
What did you order at the restaurant?	●	Good question.
How did you pay for your bill?	●	This question did not have relevance to the case.
Did you order an alcoholic beverage while dining?	●	Good question.
What did you see?	●	This question was not specific enough.
What did you see at the restaurant?	●	This was a critical question that yielded vital information to the case.
Who was Chief MANLEY with?	●	This was a critical question that yielded vital information to the case.

The second type of feedback that the WBT gives to the learners is an AAR. This is a detailed report at the end of each interview and provides corrective information. Shown in Figure 4 is a sample of the AAR from the 97B10 WBT. On the left-hand side, the report outlines every question that the learner asked. The right-hand side contains the feedback that the learner was given about the question.

It is important to note that the learner is not given the answers to the questions in the AAR. This is a requirement that the army outlined in the statement of work for this project. The learner is simply told whether they chose questions that were critical, good, or not relevant. Although the answers to the questions are critical, it is more important that the student learn what types of questions are important to ask in order to receive the most crucial information. Not giving the learner the answer is part of assessment security that Imedia.it has implemented and is further discussed in the next section.

Problem: Assessment Security

Test item security is a problem in both the classroom setting and WBT. In both situations, some students will know people from a previous section and will ask for information regarding tests. Although some students may be able to offer only general advice about what to study, others may hand over a copy of the test. Toward the extreme side, there have even been cases of students sitting in for another student and taking a test on his or her behalf. Because of these issues, many schools and universities have implemented the proctoring of exams. Identities are checked upon entering a test center, and test packets are picked up after the test. In WBT, proctoring can be accomplished by having students come to a testing center to take the online assessment. Identities are checked and the students are monitored as they take the exam on the computer. Although proctoring reduces test compromises, it is not always practical for all assessments. Beyond testing, assessment compromises can be an issue with papers and reports. Many students have started downloading papers from the Internet and turning them in as their own. The passing of reports from previous students to current students and the current students turning reports in as their own, which is sometimes referred to as ghostwriting, can also be a problem. Luckily for instructors, the students will typically forget to change some detail, such as the date, and instructors can confront the student about the problem. The same issue can and does happen with online assessments.

Solution: Detailed Tracking of Performance and Ghostwriting Capabilities

With online training, many security issues must be taken into consideration. In order to access the training, the student must use a login with a username and password. Although students may not always protect their passwords, this is the first step in online security. The second step in reducing compromises of test content is to randomize which scenarios the student receives. In this way, not all students receive the same scenario and therefore have a more difficult time tracking down the answers from another student. For the 97B10 WBT, learners are assessed on both the interview questions they choose and on multiple choice tests. The multiple choice test, at the end of each scenario, makes certain that the learner obtained the most critical information pertaining to the case. This information must be contained in the learner report written after the interview. In regard to assessment security, the learner is shown only one question at a time. The learner is not allowed to return to a previous question and cannot exit from the program until he or she is finished with the test. Almost all print functionality has been removed from the courseware to keep students from printing the questions and passing them on to others. However, if a student is computer savvy, he or she will be able to print the page anyway. When a student is finished with the test, a bookmark is set. If the learner goes back into the program, he or she will be placed at a point beyond the assessment.

As mentioned in an earlier section, the database associated with the courseware is capable of tracking which questions the learner asked the interviewee. The ghostwriting functionality tracks the student's performance, including each question asked. If a learner does not ask enough questions during the interview and therefore cannot answer the test questions, the student fails the training. If the learner asks every question in the interview in an attempt to get to the multiple choice test faster, he or she earns points for the right questions but is penalized for the incorrect questions. This method will cause a learner to fail the course without being able to attempt the assessment, because there are more incorrect than correct questions.

If a student tries to answer a multiple choice test question but did not receive that information in the interview, the ghostwriting functionality activates, and an avatar appears, offering a warning to the student. During the multiple choice test, the learner has five possible responses. The first four have the right and wrong answers. The fifth response is "I don't know." The learner can respond with the fifth choice if he or she did not receive that information from the interviewee. Although the answer "I don't know" does count as an incorrect response, the student is not falsely accused of cheating and can proceed to the next question. If this process happens a second time, the learner is automatically logged out of the program and instructed to see a course manager or instructor. The instructor is notified of the incident in the instructor section that outlines each student's performance. At this point, the learner can no longer access the training program. The course manager has the ability to determine if the learner should be allowed back into the course or if the learner must repeat the course. Learners must pass both the traditional assessment and the performance assessment in order to pass their current scenario.

Validation Results

The validation of the 97B10 course took place at Fort McCoy in July 2003. The control group was a class prior to the validation group, who had completed the course and all interviews face-to-face. The validation group had been at Fort McCoy for several weeks attending the face-to-face classes and was ready to begin the WBT interviews. It comprised 20 students whose time in service ranged from 2 to 16 years. The education levels ranged from General Equivalency Diplomas (GEDs) to master's degrees. The validation group was split into two groups because of the number of computers. The students would spend half the day in a classroom listening to lectures and the other half of the day in the computer lab working on the simulated interview training. After the validation group completed the WBT, the students were required to conduct live interviews with the instructors playing the interviewees. The control group also had to conduct live interviews after completing the classroom training.

Figure 5. Live interview test scores

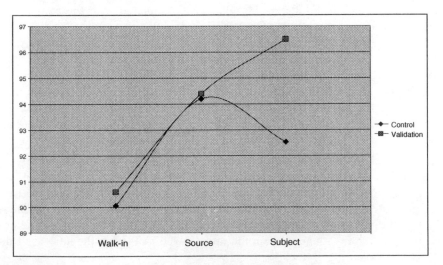

Table 1. Final live interview results

	Validation Group	Control Group
Walk-in		
Average	91	90
Standard Deviation	5.01	8.82
Source		
Average	94	94
Standard Deviation	4.94	4.77
Subject		
Average	97	93
Standard Deviation	3.08	3.34
Average of Three Student Interviews		
Average	94	92
Standard Deviation	2.07	4.35

"The most important measure of the validity of the courseware is the transfer of skills to a live interview" (Imedia.it, 2003, p. 15). Figure 5 "compares the average of the actual interview scores of the control group, who took the course in February 2003 and did not use the online courseware, to the average of the actual interview scores of the validation group who participated in the study" (Imedia.it, 2003, p. 15). As displayed in Figure 5, the validation group performed better on the live interview portion than the control group.

As shown in Table 1, "average student scores on the final live interviews for the validation group were equivalent to those for the control group" (Imedia.it, 2003, p. 16). "The average of all scores by the validation group for the walk-in, source, and subject were higher than the control group, 94 as opposed to 92" (Imedia.it, 2003, p. 16).

More importantly, the validation group using the WBT not only outscored the control group, but also their scores were generally more tightly grouped than those of the control group. With all the validation learners getting consistent feedback and remediation, the standard deviation of their scores was much lower. The control group did not have this consistency and, therefore, the standard deviation of their scores is generally higher.

Based on the results of the preassessment, the validation group fell into one of two categories, as shown in Table 2. The remedial group consisted of the students who started their training on Level 1. The competency group (shaded columns) consisted of the learners who started their training on a Level 2. The remedial group had less experience and education than the competency group. After the remedial group finished their Level 1 training and moved into Level 2 training, their scores were about the same on average as those of the competency group. It can be assumed that because the students' skill levels were assessed in the pretest and the learners were put into training that was appropriate to their learning needs, adaptive learning was successful in bringing all students to an equivalent level of achievement.

Table 2. Comparison of validation groups

	Manley Preassessment		Level 1		Level 2		Final Interview	
Posttest								
Average	51	86	83		88	88		
Standard Deviation	27.67	5.02	7.77		5.26	4.00		
Interview								
Average	63	77	83		82	82	94	94
Standard Deviation	17.14	6.9	4.44		5.64	2.15	2.28	1.87
Educational Level								
Mode	6	8						
Equivalent	High school + 1 year of college	Bachelor's degree						
Time in Service								
Mean	6.4 years	10.3 years						

Future Trends

More and more statements of work from the U.S. Army are mandating the use of adaptive learning. Hopefully, as people become more aware of the benefits of adaptive learning, its use in WBT will become a standard methodology.

An *assessment rubric* is a form of evaluation that graphically depicts the conditions and standards for a training product. In another WBT that Imedia.it is creating for the U.S. Army, a rubric is being used for the assessment of the learner's performance. As stated by Pickett and Dodge (2001), "The rubric is an authentic assessment tool which is particularly useful in assessing criteria which are complex and subjective. Authentic assessment is geared toward assessment methods which correspond as closely as possible to real world experience." However, a rubric is not the appropriate tool for every assessment situation. Rubrics are meant to be used toward the evaluation of portfolios, essays, multimedia presentations, and comparable deliverables; "where and when a scoring rubric is used depends... on the purpose of the assessment" (Moskal, 2000). When an assessment rubric is the most appropriate evaluative solution, the primary concern is to "address the aspects of student work that you feel are most important" (Chicago Public Schools, 2000). One of the advantages of using a rubric is that it...offers the learner and the instructor the ability to review the expectations of any assignment so that everyone has a clear understanding of the final product as well as the expected grading criteria that will be in place for each assignment. (Crawford, 2001)

For an instructional designer, the rubric is an excellent way to lay out all the objectives and grading criteria. A rubric keeps the student feedback consistent. The rubric should be presented to the student at the beginning of the training, accessible at any time during the training, and used as the AAR at the end of the training. Using the rubric as the AAR, the student can look at his or her performance level and what could be done to advance to the next higher level.

An additional possibility that blends seamlessly with adaptive learning is computer-adaptive testing (CAT). As a learner is taking a test, the assessment adapts itself to the learner by selecting the next test item based on the performance on a previous item. In this way, CAT could be used as a preassessment to determine the knowledge that the learner already possesses. After the preassessment, the training could utilize adaptive learning and place students in a performance level that is equal to their skill level. Another option would be to design the training so that the student has to take only the sections that he or she did not pass in the preassessment. In this way, training can be built based on the needs of the individual student.

Another emerging trend is in the assessment security realm. Some places are asking distance education learners to answer biographical questions during an assessment. The student has only a short amount of time, 10 to 15 seconds, to answer these biographical questions. This method is being used in the Texas defensive driving online course offered by DefensiveDriving.com. The assumption is that only the learner who is supposed to be taking the test would know the information. The time limit is put in place so that in case someone else is taking the test, that person would not have enough time to find the answer. Sometimes the question is repeated to ensure the same answer is given. If the question is not answered quickly or correctly, a consequence ensues.

Conclusion

The lack of instructors, diverse audience, consistent and immediate feedback, and assessment security were some of the problems that the U.S. Army encountered in delivering this course. Imedia.it was able to remedy these problems in several ways. Using WBT that included a database to track the performance of the learner, offering consistent and immediate feedback and providing assessment security measures, relieved many of the problems encountered. To address the diverse audience that would be taking this course, Imedia.it decided to use adaptive learning. Adaptive learning approaches help all students to succeed at their skill level. Incorporating all these aspects into online courseware helps emulate the real job situation and aids the learner in completing training with the necessary skills to move ahead in his or her career field.

References

Auld, C., Brown, J., Duffy, M., Falter, N., Hammond, T., Jensen, D., et al. (2000). *Promising curriculum and instructional practices for high-ability learners manual*. Lincoln, NE: Nebraska State Department of Education. (ERIC Document Reproduction Service No. ED448562)

Carpenter, D., Holmes, D., Henderson, J., & Malloy, K. (2003). *Validation report: 97B10 Counterintelligence Agent Interactive Multimedia Course*. Houston, TX: Imedia.it.

Chicago Public Schools. (2000). *Ideas and rubrics*. Retrieved June 7, 2004, from *http://intranet.cps.k12.il.us/Assessments/Ideas_and_Rubrics/Rubric_Bank/Other_Rubrics/other_rubrics.html*

Crawford, C. (2001). Rubrics: Models of evaluation within a constructivist learning environment. Paper presented at the spring conference of the *National Council of Teachers of English*, Birmingham, AL.

Dabbagh, N. (2003). Scaffolding: An important teacher competency in online learning. *TechTrends, 47*(2), 39-44.

DefensiveDriving. (2003). Retrieved June 7, 2004, from *http://www.defensivedriving.com /ddo/index.html*

Gregory, G. H., & Chapman, C. (2002). *Differentiated instructional strategies: One size doesn't fit all*. Thousand Oaks, CA: Corwin Press.

Gregory, G. H., & Kuzmich, L. (2004). *Data driven differentiation in the standards-based classroom*. Thousand Oaks, CA: Corwin Press.

Moskal, B. M. (2000). Scoring rubrics: What, when, and how? *Practical Assessment, Research & Evaluation, 7*(3). Retrieved June 7, 2004, from *http://PAREonline.net/getvn.asp?v= 7&n=3*

Pickett, N., & Dodge, B. (2001). *Rubrics for Web lessons*. Retrieved June 7, 2004, from *http://webquest.sdsu.edu/rubrics/weblessons.htm*

Rothwell, W. J., & Sredl, H. J. (2000). *The ASTD reference guide to workplace learning and performance: Present and future roles and competencies*. Amherst, MA: Human Resource Development Press.

Smith, P. L., & Ragan, T. J. (1999). *Instructional design*. New Jersey: Prentice-Hall.

Stolovitch, H. D., & Keeps, E. J. (1999). *Handbook of human performance technology: Improving individual and organizational performance worldwide*. San Francisco: Jossey-Bass.

Chapter XVII

The Seven C's of Comprehensive Online Assessment:
Lessons Learned from 36 Million Classroom Assessments in the Cisco Networking Academy Program

John T. Behrens, Cisco Systems, USA

Tara A. Collison, Cisco Systems, USA

Sarah DeMark, Cisco Systems, USA

Abstract

During the last 6 years, the Cisco Networking Academy™Program has delivered online curricula and over 36 million online assessments to support instructors and schools teaching computer networking skills to students. This chapter describes the context of this work and lessons learned from this endeavor. Through discussions with stakeholders concerning the central aspects of the Cisco Networking Academy Program assessment activities, seven themes have evolved, each starting with the letter C: claims, collaboration, complexity, contextualization, computation, communication, and coordination. These themes address many aspects of assessment, including design, development, delivery, and the management of assessment resources, which are all necessary to ensure a quality assessment program.

Background

The Cisco Networking Academy Program was funded as a collaborative effort by Cisco Systems, Inc., and the Cisco Learning Institute and partnered with educational institutions to support schools and instructors teaching networking technology skills. The program contains many notable aspects, including (a) online curriculum materials designed for high interactivity, (b) comprehensive instructor training through partnering educational institutions, (c) a Quality Assurance Plan that helps schools monitor and improve program implementation, and (d) online assessments for in-class delivery by instructors. This program provides online curriculum and online assessment access along with support tools and staff at no cost to participating not-for-profit educational institutions.

Teacher training is provided in a tiered structure in which instructors at local academies (lowest in the structure) obtain training and mentoring from instructors at regional academies, which, in turn, obtain their instruction from Cisco area training centers. School personnel in this system provide instruction and guidance to other schools on a cost-recovery basis. Schools desiring to participate in the Cisco Networking Academy Program agree to a number of quality assurance practices, including sending instructors to instructor training, monitoring course feedback, and including a high degree of hands-on activity in the class.

In essence, the academy program offers teaching aids to the instructors. The instructors receive suggestions and some guidance from the Networking Academy Instructor material, but they are directed to implement their instruction following their own local conditions, constraints, and resources. For example, schools participating in the program are required to purchase a small amount of networking hardware so that students can have hands-on in-class experience with real networks, but the actual amount of this activity varies by teacher and school.

The prototypical instructional format is for instructors to assign students Web-based reading and activity lessons in the online curriculum. Students have unique login names and passwords to a curriculum and assessment portal. Interaction with the curriculum is followed by class discussion and hands-on activities and exercises. A key component of the academy program has been the notion that the instructor is present and facilitating the learning. Students are not simply dumped into online curricula. Courses are composed of modules that segment the curriculum as chapters in a book do. At the end of each module is a quiz designed to give detailed performance feedback and a module exam intended to give feedback regarding student strengths and weaknesses as well as to help prepare the student for the final exam. Module and final exams are often embellished with a feature called a *personalized feedback report*. This report creates a customized listing of curricular content based on tasks on which the student did not perform well. Assessment tasks can be tagged to correspond to a

Figure 1. Example drag-and-drop task from Cisco Networking Academy Program quiz

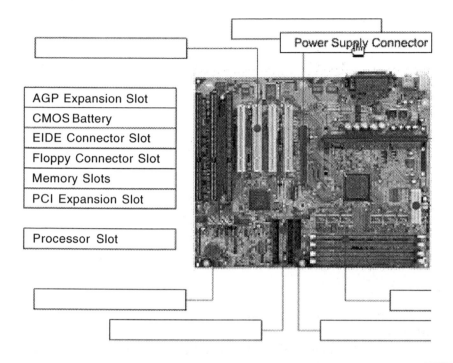

single page in the curriculum, section, module, or course, or multiple instances of these objects in the course. This gives the student a personalized subset of curricular content to review. This subset is created dynamically by the delivery system.

The Networking Academy Program has two delivery mechanisms for assessment activity. Quizzes are embedded inside the curricular materials and are developed in the FLASH interactive media system, which is a common application on the Internet. These activities give feedback on question correctness and, in some cases, employ personalized feedback reports as well. Quizzes generally consist of 10 to 20 tasks including multiple choice questions, drag-and-drop tasks, and point-and-click activities. Figure 1 is an illustration of a drag and-drop task from a quiz in one of the academy program's courses. No data are recorded from quizzes. Other assessments, such as module and final exams, are provided through an assessment server that presents the tasks and stores the results. Instructors must activate exams in advance for students to access them, and instructors and students have access to results through grade books after the completion of the assessments.

The most frequently used curriculum in the Cisco Networking Academy Program is targeted to help students prepare to take the Cisco Certified Network Associate® exam. This is an industry standard for certified entrance into the networking profession. For courses preparing students for industry certification exams, additional practice certification exams or voucher exams may determine if a student is eligible for discount vouchers for that exam. Industry certification exams are always administered

Table 1. Summary of seven C's of Networking Academy comprehensive assessment model

Area	Goal	Examples
Claims	Clarity of design	Develop content following claims implies evidence implies tasks model. Make delivery system flexible to match different assessment goals.
Collaboration	Embed development in instructional community	Involve instructors in content development via online authoring tool. Establish online feedback mechanisms.
Complexity	Leverage digital technologies to make assessments as complex as appropriate	Flexible scoring technologies. Use of simulations and automated scoring of hands-on tasks. Linking to curricula.
Contextualization	Translate and localize content for stakeholders around the world	Authoring and delivery tools that support complex language formats. Localization and review processes to ensure appropriate translation and delivery.
Computing	Analyze data to improve and revise content	Use of classical and IRT models to analyze results. Flexible delivery system allows fast revision.
Communication	Empower stakeholders with data	Multilevel grade book. Item information pages and summary reports.
Coordination	Develop assessment system in context of other assessment and learning activities	Linking of curricular assessments with external capstone assessments by design and statistics.

by organizations independent from the schools administering the academy curriculum-based assessments.

The reader is referred to Murnane, Sharkey, and Levy (2004) for a discussion of the origin of the program, while Levy and Murnane (2004) describe issues related to technological application of the curriculum and assessment. Porter and Kramer (2002) discuss the business and social rationale for such work occurring in a philanthropic context.

In the course of developing our assessment procedures to meet this global need, our work has emerged around multiple themes, which we have come to call the Seven *C's* of comprehensive assessment. These seven themes are claims, collaboration, complexity, contextualization, computation, communication, and coordination. An overview of these key features is presented in Table 1. Each is discussed in turn in this section.

Claims

In this context, the word *claims* refers to the claims we want to make about what our examinees know and can do. Claims are the core objects in our assessment system because they drive the design and development of all assessment work. This focus on claims and purpose comes from the assessment framework called Evidence Centered Design (ECD; Mislevy, Steinberg, & Almond, 2003). We adopted ECD because it provides a rich language for describing assessment activity in a way that is not tied down to old technologies or delivery formats. Evidence Centered Design encourages assessment practitioners to (a) consider the claims they would like to make about examinees, (b) articulate the evidence that would be needed to support such claims, and c) construct tasks to directly obtain the evidence needed to make the desired claims. Although this sounds like common sense, we have found that the specific endeavors of reflection, discussion, and documentation involved in this practice are extremely beneficial.

Our early efforts focused on exam designs that very tightly matched the structure, scope, and level of integration of the curriculum. Accordingly, the chapter exams were more likely to follow a uniform distribution of content in which a global rule was applied, such as "one question for each html page" or similar unit. Although such a design does ensure that coverage is broad, it may lead to questions that are aimed at the lowest level of the skill hierarchy. Claims development workshops were held that started with discussion of the nature of the domain, and continued with the generation of highly integrative claims. This led to claims implying rich real-world tasks, such as "the student can troubleshoot the network," to supplement the more focused instructional tasks that are elemental subskills, such as "the student can identify a type of cable."

The generation of highly integrative claims has direct impact on the architecture of the delivery system. For example, the original personalized feedback mechanisms were based on the linking of each task (primarily multiple choice questions) being linked to an individual page in the curriculum. This, however, limited the scope of the assessment tasks to small chunks of content. The call for more integrative claims, and therefore more integrative tasks, led to a change so task-curriculum linking could occur at the page, section, or module level. This allows for much richer tasks and corresponding feedback.

Table 2. Feature by exam type assessment design matrix

Feature	Quiz	Module Exam	Practice Final	Final Exam	Voucher Exam	Practice Certification Exam
Organizational purpose	Feedback to learner	Feedback to learner, teacher, administrator	Provide feedback and practice to learner	Feedback to learner, teacher, administrator	Provide minimum level for discount voucher	Provide feedback and practice to learner
Instructional purpose	Formative	Formative or summative	Learner feedback	Primarily summative	None	Learner feedback
Grain size of feedback	Task or option level	Task level, task area, overall proficiency	Task area, overall proficiency	Task area, overall proficiency	Overall proficiency	Task area, overall proficiency
Grain size of claims and tasks	Small to medium	Small to medium	Medium to high	Medium to high	Medium to high	Medium to high
Level of task complexity	Varies	Varies	High	High	High	High
Level of content security	Low	Low to medium	Low to medium	High	High	Low

The Variety of Needs

In our online world, we are attempting to provide a comprehensive assessment system that serves many instructors with varying instructional backgrounds. Accordingly, we require different assessment activities for different purposes and claims. In some cases, instructors wanted detailed feedback and repeated practice for their students. In other cases they wanted highly secure exams with frequently changing content. In some cases, highly integrative tasks are sought; in other cases, more detailed feedback on focused tasks is desired. To accommodate these varying uses, we established a matrix of assessment attributes and desired features. The current version of this matrix is shown in Table 2. As the reader can see, the variation in instructional purpose requires a wide variety of design and deployment options in the assessment implementation.

To be able to provide assessments with these many characteristics, our delivery system has been designed so that a wide range of presentational attributes can be authored along with the task content itself. For example, when creating a practice final exam, its content will be considered to have a low-security requirement, and the presentation of the exam will be authored to allow the instructor to choose whether he or she wants the students to see the exact questions after the exam. Such a choice is not made available for the secure final. All these settings are specified in a rich IMS compatible XML structure that is interpreted by the delivery system.

Although the Evidence Centered Design framework is only mentioned in broad strokes here, it runs throughout our language, conceptualizations, and implementations. The interested reader is referred to Behrens, Mislevy, Bauer, Williamson, and Levy (in press) for additional treatment of the impact of ECD in the Cisco Networking Academy Program.

Collaboration

From its inception, the Networking Academy Program was designed as a collaborative activity between Cisco Systems, Inc., the Cisco Learning Institute, and educators in the partnering educational institutions. In the assessment arena, this is done in three ways. First, the content development for assessments is accomplished primarily by active academy instructors working at universities, colleges, and secondary schools around the world. Second, a number of academy instructors are engaged to review assessment content prior to their release to the public. Third, there are ongoing mechanisms for feedback to the assessment team from the instructor community.

Online Content Development

Because Cisco Systems, Inc., is a networking solutions company, it was natural that we conceptualized and developed our authoring tools as online tools to engage a geographically distributed community[1]. Instructors that are invited to work on the assessment teams go through leader-led training, using online presentations and voice-based conference calls. The training covers topics related to Evidence Centered Design, task design and creation, and the use of the assessment authoring tool. These training sessions are now being formalized as video segments that can be downloaded for review or initial training by using the Video on Demand (VOD) technology over the World Wide Web.

Our assessment authoring tool is a Web-based application that content developers, editors, and administrators log into to assign or complete tasks, monitor progress, and create content and exams as needed. Reports are available to help monitor the progress of work through an assessment development process with specific workflow stages. For example, after questions are written, reviewers comment on recently completed tasks. Editors must acknowledge each comment that is written before tasks can be passed on to subsequent phases in content development. These types of workflow processes are intended to facilitate activities similar to "passing the first drafts around." When appropriate, groups meet in an online forum and share a common view of the application to discuss certain questions that are deemed unusually suitable or unsuitable.

Review and Feedback

In addition to involving academy instructors directly in the content authoring, focus groups and preliminary training sessions are held in which instructors validate the assessment content in a special preview mode. In this view, instructors are presented the questions and asked to answer them. Data on their responses are collected (again, easily accomplished in an online situation) and analyzed to determine where instructors differed in opinion on the correct answer. This allows identification of possibly problematic tasks before they are placed on scored assessments. We are careful not to indicate the intended correct answer in this mode, because we have found that such review tends to lead to greater acquiescence to the original answer.

Despite these many methods to ensure quality before the exams go live, we still have an online and call-center-based help desk. Instructors can open a help desk ticket online to raise concerns or ask for additional information. Personnel focused on maintaining this feedback loop pass concerns back to the content development team for appraisal and possible action. These tools for receiving feedback and communicating to customers are all Web-based, allowing us to employ a large part-time contingent that is geographically distributed. The absence of these tools would lead to an enormous amount of time and expense for content management and individual communication.

Complexity

Having established clear goals regarding the purpose and scope of the assessments (claims) and having enlisted and supported instructors in the endeavor (collaboration), the next aim is to create sufficiently complex and appropriate tasks to elicit the desired evidence of student knowledge and skills.

Figure 2. Schematic of Four Process Model for assessment delivery

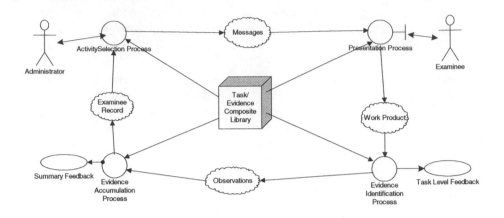

The world has changed dramatically because of computers and computer networks. Using the World Wide Web, the presentation and collection of complex information can occur in remote and under-resourced locations as well as in easily accessible population centers. By using advanced server technologies as well as sophisticated presentation and scoring approaches, the academy program is providing state-of-the-art e-learning to students around the world. Assessments in the academy program are composed of tasks that can be as simple as asking a multiple choice or fill-in-the-blank question or as complex as troubleshooting a simulated network.

The delivery system used in the Networking Academy Program follows the architectural elements of the Four Process Model suggested in the ECD framework (Almond, Steinberg, & Mislevy 2002). This view divides the delivery aspects of assessment into four components, as illustrated in Figure 2. Task selection concerns the choices about what the examinee will be presented. This may be as simple as a rule to show the next question or may be based on a complex mathematical model of examinee knowledge and dispositional states. The next process is called *presentation,* which considers the display of information to the examinee and the capture of information from the examinee. Behrens, Reinert, Mislevy, and Levy, discuss how the digitization of psychological representations and activities offers new opportunities to exploit computing in this realm.

The result of the presentation process is a work product that must be examined and scored. This process is called *response processing* or *evidence identification* and constitutes the third of the four processes. The ECD literature discusses the idea of looking for features in the work product and characterizing the work product according to one or more observables. Observables are variables that characterize some dimension of the work, such as correctness or efficiency. In this approach, most multiple choice questions are scored on a single observable of correctness. However, more complexity is relatively easy to add. For example, questions can be written with scoring rules such that if a student chooses option A, he or she may receive 1 point each for correctness and efficiency, while option B may represent an answer that receives 1 point for correctness and 0 points for efficiency. In some cases, multiple choice multiple answer questions are scored by using both binary (right/wrong-0/1) and partial credit observables (0-number possible).

By creating a delivery architecture that allows for multiple observables, a wide door of possible information can become available. This is an important and fundamental shift in delivery and data architecture, because it moves the basic unit of analysis from "the item" to a scoring result on a task. This offers room for growth as presentation processes become increasing complex and end users look for correspondingly complex scoring information.

The fourth process is called *evidence accumulation*. It is the statistical process of combining information from all the observables and updating the ability and student models. Evidence Centered Design includes a comprehensive use of Bayesian inference networks for thinking about statistical information in the assessment context (cf. Jensen, 1996; Mislevy, Almond, Yan, & Steinberg, 1999).

A Complex Example

Although the delivery portions of the Networking Academy systems have been designed around the Four Process Model and allow complex scoring of any task, we are currently in the process of extending this to include complex tasks that occur in simulated network microworlds. In this scenario, an instructor activates an exam that is denoted as containing network simulations. The learning management system then passes the examinee to the delivery system, which passes the examinee to an external simulation and scoring application. The movement between these systems is completely hidden to the examinee, who does not know that multiple computing environments are involved. The student is presented with a diagram of a computer network, a statement of a problem with the network, and access to a network simulation that most examinees would not be able to detect is a software simulation of a computer network (the presentation process). Figures 3 and 4 depict one version of the interface as it may appear to an examinee in this context. Note the tabs for navigating the different types of information required and the different parts of the network involved in the simulation.

After the task is completed, the relevant states of the network and information from any relevant activities of the student are examined by automated scoring rules (the evidence identification process). These give values to the multiple observables, diagnostic feedback is created, and this information is passed back to the delivery software, which will be shown to the student in his or her own, and the instructor's grade book when desired. These attributes are summarized as needed (the evidence accumulation process).

Williamson, Bauer, Steinberg, Mislevy, and Behrens (in press) describe research in the application of the principles of ECD and the Four Process Model technology that led to online performance-based assessments in the Networking Academies. Levy and Mislevy (in press) discuss the development of statistical models using Bayesian

Figure 3.User interface as it appears for networking task that uses simulator when the user has clicked on the "description" tag. The bottom half of the interface is constant, regardless of the tab chosen.

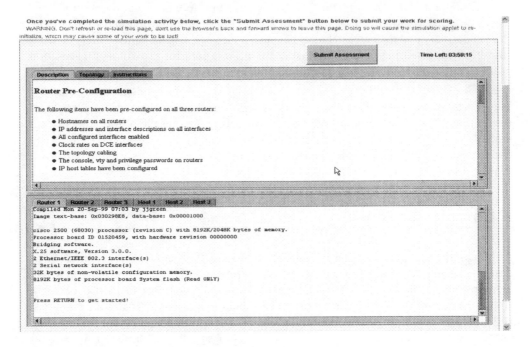

Figure 4. Top half of user interface for networking tasks using simulator when user has chosen the "Topology" tab

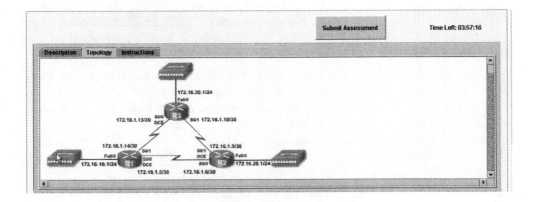

Inference Networks to support such rich data, while DeMark and Behrens (in press) report on efforts to statistically validate complex scoring rules from open-ended performance-based tasks.

Contextualization

Given appropriately complex tasks to make the desired claims about students in English, the Networking Academy Program translates and localizes curricular and assessment content to other languages. Translation concerns mapping meaning from one linguistic system to another. Localization concerns expressing language in a manner that meets the intent of the original author while making it appropriate for the local context. For example, a question about running network cables through walls in the United States may reference the common building material called "drywall". Drywall is not a universal building material, and a direct translation would not be meaningful to many examinees outside of the United States. Accordingly, the content needs to be localized to reference building material appropriate to the many local contexts in which the academy program works.

Computing Issues

The most important aspect of localizing assessment or curricular content from a computational perspective is to plan ahead and build systems with an awareness of the complexity that may come ahead. For example, although many computing environments now support the display of non-English characters, not all systems support pictorial languages that require double-byte representation, such as Chinese or Japanese. Likewise, a system may support individual characters in Arabic but may not have appropriate mechanisms to display from right to left as required by the end user.

Apart from the typographic issues in computing, languages may differ dramatically in the size of the display needed to communicate equivalent meaning. For example, the phrase "wiring closet" in English has 13 letters, while the corresponding token in German is "verdrahtung wandschrank." Such differences can lead to great difficulty in the localization of labels on graphics or Web pages. Although the English word may fit on the graphic, the localized word may not. Accordingly, the computing systems need to allow not only for easy manipulation between languages but also for editing and revision as needed.

Content Issues

Even if the computational issues are sufficiently addressed, an equally insidious difficulty comes from the improper translation of assessment content. To address this difficulty, we instruct native speakers in the target non-English language in the basics of task design and employ them as content validators in the same way the English content is validated. This involves a process of exporting exams to translators from

English, allowing translation in the target language, and then importing the translated content back into the assessment authoring and content management tool. Next, validators fluent in the target language and subject-matter experts in the curriculum review the translated tasks and track possible errors. An assessment professional with international experience consults with the validation team, and final edits are made. A final deployment QA occurs before the exam goes live to make sure scoring rules, presentational aspects of the tasks, and supporting materials such as exam names are all displaying or acting properly.

Numerous logistical issues need to be anticipated. For example, if two exams have overlap in content, the system should be able to know which items have already been translated and which have not. In our authoring and content management system, the exporter checks to make sure no previously translated items are sent out for translation again.

Central to the localization process is the idea that literal translation is not the goal, but rather that the translator should work to be authentic to the intent of the original task writer. Here, again, the online tools are used so the validators can log in from their home countries and the progress of the work can be monitored by geographically distributed teams. Reports created at the time of the import of translated material provide metrics for the number of tasks translated and the number of words across all the tasks. These help monitor costs for translation as well as provide the first level of process checking.

Computation

Despite the extensive design and review work discussed in the preceding section, there is no substitute for analysis of performance data. Because the delivery systems maintain the responses to all exams, we have the opportunity and responsibility to statistically track the quality and difficulty of assessment tasks and their aggregation in specific exams. To accomplish this, a largely automated process is used to extract data, compute statistics, and analyze data collected from all participating schools. Following our Internet-centric strategy, results are stored, searchable, and accessible through Web-based tools.

Despite 50 years of startling computing advances, most software for measurement and psychometrics continues to emphasize individual point-in-time exams whose description needs to be input by hand. This model is quite different from the ongoing production model of thousands of schools operating continually around the world. To deal with this disparity, we have created a number of scripts that automatically read the appropriate data and write the computer code needed to obtain the desired statistical results. Additional scripts submit the programs for processing and run follow-up programs that process results and post them on the Internet. After this is done, content experts designing subsequent tasks or forms have a library of information about item performance that can be used to support decision making.

For example, the graphic displayed in Figure 5 is a series of Item Characteristics Curves following the display suggested by Lord (1980) with the addition of the fact that the

Figure 5. Graphical interface of ICC map presented on the Internet for remote task designers to view. Example items depicted are not from Networking Academy exams.

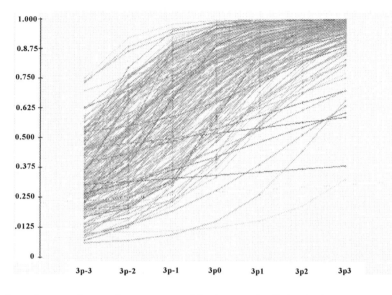

display is an interactive exploratory graphic that can be linked with other data for rapid exploration (Behrens, 1997; Behrens & Smith, 1996; Behrens & Yu, 2003). By clicking on one of the lines in the graphic, the user can obtain the item identifier and background information regarding the item. Such a display is created with relatively little human involvement, though, of course, any model-based approach requires human oversight and judgment. Classical statistics (which are not model based) typically require dramatically less oversight.

Using these automated scripts and programs, we believe we have freed the psychometricians from much of the tedious programming and have allowed them to spend time on model refinement and consultation with end users. This is possible because the data are collected in digital format on the World Wide Web, and our use of Web servers allows remote access of these many results. Furthermore, the transformation of this type of information into easily interpreted graphics or other representations helps bring the content expert into conversations about task performance in ways not previously available.

Communication

Although the collection and analysis of information regarding student performance is important, its value is determined by its use to relevant stakeholders. As noted in the previous section, a key element of our statistical computing strategy is the availability of the statistical results to task designers using the World Wide Web. Likewise, we see the *communication* of student results as an essential aspect of online assessment.

All the complexity in design, construction, and analysis is useless if results are not communicated in a way that the end user finds useful.

In the Networking Academy Program, this means making sure reporting and interpretation aids are available for students, instructors, and administrators. For students, exam results are presented within a few seconds of task completion. Assessment-level reports provide the percentage correct and, at times, characterizations of performance according to predetermined proficiency levels: novice, partially proficient, proficient, and advanced. These categories are chosen by a team of instructors and are given as guidelines, not as invariant dictates. These proficiency categories were established to help schools create pre-post descriptions of shifts in proficiency. In some simulation-based performance assessments, students are also given detailed diagnostic feedback reports that point out specific strengths and weaknesses in their performance.

For instructors, a comprehensive grade book is available with detailed scoring and performance information on each of their students. The grade book functions at three levels. The top level of the grade book lists students by rows and exams by column, with percent correct in the cells. When an instructor clicks on a column heading representing an exam, he or she drills down to the exam details page, which summarizes performance with rows for students and columns for tasks, again with an indication of level of performance in each cell. This is typically an integer number, such as 0 for no credit, 1 for binary credit, or a larger integer such as numbers from 2 to 6 for partial-credit items.

A third level of the grade book is obtained by clicking on the task header in the exam details page. This brings the instructor to the item information page. This page presents the content of the task and the scoring rules. In a straightforward multiple choice task, the scoring rules may be as simple as "Option D is correct; all others are wrong" or may include more detailed scoring rules for more complex tasks. For example, in a network troubleshooting task, the scoring rule may say, "Three points are given if Computer A can communicate with Computer B."

Although grade book data are automatically filled in for instructors, instructors have the flexibility to add additional columns for their own exams and to apply weight to different exams according to their preference. All students must complete a course feedback evaluation at the end of each course.

For administrators, online reports are available by class or across classes, summarizing students' performance as well as course-related comments and student feedback about class activities. By combining all these different types of assessment activities, the program supports immediate instructional goals and the more global policy and accountability needs of an educational institution.

Coordination

Like all educational activities, assessment is embedded in a larger context. In the context of the Cisco Networking Academy Program, the capstone certification exams provide a valuable goal for the students. The widely recognized industry certifications are obtained independently from the assessment system of the Networking Academy

Program. However, for certification exams administered by Cisco Systems, Inc., it opens the possibility of a comprehensive assessment ecosystem linking the certification and curriculum programs. In the cases where the academy curricula lead to certification exams, these two systems are linked in three ways. First, the exams are linked conceptually insofar as they follow the same ECD model and flow from the same claims. Second, they are linked developmentally insofar as there is considerable overlap in the staff developing the curricular and capstone exams. Third, the item pools are linked statistically through statistical analysis of person and item equating. These processes help ensure comprehensive alignment of the curricula and assessment activities. The goal of this approach is to make sure that the in-class assessments are aligned with the external capstone assessments. By working across all stages of assessment, we aim to avoid disconnections between classroom and capstone activities.

Summary

In our journey to create a comprehensive and global online educational assessment system, we have emphasized assessment activities around the seven *C*'s: claims, collaboration, complexity, contextualization, computation, communication, and coordination. Each one of these emphases has led to the construction of Web-based tools and processes that have provided access to human resources around the globe, great gains in efficiency, and advances in community making by opening doors to involving individuals across geographic and political borders.

We believe that, at present, most assessment activity is largely constrained by continued thought in terms of pre-computer-based assessment, and we are just beginning to have a small idea of the real extent of the possibilities for online assessment. As the world continues to become more digital and representations and tasks continue to be more natural in digital situations (e.g., on the computer), we will see a revolution in the sophistication of computing to bring rich tasks, rich scoring, and rich information to students around the globe via the Internet (cf. Behrens, Mislevy, & Bauer, 2001).

In the final account, online assessment is first and foremost assessment, and we must remember that all the computational sophistication available is unimpressive if the design, development, and analysis of assessment tasks and data do not lead to the valid inferences desired. As assessment professionals continue to become more Web savvy, we must keep our eye on the logic of good assessment practice.

References

Almond, R. G., Steinberg, L. S., & Mislevy, R. J. (2002). Enhancing the design and delivery of assessment systems: A four-process architecture [Electronic version]. *Journal of Technology, Learning, and Assessment, ý(5).*

Behrens, J. T. (1997). Principles and procedures of Exploratory Data Analysis. *Psychological Methods, 2,* 131-160.

Behrens, J. T., & Yu, C. H. (2003). Exploratory Data Analysis. In Schinka, J. A., & Velicer, W. F. (Eds.). *Handbook of Psychology. Volume II: Research Methods in Psychology* (pp. 33-64). New York: Wiley & Sons.

Behrens, J. T., Mislevy, R. J., Bauer, M., Williamson, D. W., & Levy, R. (in press). Introduction to Evidence Centered Design and lessons learned from its application in a global e-learning program. *International Journal of Testing.*

Behrens, J. T., Mislevy, R. J., & Bauer, M. (2001, August). Future prospects for assessment in the online world. Paper presented at the *University of Maryland Conference on Assessment and Cognition,* College Park, MD.

Behrens, J. T., Mislevy, R. J., Bauer, M., Williamson, D. W., & Levy, R. (in press). Introduction to evidence centered design and lessons learned from its application in a global e-learning program. *International Journal of Testing.*

Behrens, J. T., Reinert, P., Mislevy, R. J., & Levy, R. *Assessment design in an age of digital information and computing.* Manuscript submitted for publication.

Behrens, J. T., & Smith, M. L. (1996). Data and data analysis. In D. C. Berliner & R. C. Calfee (Eds.), *Handbook of Educational Psychology,* 945-989.

Behrens, J. T., & Yu, C. H. (2003). Exploratory data analysis. In J. A. Schinka & W. Velicer (Eds.), *Handbook of Psychology. Volume II: Research Methods in Psychology* (pp. 33-64). New York: Wiley.

DeMark, S., & Behrens, J. T. (in press). Using statistical natural language processing for understanding complex responses to free-response tasks. *International Journal of Testing.*

Levy, F., & Murnane, R. J. (2004). *The new division of labor: How computers are creating the next job market.* Princeton, NJ: Princeton University Press.

Lord, F. M. (1980). *Applications of item response theory to practical testing problems.* Hillsdale, NJ: Earlbaum.

Mislevy, R. J., Steinberg, L. S., & Almond, R. G. (2003). On the structure of educational assessments. *Measurement: Interdisciplinary Research and Perspectives, 1,* 3-62.

Murnane, R. J., Sharkey, N. S., & Levy, F. (2004). A role for the Internet in American education? Lessons from the Cisco Networking Academies. In P. A. Graham & N. G. Stacey (Eds.), *The knowledge economy and postsecondary education: Report of a workshop* (pp.127-158). Washington, DC: National Academies Press.

Porter, M. E., & Kramer, M. R. (2002). The competitive advantage of corporate philanthropy. *Harvard Business Review, 80*(12), 56-68.

Williamson, D. M., Bauer, M., Steinberg, L. S., Mislevy, R. J., & Behrens, J. T. (in press). Design rationale for a complex performance assessment. *International Journal of Testing*.

Endnote

[1]   Oftentimes people refer to such groups as ours as *virtual*. We prefer to describe our teams as *geographically distributed* instead, because *virtual* connotes an attempt to recreate something that is otherwise more real. We believe our teams are already perfectly real, differing primarily in geographic proximity.

Chapter XVIII

Feasibility Studies on Transitioning Assessment Programs from Paper and Pencil to CBT Delivery

Sandra Greenberg, Professional Examination Service, USA

I. Leon Smith, Professional Examination Service, USA

Abstract

A wide range of decision points is described in determining if, how, and when an assessment program should be transitioned from paper and pencil administration to computer-based delivery. The key factors in making effective strategic policy decisions regarding a transition are described on the basis of experiences gained in conducting feasibility studies over the past decade. The feasibility study is conceptualized as a five-phase, partially sequential process in which information learned in one phase can trigger reinterpretation of previous understandings and impact directions taken in subsequent phases. No claim is made that the conduct of a feasibility study will guarantee a seamless transition; instead, a strategic roadmap is provided for navigating bumps in the transition road.

Introduction

The sponsoring agencies (sponsors) of assessment programs frequently espouse the fallacy of simple substitution when thinking about shifting the delivery of examinations from paper and pencil to computer-based testing (CBT). The fallacy goes something like this: "By going to CBT, all costs and concerns associated with paper and pencil administration go away. We simply substitute the computer for paper and pencil and we can keep all our regular procedures and costs the same." This way of thinking is clearly unrealistic, for reasons described in this chapter.

Even as the applications of computer technologies have changed the way we live, work, and play, we have come to realize that the changes affect not just *what* we do, but *how*, *when*, and *where* we do it. For example, making a simple transition from the paper and pencil administration of an assessment to CBT delivery can impact what we assess, how we design the assessment, when we administer the test, where we administer the test, and importantly, how and when scores or the status of pass or fail are communicated to the candidates and other stakeholders. These considerations will also impact the proverbial question "How much will it cost?" and its answer.

This chapter identifies a wide array of decision points to be considered in determining if, how, and when to transition an assessment program to CBT. Relying on the experience gained in the conduct of multiple CBT feasibility studies conducted over the past 10 years, we illustrate the key factors to consider in making effective strategic policy decisions about the transition. Note, however, that this chapter does not claim to provide instruction about making a seamless transition to CBT; instead, it provides a roadmap for navigating bumps in the transition road.

An overall approach to the conduct of CBT feasibility studies is presented, including the expertise required to formulate the major study questions to be addressed, to obtain meaningful input from experts and providers, and to synthesize and evaluate this input in developing the CBT feasibility report, including recommendations, cost estimates, and timelines, if appropriate.

Technical and implementation issues are largely bound together. We have learned in evaluating options for CBT that a transition may be attainable only at a cost that outweighs the benefits. Accordingly, we describe many variables that must be considered in the transition of each of the assessment components. Equally important, however, is the ability to understand the interrelatedness of the components, the overall program context, and the needs and interests of the major stakeholders of the program.

The chapter presents our real-world experiences in dealing with the computerization of large-scale assessment programs in order to demonstrate how a project team can synthesize a variety of elements to produce a realistic appraisal of the transition to CBT. The examples are based on feasibility studies conducted for the sponsors of three high-stakes licensure and certification programs in the professions. One program administered only a multiple choice examination (Professional Examination Service, 2000). The second program administered an essay and short-answer examination in addition to the multiple choice examination (American Institute of Certified Public Accountants, 1999). The third program administered a performance examination in addition to a multiple choice examination and a simulation examination (Board of Certification, 2004). As might be expected, a feasibility study that considers the transition of multiple examination components is more complex than one that concerns transition of one multiple choice examination from paper and pencil administration to CBT delivery.

We describe procedures designed to facilitate the following processes: (a) the investigation of the impact of CBT on candidates and other key stakeholders, including state boards, professional and membership associations, and education and training programs; (b) the evaluation of vendors' capabilities with regard to the delivery and scoring of examinations; and (c) the integration of all information, leading to the development of a recommendation about the transition—including either a *go* or a *no-go* decision.

Feasibility Study Process

A feasibility study is conducted through a five-phase, partially sequential process. Although the five components of the study are described as phases, they are largely synchronous and interconnected. In fact, they are probably more accurately portrayed as points on a feedback loop; for example, the information gathered from one source will impact the direction of the questioning of other sources.

Phase 1: Strategic Planning with the Sponsor

In the first phase, the objectives are to clarify the expected outcomes of the study, locate key sources of information, and identify similarities and differences in the beliefs and expectations of key stakeholders.

Regardless of the specific nature of the sponsor's examination program, a comprehensive feasibility study should target four areas for investigation:

1. The technical viability of the computerized examination, including a psychometric evaluation of the examination model underlying each component of the examination program (for example, the multiple choice, the simulation, the constructed-response, and/or the performance components)

2. Stakeholder reactions to computerization of the testing program, including the reactions of members of the sponsor's board of directors and committees, candidates, members of the profession, and state boards

3. Timeframes for computerizing the examination, including milestone dates and key deliverables in order to implement the transition

4. Financial viability of CBT delivery, including costs to develop the required numbers of items (test questions) and examination forms, to computerize the examination (including hardware and software), to administer and score the examination, and to report examination results to the relevant parties

Sponsors usually have a definite conception about the transition to CBT. For example, they may want to administer the current examination *just as it is,* modify the content and format of the current examination, or deliver the examination more frequently—either daily or within prescheduled windows. Each *want* impacts the assessment of psychometric acceptability, stakeholder reaction, timeframes, and financial viability.

Gathering information from key decision makers (such as the sponsor's board of directors) can surface similarities and differences in the personal perceptions and understandings of the people who will make the final decision about the transition. In one case, about half of the board members strongly supported CBT on the assumptions that the current type of examination would be less expensive to develop and administer and that the fees charged to candidates could be reduced. The remaining board members supported CBT on the assumptions that enhanced item types could be introduced into the examination and that candidates would be willing to pay more for a *better* and more frequently administered examination. One goal of the CBT feasibility study for this sponsor was to investigate the assumptions being made and provide feedback to the decision makers so that a final determination could be based on a realistic appraisal of the situation.

We have used both telephone interviews and focus panels with a sponsor's board members to verify support for the proposed CBT examination, and document their perceptions about such issues as the ease of the transition, the costs of the transition and implementation phases, the advantages and disadvantages of CBT, and the beliefs and expectations of the candidates.

Board members may vary widely in their degree of support for a proposed CBT examination, ascribing advantages to CBT that may be more or less realistic. They may correctly or incorrectly believe that the majority of candidates share a common set of understandings about CBT. Knowledge of the differences in views among these key stakeholders at the beginning of the study is crucial in developing consensus as the study proceeds. After consensus has been achieved regarding the proposed CBT examination, the four areas of investigation identified earlier in this section can be evaluated in a reasonably straightforward manner. Lack of consensus suggests that the feasibility study should be broadened to include the investigation of alternative *wants* in regard to the proposed CBT examination.

Phase 2: Extended Data Gathering

In this phase, the objective is to gather information from subject-matter experts in areas such as psychometrics, the use of multiple types of assessment events (multiple choice examinations, simulations, performance examinations, etc.), and CBT delivery systems, including both hardware and software components. In addition, it is critical to identify and document the perceptions and concerns of key stakeholders other than the members of the sponsor's board of directors. Resolving areas of conflict involving board members and other stakeholders is important in ensuring the success of any transition.

Extended data gathering must first begin with the verification of all information and assumptions regarding the current examination components. Exhibit 1 lists general and specific information to be verified about the current examination program.

Exhibit 1. Information to be verified about the current examination program

General Information
- Current total testing time per candidate
- The sequence of events involved in current candidate registration and testing
- The use of scheduling software for the administration of the current testing program
- The number of candidates in the testing system
- The number of candidate retries permitted per year, and in total
- The average number of total tries per candidate
- The percentage of candidates who currently retest as frequently as is permissible
- In the case of multiple examination components, the number of first-time candidates who pass one or more but not all components of the examination
- The percentage of candidates who drop out of the testing process before passing all components of the examination

Specific Information
- Number of operational and pretest items on each examination
- Number of different forms of the examination in use each year
- Number of pretest blocks administered in connection with each form
- Total number of operational and pretest items in the bank
- Psychometric characteristics of each item in the bank, including item statistics and usage history, in relation to item exposure rules
- Psychometric characteristics of the examination forms, including evidence of content validity and reliability
- Strengths and weaknesses of the bank in regard to each category in the test specifications
- Anticipated volume of candidates, including fluctuations in the annual scheduling cycle and the potential for changes in candidate numbers
- Number of administration dates each year
- Number of sites used to administer the examination on each date
- Item and examination development and review procedures, including the use of operational and pretest items, and the percentage of overlap between forms
- Evaluation of recently administered examination components to determine the degree to which the various components provide overlapping and/or redundant information
- Psychometric characteristics of each examination form, including reliability and validity
- In the case of multiple examination components, comparability of components in regard to content coverage, scoring, and standard setting
- Time and resources required to develop each item and each examination form (including all travel and per diem costs for staff, volunteers, consultants, and contractors)
- Time and resources required to administer each examination via paper and pencil (including all proctoring costs, room rentals, shipping, etc.)

The goal of this phase of data gathering is to verify the resources required to support the current examination program. This information is used as a benchmark against which any proposed CBT examination program information can be compared. If the current examination program includes only a multiple choice examination, then the collection of information is far easier than with a program including multiple examination components. It has also been our experience that obtaining accurate information about the current cost of line items such as item development, examination construction, scoring, and reporting is not easy. When a sponsor develops multiple examination components, pinpointing the cost of individual line items becomes even more complex.

Key Decision Points and Assessment of Stakeholder Perspectives

In determining the feasibility of implementing CBT, a sponsor must make key decisions concerning the form and content of the examination and the manner in which it is to be delivered. Six key decision points are required: (a) selection of a testing model, (b) selection of a CBT administration model and score-reporting schedule, (c) selection and implementation of item calibration procedures and the construction of pre-equated examinations, (d) use of eligibility requirements to facilitate timely scheduling, (e) selection of item types and enhanced formats, and (f) selection of CBT vendors. It is also critical that stakeholder perspectives be identified and considered with regard to the six key decision points.

In some cases, a sponsor makes initial decisions about one or more of these key decision points. Our experience suggests, however, that information about all the points, in addition to the stakeholders' perspectives, must be considered prior to making final decisions about each point. Accordingly, the collection of information in Phase 2 is a dynamic and iterative process.

Selection of a Testing Model

Currently, at least six different testing models are available for the administration of multiple choice examinations. Brief descriptions of six different testing models follow (Hadidi, Swanson, & Luecht, 1999; Luecht, 1998; Mills & Stocking, 1996; Parshall, Spray, Davey, & Kalohn, 1998; Van der Linden, 1998; Wainer & Kiely, 1987). All the models have useful features and limitations and may be employed in a CBT environment.

1. **Linear (L):** This model consists of the computer administration of one or more fixed forms that are directly analogous to paper and pencil multiple choice tests. Items may be administered in randomized order, but all candidates taking a form will see the same set of operational items. Different forms of a linear examination may contain overlapping operational items. Individual scores are provided.

2. **Domain Sampling (DS):** This model is very similar to the linear model, except the number of forms is much larger. The large number of forms is made possible by the use of automated test assembly procedures to construct multiple forms to

the same content and statistical specifications. Forms are generally assembled in advance so that they may receive the usual test form reviews. Again, candidates taking a form will see the same set of items, but many fewer candidates see each form. As with the linear examination, forms may have item overlap, though the larger the item pool, the more limited the overlap. Individual scores are provided.

3. **Computer-Adaptive Testing (CAT):** The test is tailored to each candidate. After an initial item is administered, a candidate responding correctly to the first item will receive a more difficult item, while a candidate responding incorrectly will receive a less difficult item. Testing continues in this way, with each successive item chosen to provide the most information about the candidate's ability. Administration may continue for a fixed number of items or may be ended when the estimate of the candidate's ability is sufficiently precise for confidence about the score to be assigned.

4. **Computer Mastery Testing (CMT):** Short item sets (testlets) that are parallel in content and difficulty are randomly selected and successively administered until there is sufficient confidence about the status of a candidate as passing or failing according to a preset cutting point. In this model, the number of testlets administered is different for candidates of differing abilities, with the smallest number of testlets administered to those whose performance is furthest from the cutting point. Individual scores are not provided.

5. **Computer-Adaptive Mastery Testing (CAMT):** In this model, items are administered as in CAT, but testing continues only until a decision can be made about the pass/fail status of the candidate. The examinations typically have a minimum number of items that must be administered to all candidates but otherwise are variable in length, with shorter exams administered to candidates whose performance is furthest from the preset cutting point. Individual scores are not provided.

6. **Computer-Adaptive Sequential Testing (CAST):** Short item sets (modules) are developed with parallel content but different levels of difficulty. Testing is begun with a first-stage medium-difficulty test and a candidate is routed to an easier, more difficult, or (possibly) similar second-stage module, depending on performance at the first stage. A candidate would then be routed to a third-stage module in a similar fashion, depending on his or her performance at the second stage. Individual scores are provided.

We have developed a strategy to facilitate the selection and evaluation of a testing model. The method includes consideration of up to 24 features in comparing the models and making a final selection. Various psychometric-, stakeholder-, and cost-related drivers that interact with these features are identified and reviewed in the process of evaluating the testing models.

The features associated with the testing models are identified and organized within four topics—item and form development, test administration, psychometrics/validity, and cost. The features can be used to highlight the strengths and weaknesses of each testing model and facilitate decision making regarding the selection of the ideal or best approach.

1. **Item and Form Development:** Salient features are the size of the initial item pool, item maintenance and replacement requirements, pretest requirements, the review of forms, the use of diagnostic subscores, and the impact of changing test specifications. In evaluating the interactions between each testing model and the features related to item and form development, consider the following: statistical characteristics of the items; requirements for security; candidate volume; administration model; item calibration; content and statistical specifications; rate of pretesting loss; preferred test assembly procedures; program credibility and perception of fairness; and acceptability of testing program to candidates, sponsoring boards, and members of the profession.

2. **Test Administration:** Salient features are overall testing time, fixed versus variable length of the examination, candidate item review, item exposure, and item challenges. In evaluating the interactions between each testing model and the features related to test administration, consider the following: seat-time capacity of test delivery facility; requirements related to measurement precision and diagnostic subscores; pool size and item maintenance; administration model; perception of fairness; and acceptability to candidates, sponsoring boards, and members of the profession.

3. **Psychometrics/Validity:** Salient features are the degree of measurement precision required, item selection algorithms, decision accuracy, content coverage, scale score continuity, model robustness, and standard setting. Consideration should be given to the interactions between these features and testing purpose; test length; statistical specifications; candidate volume; item exposure; pool size; test validity; test specifications and anticipated rate of change in the content domain; perceived fairness; and acceptability to the candidates, sponsoring boards, and members of the profession.

4. **Cost:** Salient features are item development and pretesting requirements; form development; hardware and software systems requirements for CBT delivery, scoring, and reporting; and candidate education. For each testing model, consider interactions in terms of statistical and content specifications; security; item development procedures; the use of new item formats; candidate volume; item exposure; item replacement rate; administration model; test delivery facility requirements; perception of fairness; and acceptability to candidates, sponsoring boards, and members of the profession.

Each of the six testing models has different cost requirements, but all are likely to be more expensive than conventional paper and pencil testing. The critical issue in model selection is balancing the array of psychometric-, stakeholder-, and cost-related drivers.

In our experience, sponsors may make an initial decision to implement either the L or the CAT model, the former on the assumption that the item development and test construction efforts will not change as a result of a conversion to CBT, and the latter on the assumption that item exposure will be minimized, computer testing time will be reduced, and stakeholders will easily understand the model's complexities. Although the results of the data collected in Phase 2 may not change the initial decision about the testing model, the assumptions made about the model must be tested, verified, and/or modified.

Selection of a CBT Administration Model and Score Reporting Schedule

Traditionally, organizations computerize their multiple choice examinations because of the enormous benefits of enhanced accessibility. The implementation of either a windows testing or a continuous or on-demand testing CBT administration model for scheduling provides candidates with many more opportunities to test than a paper and pencil testing administration. Brief descriptions of the two administration schedules follow. Both schedules have useful features.

1. **Windows Testing:** Candidates are allowed to test at any time within predetermined windows; for example, each testing window may range from 1 to 2 days up to 6 to 8 weeks. A sponsor may schedule one or more windows per year. Candidates are permitted to take each available examination one time during each window. Generally, the length of each testing window and the number of testing windows per year is established with reference to the number of candidates testing each year and the ability of the CBT vendor to provide sufficient seat time for the volume of candidates. Finally, it is not necessary that each testing window be of the same duration.

2. **Continuous or On-Demand Testing:** Candidates are allowed to test at any time that the CBT center is open and seats are available. Should a sponsor select a continuous testing model, policies and procedures regarding frequency of retesting must be established.

Issues related to item exposure and examination security are clearly related to the selection of an administration schedule. Long testing windows and continuous testing lead to greater item exposure and increased risk to the security of the examination.

The selection of an administration schedule has a direct bearing on issues such as cash flow and staff workload. Experience reveals that candidates do not schedule their tests evenly across a window; rather, they tend to delay scheduling the testing event until the end of a window or even wait for the next or last window. Candidates also procrastinate with continuous testing because the administration has no closing date. Sponsors can exert some control over the process by establishing eligibility periods. After the eligibility period has expired, the candidate has to reapply and pay the per-candidate fee again. Finally, our experience suggests that more-able candidates test earlier in the window than less-able candidates—a factor that can influence standard setting for examinations that are not pre-equated prior to administration.

Regardless of the length of the testing window, the sponsor will have to establish a schedule for the transmission of examination data from the CBT vendor to the sponsor. We recommend that the sponsor receive performance data on a daily basis in order to monitor the CBT vendor's processes and quality control procedures.

The sponsor will also have to establish a score-reporting schedule. The obvious goal is to report scores in a very timely way, certainly not less timely than in the case of the paper and pencil administration. We recommend that scores be reported to candidates on a relatively frequent basis, for example, every two weeks. This practice, however, will be more costly than reporting scores once per month and more expensive than reporting scores after the large-scale, paper and pencil administration that may be offered once or twice per year.

The decision to transmit scores to candidates more or less frequently is generally influenced by a number of factors, including the use of pre-equated examinations with known passing points, expectations regarding the timeliness of score reporting, contingencies related to scheduling retake examinations, and the use of a preliminary score report provided to candidates at the CBT testing centers. Although considered unofficial, preliminary score reports provided by the CBT vendor are useful to candidates in that they alert failing candidates to the requirements to continue to study and schedule retake examinations. Although failing candidates may be disappointed, passing candidates should be pleased. Since, in most cases, an absolute majority of first-time candidates passes an examination, a greater number of these candidates will receive good news rather than bad news. In our view, selection of an effective CBT administration model and reporting schedule requires balancing tensions between the desire to make the examination more accessible to candidates and the need to protect against threats to the security of the sponsor's intellectual assets in relation to the financial resources available to support the additional costs of items and test forms needed for CBT.

Selection and Implementation of Item Calibration Procedures and the Construction of Pre-Equated Examinations

Sponsors modify the procedures they use to review items, assemble examinations, and score candidates' performances on the examinations to take full advantage of CBT. For example, sponsors may use Item Response Theory (IRT) to calibrate all the items in their banks and construct pre-equated examinations with known psychometric properties and pre-equated passing points. Through the implementation of IRT methodology, the difficulty level of multiple forms can be controlled and candidates can be given immediate test results. Alternately, if the items are not calibrated, the candidates' scores can be verified after a minimal amount of test data is collected, and candidates can be sent score reports on a timely basis. It would not be necessary to wait for the end of a testing window to review performance.

Model-fit studies should be conducted to determine which IRT model best fits the item data. It is necessary to assess how well each of the three commonly used IRT models, that is, the one-, two-, and three-parameter logistic models, fits the data. It is also important to evaluate the impact of any identified model-data misfit on the intended IRT applications, such as item-bank calibration and test equating. The goal of these studies is to create a pre-equated item bank that will support the construction and scoring of the multiple choice examination with a known passing point equated to the current passing point.

Decisions about the selection of item calibration procedures are largely determined on the basis of psychometric investigations regarding the item characteristics and the size of the candidate pool. The decision to pre-equate all examinations means, however, that all items must be pretested, and that pretest items as well as operational items will be included in all test forms. Accordingly, the number of items on an examination and the time required to complete the examination may increase. Alternately, sponsors may decide to reduce the number of operational items on an examination in order to maintain the overall test length and time.

Use of Eligibility Requirements to Facilitate Timely Scheduling

As long as the sponsor implements infrequent paper and pencil administrations, decisions about eligibility requirements may not be important. That is, exposure of the item bank and/or the test forms is minimal. There is, however, increased exposure of the item bank and/or the test forms in either a windows or a continuous testing administration model. Accordingly, the sponsor may wish to enhance eligibility requirements to reduce access to the intellectual assets of the agency and to ensure timely scheduling for legitimate candidates.

The introduction or tightening of eligibility requirements for an examination will affect the volume of candidates taking the examination and the cash flow to the sponsor. If access to CBT resources is limited, however, the authors recommend that the sponsor review the eligibility requirements for the examination in order to ensure that only those candidates who have completed all other licensure or certification requirements have scheduling preference. On the other hand, if the sponsor requires that candidates complete a non-CBT examination such as an oral interview or a performance-based test in addition to the CBT examination, the authors recommend that candidates be required to successfully complete the CBT component prior to scheduling any other component. By restricting access to the most labor-intensive examination components to those candidates who have successfully passed the CBT component(s), the sponsor can minimize the burden of administering nontraditional examinations.

Selection of Item Types and Enhanced Formats

The use of the computer to deliver examinations expands the types of items and the content that can be tested on an examination. Even within the context of the multiple choice examination, items can be enhanced through the use of graphics and audio to include still pictures and videos. New item types and enhanced item formats require the sponsor to implement new procedures for item development and review, item banking, examination construction, and scoring. Moreover, CBT vendors must be able to support the delivery of the new item types, and candidates must be provided with opportunities to become familiar with the new types. Customized tutorials and sample questions should be available at the CBT testing center and/or via the Internet. Finally, should the sponsor support the use of new item types, the academic community should be given the opportunity to preview them so that their students can become familiar with the new formats.

Selection of CBT Vendors

High-stakes examinations such as those associated with licensure and certification are administered under secure, proctored conditions in either special CBT commercial testing centers (known as bricks and mortar centers) or in a variety of networked centers, such as those located in colleges or other wired facilities. An essential element in the conduct of a feasibility study is the evaluation of the potential CBT vendors' capability of delivering the testing program. Exhibit 2 identifies the features to consider in gathering data from various CBT vendors.

Exhibit 2. CBT vendor interview topics

Key Topics for CBT Vendors
- Ability to administer various item formats, including graphically enhanced items and video clips
- Ability to administer and score examinations constructed by using various testing models
- Ability to administer examinations in English and other languages
- Availability of generic or customized tutorials for candidates
- Test item review features
- Number and location of testing centers available in relationship to geography of candidate population
- Availability of international testing centers (if required)
- Staffing configuration at testing centers, including the training of personnel
- Business model of testing centers: owner operated, franchised, or leased?
- Nature of all other businesses transacted at the testing center and their effects on security and seat time
- Uniformity of testing centers throughout the network regarding staff configuration, physical layout, and hardware and software
- Receptivity to the use of third-party software and test drivers
- Availability of portable sites for special test administrations
- Days and hours of operation
- Facilities for testing candidates requiring special accommodations mandated by the Americans with Disabilities Act
- Availability of scheduling software
- Availability of preliminary scoring and reporting
- Level of security, including candidate-to-proctor ratio, video surveillance, and the use of biometric identification
- Use of secure network and/or the Internet to deliver examinations
- Availability of special hardware and/or proprietary software and drivers
- Procedures for securely and reliably uploading and downloading data between sponsor and CBT vendor
- Data management and storage facilities
- Costs to deliver services, including seat time, publication, examination review and modification, special accommodations, and network delivery versus Internet delivery

Assessment of Stakeholder Perspectives

An essential element in the conduct of a feasibility study is the assessment of stakeholder reactions to the computerization of the testing program. Key stakeholders include current and recent candidates, volunteers (such as item writers and members of the examination development committee), education and training program directors, state regulatory agencies and board members, members of the profession, and employers.

Data may be collected in person through focus panels and interviews or impersonally through electronic or printed surveys. Evaluation of stakeholder perspectives requires

Exhibit 3. Information to be collected from key stakeholders

Current and Recent Candidates
- Advantages and disadvantages of current and proposed testing models, including frequency of test administration and availability of test sites and testing centers
- Knowledge of and experience with CBT
- Desire for immediate scoring and performance feedback
- Concerns about scheduling initial and retake examinations
- Perceptions about current and proposed fees
- Actual cost of current test (including testing fees, travel, per diem, and time off)
- Overall level of support for current and proposed testing models

Education and Training Program Directors
- Advantages and disadvantages of current and proposed testing models
- Relationship between test preparation initiatives and current and proposed test delivery schedule
- Relationship between curriculum content and both current and proposed content specifications
- Use of computer-based training or testing in education or training programs
- Perceptions about current and proposed fees
- Overall level of support for current and proposed testing models

State Regulatory Agencies
- State board policies and procedures impacted by proposed changes in delivery mode, test content, frequency of administration, and test fees
- Feasibility of the CBT alternative given the existing regulations in the state
- Procedures and time required to modify regulatory act, if necessary
- Overall level of support for current and proposed testing models

Members of the Profession
- Knowledge of and experience with CBT
- Overall level of support for current and proposed testing models

Employers
- Perceptions about current and proposed fees
- Perception regarding strengths and weaknesses of recently credentialed candidates
- Overall level of support for current and proposed testing models

careful description of the current paper and pencil examination and the proposed CBT examination. Exhibit 3 documents the logical areas of inquiry. Data collection efforts generally become more extensive when the sponsor proposes a CBT examination format that differs from the paper and pencil format.

Regardless of the data collection methodology, it is important to elicit a discussion of the strengths and weaknesses of the proposed CBT format as well as suggestions for modifying the proposed format. The discussion of strengths and weaknesses should reveal the components of the proposed CBT format that are most and least desirable. This strategy should also surface any confusions or misunderstandings about the CBT format so that clarification can be provided. The demographic and professional background of participants in each stakeholder group should be documented to ensure that all key constituencies are represented.

In our experience, the perspectives of the educators and training program directors are especially critical. We have found that these professionals have strong feelings about testing in general and about assessing their own students in particular. Moreover, as educators, they are likely to be among the most respected individuals in the profession, occupying key leadership roles and maintaining extended spheres of influence. It has also been our experience that educators may have perspectives that differ from those of the sponsor. For example, educators may support more or less stringent assessments than those currently implemented or proposed. In addition, they may support more extensive testing in the areas of interpersonal skills, work ethics, and attitudes — areas that are not typically the focus of licensure and certification examinations.

Phase 3: Integration of Data Gathered and Analysis of Costs and Timeframes

The focus of Phase 3 is on the integration of all information gathered in order to asses the following factors: (a) the technical viability of the computerized examination, (b) the level of stakeholder support for the proposed examination, (c) the timeframes for preparation and implementation of the transition, and (d) the costs of developing and implementing CBT. The outcomes of this phase include cost comparisons of continued delivery of the examination program in paper and pencil format versus delivery by CBT.

During Phase 3, the iterative aspects of the feasibility study become obvious. As described above, consensus among the key stakeholders regarding the proposed CBT examination means that the feasibility study can be conducted in a reasonably straight-forward manner. Lack of consensus suggests that the feasibility study should be broadened to include the investigation of alternative *wants*. For example, it may be necessary to investigate stakeholder reactions to more than one proposed testing model or CBT administrative model and reporting schedule. If the sponsor administers multiple examination components, it may also be necessary to investigate the utility of each component and the contributions each one makes to the final credentialing decision.

Support for the key decisions reached in Phase 2 and stakeholder acceptance of the proposed CBT plan impact the assessment of the technical viability of the examination as well as the projected timeline and costs. For example, the selection of a particular testing model, a CBT administration model, and a reporting schedule impact the level of human and financial resources required to develop, implement, and maintain the testing program. If the examination program includes more than one examination component, then the study must be expanded to investigate the utility of the separate components and/or the impact of modifying and/or combining the components.

In one investigation, the integration of findings from the CBT feasibility study resulted in the development of recommendations for the transition of one examination component to CBT and the discontinuation of a second examination component. Statistical analyses had been implemented to determine whether each component was independently contributing to sound credentialing decisions. Although these analyses might have been conducted at any time (and outside the realm of the CBT feasibility study), it became clear that only in the context of major changes (the transition from paper and pencil administration to CBT) could the utility of one of the examination components be investigated and a recommendation for discontinuation be put forward successfully.

In a different investigation, the feasibility study findings highlighted the desire of the stakeholders to enhance the existing multiple choice examination, using CBT technology to expand the range of content to be assessed. As a result, recommendations were developed to implement an L testing model, including complex scenario- or case-based test questions and enhanced graphical presentations in the stems of the items. The goal was to use multiple choice items to assess content that is more typically assessed with simulation items.

To determine the human and financial impact of the transition, it is necessary to finely delineate the terms and conditions of the proposed CBT program, including all aspects related to the key decisions. In general, the accuracy of the cost estimates for the proposed CBT examination will be limited by the accuracy of the cost estimates for the current program. All assumptions used to make the cost estimates should be documented, and all doubts about the cost estimates should be highlighted. We also recommend that sponsors conduct cash flow analyses in relation to anticipated CBT costs and projected candidate revenue, considering different configurations of candidate volume and scheduling under CBT.

The projected timeline and cost estimates interact with each other as well. For example, if more test items are required to support the development of additional forms of the examination with CBT, the sponsor may elect to speed up the production of new test items and examination forms or to maintain the current rate of production and delay the transition. Assuming that the sponsor can achieve certain economies of scale by intensifying current development efforts, it will be necessary to project per-item and per-examination development costs in the context of multiple development schedules.

Phase 4: Integration and Interpretation of Data to Identify Deal Breakers

One important outcome of Phase 3 is the development of a draft feasibility report, including the results of the initial investigations, interpretations, and recommendations. The focus of Phase 4 is on the review of the report by the sponsor to identify problems with the proposed CBT transition. At this time, the sponsor has a chance to verify the assumptions and interpretations that have been made and make both mid-course corrections and suggestions regarding the transition.

The draft report may contain deal breakers. Some state boards impose limits to the fees that can be charged to licensure candidates. Other state boards specify the mode of examination delivery in the regulatory act. In those cases, changing the fees charged to candidates or the delivery mode of the examination may require that the state board open the regulatory act governing the profession. We have seen instances wherein changes required in the regulatory act can take several years to implement. Although this type of revision need not be a deal breaker, remember that not all states move at the same speed, so it may be essential to modify the timeline.

More serious deal breakers relate to the psychometric evaluations of the proposed examinations. In one instance, the sponsor proposed an ideal CBT examination to replace a national examination that had exemplary psychometric characteristics. At face value, the ideal examination was appealing, as it included new item types and enhanced test formats that closely resembled the requirements of actual practice. However, investigation of the ideal examination raised serious security concerns because the items would be highly memorable thereby compromising the validity of the proposed examination program. It was also determined that it would be very difficult to develop, pilot test, and score enough new items to support the continuous testing model that the sponsor desired. This feasibility study resulted in a set of recommendations that enhanced the security of the examination program and facilitated the development of multiple items that were cloned from item templates.

Other serious deal breakers relate to recommendations to change the format of existing examinations or to combine multiple examination components. In one study, the sponsor desired to transition only the paper and pencil examination components to CBT. Results of various data-collection initiatives demonstrated strong support for the transition; however, the sponsor also administered a practical examination component that required face-to-face contact with the candidates. In the case of the practical examination, the results from the feasibility study were mixed. Some key stakeholders were not willing to eliminate the practical examination, although continuing to administer the practical component would have become problematic if the other examination components were delivered via CBT. In order to secure approval for the transition to CBT, the final recommendations for this sponsor had to address the revision of all procedures related to the practical examination component, including a shift in the responsibility for the systematic assessment of performance competencies to the education and training community.

Ideally, the identification of potential deal breakers should result in a revised transition plan—one that accounts for the needs of all key stakeholders and reflects a consensus opinion about moving forward. The revisions may focus on a modified timetable for implementation. Occasionally, deal breakers may highlight the need to rethink the transition. In that case, it may be necessary to examine and modify the key decisions developed in Phase 2 and then resolicit stakeholder perspectives about the revised plan.

Phase 5: Development and Presentation of a Feasibility Report, including a *Go* or *No-Go* Decision and Follow-Up Activities

The objective of the final phase of a feasibility study is the development and presentation of the feasibility report to the sponsor, at which time the agency may make a *go* or *no go* decision about the CBT transition. In our experience, the sponsor generally decides to go forward with the transition. The real focus in Phase 5, then, is on the terms and conditions of the transition. A timeline must be developed and announced, including dates for key milestones and deliverables. The sponsor's spending budgets must be revised to include expected expenditures across the duration of the transition and initial implementation phases. A detailed transition and implementation plan that is aligned to the approved recommendations contained in the feasibility report must be developed. Depending on the degree of consensus among the key stakeholders and the nature of the changes to the testing program, the timeline may be fast tracked. Similarly, the availability of human and financial resources may impact the speed of the transition. Finally, both candidate and professional acceptance must be secured, and the speed of transition may be impacted by the extensiveness of the educational outreach efforts implemented by the sponsor.

In the less likely event that the sponsor decides to not go forward with the CBT transition, the focus may turn to the development of other contingency plans—either modifying or enhancing the paper and pencil examination or reconceptualizing a future CBT transition.

Because the final report becomes the basis for the implementation plan, it is important to achieve consensus on the actual contents of the report, including the level of detail in regard to the documentation of the information gathering initiatives, the initial and modified recommendations for the transition, and the rationale for each of the key decisions. The actual contents of the report depend on the scope of the study and the number of examination components that are reviewed. We recommend, however, that the level of documentation be sufficient to support the rationale for each of the major changes in policy and procedure that the CBT transition will require.

References

American Institute of Certified Public Accountants. (September, 1999). *Final report of the conduct of a feasibility study for the computerization and implementation of a uniform CPA examination in fifty-four jurisdictions.* Retrieved October 5, 2004, from *http://ftp.aicpa.org/public/download/members/div/examiner/CICstudy.pdf*

Board of Certification. (2004). *Final report of the conduct of a feasibility study regarding the computerization of the testing program for the Board of Certification, Inc., for the athletic trainer.* Omaha, NE: Author.

Hadidi, A., Swanson, D., & Luecht, R. (April, 1999). Practical issues in using automated test assembly (ATA) for large scale testing. Paper presented at the annual meeting of the *National Council on Measurement in Education*, Montreal, Canada.

Luecht, R. (1998). Automated test assembly (ATA) in the era of computerized testing. *CLEAR Exam Review, 9*(2), 19-22.

Mills, C., & Stocking, M. (1996). Practical issues in large-scale computerized adaptive testing. *Applied Measurement in Education, 9,* 287-304.

Parshall, C., Spray, J., Davey, T., & Kalohn, J. (April, 1998). Computerized testing: Issues and applications. Training session presented at the meeting of the *National Council on Measurement in Education*, San Diego.

Professional Examination Service. (2000). *HRCI feasibility study report-recommendations, transition plans & timelines*. New York: Author.

Van der Linden, W. (Ed.). (1998). Optimal test assembly. *Applied Psychological Measurement, 22,* 195-302.

Wainer, H., & Kiely, G. (1987). Item clusters and computerized adaptive testing: A case for testlets. *Journal of Educational Measurement, 24,* 17-27.

About the Authors

Scott L. Howell is the assistant to the dean for the Division of Continuing Education at Brigham Young University (BYU), USA. He assisted BYU in launching its online learning and assessment initiative (1999-2003) as the director of a new Center of Instructional Design (CID). Dr. Howell is widely published and respected for his work in distance education and online assessment. He received his PhD in instructional science, specializing in assessment and measurement, an MS in community education, and a BS in business management.

Mary Hricko is an associate professor of libraries and information services at Kent State University, USA. She serves as the library director of the KSU Geauga Campus Library. She has published and presented numerous articles and papers on academic support services in distance education, information literary, and Web accessibility.

* * *

Helen Ashton is a lecturer in the School of Mathematical and Computing Sciences at Heriot-Watt University, UK. Her specific area of interest is in the application of technology in education, and she has worked on a number of projects in this area. She has a wide range of skills and experience in both the education and technology fields. Her current work includes research into the use of online assessment and the development of online assessments and online assessment systems.

Sally Askman's professional career in technology-based learning, management systems, and software spans two decades. Before joining the Bill & Melinda Gates Foundation, USA, as deputy director of education in December 2003, Sally ran a private consulting practice for eight years, focusing on technology-based projects to improve training, learning, and management processes for a variety of public and private sector clients. She received her BA in business administration from the University of Utah.

Kristin M. Bass is a postdoctoral fellow at the Berkeley Evaluation and Assessment Research Center at the University of California, Berkeley, USA. She received her PhD from the Combined Program in Education and Psychology at the University of Michigan and has been a research associate at the University of Pittsburgh's Learning Research and Development Center. She studies the application of cognitive psychology to educational measurement and is particularly interested in the development and implementation of formative classroom assessments. Her work has appeared in the *Journal of the Learning Sciences* and the *Elementary School Journal*.

Cliff Beevers, OBE has worked on the provision of computer-based resources for 20 years, directing many projects including MathWise and the prize-winning Computer-Aided Learning in Mathematics (CALM) and developing the Interactive Past Papers software. Cliff became a codirector of the Scottish Centre for Research into Online Learning and Assessment in 2000 and since then has led an ambitious research program to investigate the impact of the delivery of online summative assessment directly into Scottish schools. Cliff remains the assessment consultant to the Learning and Teaching Support Network for Mathematics, Statistics, and Operational Research.

John T. Behrens is senior manager of assessment development and innovation at Cisco Systems, Inc, USA. John sets the strategic direction for instructional, certification, and organizational assessment while overseeing the overall implementation of assessment-related activities such as the Cisco Networking Academy Program and the Cisco Certification Programs. Prior to joining Cisco, John was an associate professor of psychology in education at Arizona State University. John has overseen the deployment of 36 million classroom assessments and hundreds of thousands of certification exams. He has published chapters in a number of widely used psychology reference books along with articles in a range of educational, psychological, and statistical journals.

Albert D. Bethke is a senior research computer scientist at RTI, International, USA. He designs and implements Web applications, database systems, computer simulation models, and various other computer programs and applications. In addition, he supervises other programmers on various projects and prepares and reviews research proposal materials. For the past three years, Dr. Bethke has been the project director and programmer/analyst for the North Carolina Computer Adaptive Testing System project. Before coming to RTI, Dr. Bethke was a senior software engineer on the Common Lisp Programming Language team at Data General. Prior to that, he was an assistant professor at the University of Kansas in the Computer Science department. Dr. Bethke has a PhD in computer and communication sciences from the University of Michigan. He is a member of Sigma Xi, the scientific research society.

Kelly Burling is a psychometrician and educational consultant at the North Carolina Department of Public Instruction, USA. She oversees the psychometric aspects of North

Carolina's performance assessments and alternate assessments, including the North Carolina Computer Adaptive Testing System (NCCATS). She does additional work for the department as the project manager, researching issues in scaling as well as student and system reporting. Prior to working for North Carolina, Kelly was an educational research consultant and a researcher at the Harvard Center for International Development, where she investigated the impact of technology use in educational programs in developing countries. She has a master's degree in educational research and measurement from Boston College, where she is also currently a PhD candidate.

Maisie Caines is the faculty development specialist at College of the North Atlantic in Newfoundland, Canada. She collaborates with six other team members in the research, development, and demonstration of technology in online learning. In 2001, she became one of the first certified WebCT trainers in Canada. Maisie is currently a candidate for the Master of Arts in Distributed Learning (2005) from Royal Roads University in Victoria, British Columbia. She is also currently enrolled in the Bachelor of Post Secondary Education program at Memorial University of Newfoundland. Maisie holds a Post Secondary Instructor's Certificate from the Government of Newfoundland and Labrador.

Tara A. Collison is an educational psychologist with specializations in school psychology and research methodology, as well as computing and statistics. As manager of the metrics, reporting, and evaluation team within the Cisco Networking Academy Program, USA, Tara oversees all reporting and program evaluation with a focus on using data to drive decisions and improve the quality of the academy program. Her responsibilities include the design and development of public and internal reports, design and implementation of surveys used to gather customer feedback, and evaluation of success and effectiveness within the academy program.

Sarah DeMark is a manager in the assessment development and innovation group at Cisco Systems, Inc, USA. Sarah manages assessment development and implementation for the Cisco Certification Program. This role includes psychometric, design, and program management oversight. Sarah has worked with the certification program for 3 years. Prior to working with certifications, Sarah worked with Cisco's Networking Academy Program. Sarah received her PhD in educational psychology from Arizona State University, has been published in several journals and books, and has presented at many conferences.

Luke Duesbery is a licensed K-12 teacher and administrator. He holds a position as distance education specialist for the College of Education at the University of Oregon, USA, and serves as an adjunct instructor for Old Dominion University in Virginia. His research interests include the development of technologically enhanced large-scale testing environments, curriculum-based measurement, and perception issues in computer-based multimedia. He teaches courses in data-based decision making, the integration of technology into the classroom and school, and instructional multimedia.

Luke Fernandez, PhD, is a software developer at Weber State University. For the past three years his main vocational energies have been focused on developing and supporting Weber's secure testing infrastructures. Before coming to Weber he worked at Campus Pipeline, a Web portal company. He received his PhD from Cornell University. Luke's research has focused on the changing nature of higher education.

Leanne Ketterlin-Geller, PhD, is the director of research projects for behavioral research and teaching at the University of Oregon, USA, where she manages several federally funded research projects that address issues relating to the measurement of academic achievement. Additionally, Leanne serves as an assistant professor for the area of educational leadership. Her research interests include universal design for assessment and instruction, large-scale and classroom-based assessment, curriculum-assessment alignment, and teacher/administrator preparation and use of data for decision making. She has presented at local and national conferences and is published in leading journals in the areas of curriculum development and assessment systems.

Stephanie Gertz, PhD, currently works at Riverside Publishing, USA, where she specializes in analyzing state and national trends in assessment. Dr. Gertz has considerable experience in all phases of assessment, data design and analysis, educational research and evaluation, program development and evaluation, project management, proposal writing and development, and survey instrument development. She has also performed a number of evaluations of educational programs. She received her BA from Wellesley College and her MA and PhD from the University of Virginia.

David Graf is director of technology support services for the Fischler School of Education and Human at Nova Southeastern University in North Miami Beach, Florida, USA. He has an extensive range of experiences in higher education and a unique insight into the instructional design elements critical to the creation and delivery of successful online courses. From 1997 to 1999, Dr. Graf was the founding director of the Center for the Advancement of Teaching and Learning at Valdosta State University. His prior academic homes have been at the University of Wisconsin-Stevens Point, the University of Wisconsin-Stout, and Iowa State University. Dr. Graf has been involved with the Webct exemplary course project since its inception in 2000.

Sandra Greenberg is vice president of research and development at Professional Examination Service in New York, USA. In that role, Dr. Greenberg has conducted strategic planning studies for professions that license or certify practitioners, resulting in the development and implementation of new credentialing initiatives, enhanced techniques to assess competency, and revisions in regard to education and experience requirements. She has conducted numerous feasibility studies to evaluate the impact of the transition from paper and pencil testing to CBT.

Cheryl Hill is a psychometrician at RTI Health Solutions. Her four years of experience in instrument development include performing item calibration, item reduction, and test scoring. She has completed many psychometric evaluations of educational and health-related instruments, which involve examining factor structure, reliability, and validity. Ms. Hill has participated in both the assembly and evaluation of the North Carolina Computer Adaptive Testing System (NCCATS) program. She is currently pursuing her PhD in quantitative psychology at the University of North Carolina at Chapel Hill, USA.

G. Eric Jenson received his PhD from Utah State University in psychology with an emphasis in research and evaluation methodologies. Eric is currently a psychometrician for Thomson Prometric, USA, specializing in standard setting, item analysis, test objective development and form balancing. Before joining Thomson Prometric, Eric was responsible for creating measures to assess the work levels of university extension personnel and for directing the testing of inner city youth for evaluations of the Junior Achievement Program. Eric also holds degrees in social work/counseling and family and human development.

Mike Keppell is principal lecturer and head of the Centre for Integrating Technology in Education (CITIE) at the Hong Kong Institute of Education, Hong Kong. His role is to oversee an educational technology centre that focuses on online learning, media production (video, audio, photography), informational technology competencies, and research. His institute-wide role encourages staff and students to utilize educational technology to enrich the teaching and learning process. His research interests cover four areas: student-centered learning (problem-based learning, case-based learning, project-based learning, and online communities); multimedia design (conceptualizing, concept mapping, design processes); processes involved in optimizing the instructional designer-subject matter expert interaction; and knowledge management (project management, systems and processes). His current interests at the institute focus on technology-enhanced authentic learning environments, online communities, problem-based learning, and learner-centered assessment.

Dhaneshwar Lall is currently employed by the College of Engineering at Pennsylvania State University, USA, as an assessment coordinator with a focus on ABET accreditation. His interests include assessment of adults in postsecondary institutions, collaborative learning, and designing online systems in education. He is a doctoral candidate in instructional systems at Pennsylvania State University.

Sang Ha Lee is a doctoral candidate in educational psychology at Pennsylvania State University, USA, and has completed the Master of Applied Statistics as a concurrent degree. He earned his BS and MEd in mathematics education from the Korea National University of Education and taught mathematics in South Korea for eight years. He is currently completing his dissertation research on a goodness of fit index in hierarchical linear modeling.

Jon Margerum-Leys is an assistant professor of educational technology in the teacher education department at Eastern Michigan University, USA, one of America's leading teacher education institutions. Jon's work has appeared in the *Journal of Teacher Education,* the *Journal of Staff Development,* and the *Journal of Educational Computing Research.* Fellowships have included a Spencer Foundation research training fellowship through the University of Michigan, selection to the California School Leadership Academy, the California Technology Project, and the South Coast Writing Project. Jon's background includes seven years as a middle and high school teacher in New Hampshire and California.

Jan D. McCoy, PhD, is an assistant professor of teacher education at the University of Oregon, teaching courses in the use of technology in instruction and assessment. A former technology specialist serving at the school building, district, intermediate district, and state levels, he has broad experience in technology-based solutions for classroom instruction and assessment. His current work addresses the application of technological tools to social studies instruction and the development of simplified techniques for inclusion of computer-based and computer-adaptive testing at the classroom level. He has published and presented nationally on topics ranging from the use of multimedia in instructional delivery to curriculum and instructional alignment.

Lori McLeod is the director of psychometrics at RTI Health Solutions, USA. She has over 10 years of experience in instrument development for both educational and health-related applications. In addition, she has conducted many psychometric evaluations of paper-and-pencil and computer-administered instruments. These investigations have included the assessment of scale reliability, validity, and responsiveness. Dr. McLeod previously directed the psychometric procedures related to a large-scale admissions test (LSAT) and contributed to research in computerized adaptive testing. Dr. McLeod has supported the North Carolina Computerized Adaptive System (NCCATS) development from concept to working system.

Colin D. Milligan is an eLearning specialist with expertise in designing, authoring, and evaluating online learning materials. An overall theme in his work has been the appropriate use of technology and the importance of supporting all online teaching on sound pedagogical principles. Current work is focused on the educational use of simulations, the opportunities for integration of learning and assessment afforded by online delivery methods, and the role that learning technology standards can play in enhancing the learning process.

Dana Offerman, PhD, is the vice provost for assessment and institutional research at Capella University, USA. Dana is responsible for assuring that assessment initiatives align with university goals and needs, leading the development of annual and long-term assessment planning, and working with the professionals in the assessment office to advocate for assessment throughout the organization. Dana received her doctorate in higher education from the University of Wisconsin-Madison. Prior to joining Capella in 2001, she was a director of academic affairs in the University of Wisconsin System Administration.

Eliza Au Kit Oi is a senior lecturer in the creative arts department at the Hong Kong Institute of Education, Hong Kong. Her major studies in the university were painting (BEd), teacher education and development (MEd), and art education (PhD). She has substantial experience in planning and teaching preservice and in-service programs for secondary schools. She is also the coeditor of the newly established *Asia Pacific Journal for the Arts Education* in Hong Kong. Her research interests include metaphor, teacher reflection, and evaluation and assessment of the art teaching. She has published articles in art journals, book chapters, and conference proceedings.

Kimberly Payne is an instructional designer for Imedia.it, USA. Prior to her job at Imedia.it, she was a professional classroom educator. Kim received her master's degree in Instructional Technology from the University of Houston–Clear Lake. Mrs. Payne was the lead instructional designer for the 97B10 Web-based training. She recently completed the Installation Force Protection Project for the U.S. Army Intelligence Center and School, located at Fort Huachuca. Mrs. Payne has presented at Training and Learning Week 2003, the Distance Education Conference sponsored by Texas A&M's Center for Distance Learning Research, and the Interservice/Industry Training, Simulation, and Education Conference (I/ITSEC) 2004.

Kimberly Pearce is the manager of assessment, and her responsibilities include conducting and reporting original institutional research and program evaluation, managing and presenting externally conducted research, and coordinating research requests. Kimberly is currently a PhD candidate in the College of Education and Human Development at the University of Minnesota. Her previous work experiences include a research position at the Tucker Center for Research on Girls and Women in Sport and an instructor at the University of Minnesota and University of North Carolina-Chapel Hill.

Leslee Francis Pelton, PhD, is an associate professor in the Department of Curriculum and Instruction at the University of Victoria, Canada, where she teaches courses in mathematics education and technology in education. Her areas of interest include numeracy, problem solving, assessment, and technology applications to enhance learning. She has codeveloped the Enhanced Instructional Presentation model (EIP) and the Classroom Interaction System (CIS). Other areas of current research include mathematics curriculum analysis, impact of teacher knowledge, computer mediated learning, and gambling and numeracy.

Timothy Pelton, PhD, is an assistant professor in the Department of Curriculum and Instruction at the University of Victoria, Canada, where he teaches courses in mathematics education and technology in education. His research interests include numeracy, measurement, and the application of technology to enhance learning. He has codeveloped the Enhanced Instructional Presentation model (EIP) and the Classroom Interaction System (CIS). Other areas of current research include the creation of meaningful measurement scales of learning and growth, the examination of learning theories and instructional practice in mathematics, problem based learning (PBL), gambling and numeracy, and computer-adaptive testing (CAT).

Dhushy Sathianathan is the department head of the School of Engineering Design, Technology, and Professional Programs (SEDTAPP) in the College of Engineering. In this position, he is also the division head of Engineering at Commonwealth College. Dr. Sathianathan joined SEDTAPP in 1991 with a PhD in mechanical engineering from Pennsylvania State University and a BS in mechanical engineering from Oklahoma State University. He has taught courses in engineering design, computer-aided engineering, and design communications and has published several books in design and computer-aided design. His research area involves developing fluid flow visualization tools by using neutron radiography.

David Schofield, after initially working as a chef and hotel manager, spent seven years working in the National Health Service, specializing in personal and organizational development for managers and clinicians at all levels ranging from graduate entry to chief executive level. David's current work is focused on the development of online assessment and reporting systems to support both teachers and students in the assessment process as part of the Project on Assessment in Scotland Using Information Technology (PASS-IT).

Peter J. Shull is an associate professor of engineering at Pennsylvania State University, USA. Dr. Shull received his undergraduate degree from Bucknell University in mechanical engineering and his graduate degrees from the Johns Hopkins University in engineering science. Dr. Shull's research has two main foci—nondestructive evaluation methods as applied to process control (NDE) and pedagogical methodology. Dr. Shull's pedagogical efforts include an interest in women's issues within the engineering environment, integrated techniques to improve engineering students' communication skills, and program assessment methods that minimize stakeholders' efforts while maximizing the effectiveness of the measurement tool.

Jacqueline B. Shrago, chief executive officer of ThinkLink Learning, USA, has 25 years in technology-based executive management positions. Working with the governor of Tennessee, she managed the implementation of the Internet in all the state's K–12 schools. Assuring effective use of the technology, she was responsible for the design of Web-based professional development tools used by 20,000 Tennessee teachers. She has served in education technology advisory capacities to the National Governor's Association, Council of Chief State School Officers, and CEO Forum. Her education projects have received recognition from the National Information Infrastructure and the Smithsonian Computer World Awards.

I. Leon Smith is president and CEO of Professional Examination Service, USA, a nonprofit organization whose mission is to benefit the public good by promoting the understanding and use of sound credentialing practices in professions and occupations. Dr. Smith has presented papers on credentialing policy and practice and published articles on issues related to competency assessment in credentialing. In addition, he has served as a commissioner for the National Commission for Certifying Agencies—an organization that accredits certification programs meeting its standards—and was selected as co-chair of a Commission Task Force charged with reviewing and revising the Commission's accreditation standards.

Michael K. Smith, PhD, is director of research and evaluation for ThinkLink Learning, USA. He is also President of TESTPREP VIDEOS, a company that produces training courses for standardized tests, such as the SAT, ACT, and PSAT. He received his PhD in psychology in 1984. Over the last 20 years, he has helped develop assessments in a variety of areas, from secondary school teacher certification examinations to selection systems for personnel in business and industry. He is author of the book *Humble Pi: The Role Mathematics Should Play in American Education.*

Christopher Tassava, PhD, the office's writer/editor, works primarily on the assessment and accreditation reports submitted by Capella to the U.S. Department of Education, the Higher Learning Commission of the North Central Association, and other organizations. Christopher divides his time between the Office of Assessment and the Office of Communication. He received his doctorate in 2003 from Northwestern University, where he studied the history of business and technology in the United States.

Ruth Thomas has been producing educational teaching and training materials for the past 20 years. She has worked as a programmer and manager within the computer-based teaching unit at Cambridge University. While at Cambridge she managed the INTER-ACT project, a major UK higher education initiative developing educational simulations in three universities. Building on the ideas of INTERACT, Ruth led the MultiVerse project in the Institute for Computer-Based Learning at Heriot-Watt University, UK, developing a set of Java-based simulation tools that were later commercialized. Ruth's current research is focused on the integration of assessment and simulation as a means of measuring higher order skills.

Gerald Tindal, PhD, joined the University of Oregon, USA, in 1984 and is currently professor and director of behavioral research and teaching (BRT) as well as area head of educational leadership. He teaches courses that focus on measurement systems for general and special education teachers and administrators. His research focuses on the integration of students with disabilities in general education classrooms by using student performance indicators to develop optimal instructional programs. Dr. Tindal publishes and reviews articles in many special education journals and has written several book chapters and books on curriculum-based measurement.

Pamela Van Dyk is a research and program evaluation consultant with Evaluation Resources, a private research and evaluation consulting firm in North Carolina. She has worked in education research and program evaluation since 1996 and specializes in projects related to education policy. Dr. Van Dyk provided oversight and management of Phase 4 of the North Carolina Computerized Adaptive Testing System (NCCATS) research and development for the North Carolina Department of Public Instruction, USA. Dr. Van Dyk received a PhD from North Carolina State University in education research and policy analysis.

Daniel Volchok, EdD, is the director of user community relations at WebCT, USA, where he is responsible for a number of programs including the WebCT Institute Program, the Exemplary Course Project, User Groups, and user conferences. Dr. Volchok has over 25 years of higher education experience, most recently as dean of students at Endicott College. He has written articles and presented numerous sessions on technology, online student services, and distance education. Dr. Volchok received a bachelor's and master's degree of business administration from Ohio University and a doctorate in higher education administration from Teachers College, Columbia University.

Ada Ma Wai Wing is the section coordinator of Home Economics Section of the Department of Information and Applied Technology, the Hong Kong Institute of Education, Hong Kong. She is currently teaching home economics, with focus on textiles for both full-time and part-time bachelor's degree programs. She is interested in various research areas, such as computer-supported collaborative learning, textiles education, curriculum innovations, and gender issues. She has actively participated in various academic activities ranging from publication of conference proceedings, journals, and book chapters to being a research investigator of some internal and external funded projects.

Paula M. Winke, a former Peace Corps volunteer in China, received her MA in linguistics from the University of Minnesota, where she taught German and worked on test development projects at the university's Center for Advanced Research on Language Acquisition. She is currently a project manager in the Language Testing Division at the Center for Applied Linguistics and is a doctoral candidate in applied linguistics at Georgetown University. Ms. Winke's doctoral dissertation, funded by the National Science Foundation, investigates native English speakers' aptitudes, motivations, and strategies for learning Chinese as a second language.

John C. Wise is the director of engineering instructional services at Pennsylvania State's College of Engineering, USA. In this capacity, he provides assistance to faculty members and teaching assistants in the areas of teaching, learning, and instructional technology. He also provides educational assessment support for the College of Engineering. He received his BA in liberal arts from University of the State of New York and his MS and PhD in instructional systems from Penn State.

Martin Youngson has been a lecturer in mathematics at Heriot-Watt University, UK, since 1978. He spent part of 1984 as a visiting professor at the University of Oregon. One of his research interests is functional analysis, and as well as publishing papers on this subject he is also a coauthor of a textbook, *Linear Functional Analysis*. His other research interest is e-assessment. He worked on Interactive Past Papers and has designed experiments to compare performance in paper-based and computer-based assessments.

Anthony Zara is vice president of testing services for Pearson VUE, USA, the computerized testing business of Pearson, plc. In his current role, he directs their product management and test development functions to provide client-focused solutions for high-stakes testing programs. He has experience on both the client and provider sides of the testing business (previously directing the national nurse licensure program, NCLEX, for the NCSBN for more than eight years). Tony earned his PhD in psychometric methods from the University of Minnesota and has worked with computerized testing research for more than 20 years. He has published research related to CAT, licensure testing, item response theory, and other topics.

Index

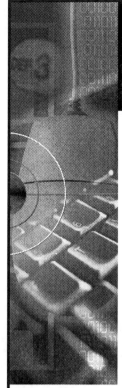